EARLY AMERICAN SILVER

Century Library of American Antiques

WALDO R. BROWNE, *General Editor*

EARLY AMERICAN SILVER
C. *Louise Avery*

EARLY AMERICAN POTTERY AND CHINA
John Spargo

EARLY AMERICAN FURNITURE
Charles Over Cornelius

EARLY AMERICAN GLASS
Rhea Mansfield Knittle

EARLY AMERICAN COSTUME
Edward Warwick and Henry C. Pitz

EARLY AMERICAN PRINTS
Carl W. Drepperd

IN PREPARATION

EARLY AMERICAN TEXTILES
Frances Little

Frontispiece   *See page 42*

STANDING CUP MADE BY JEREMIAH DUMMER
Bequeathed by Governor Stoughton to
The First Church of Dorchester, Massachusetts

Early American Silver

By C. Louise Avery

Illustrated

The Century Co.

New York   *London*

TO

MY MOTHER

ACKNOWLEDGMENTS

THE book that follows discusses early American silver in an impersonal fashion, for that is the habit of books. But my own associations with American silver have been far from impersonal, for my acquaintance with it has been made up of a long series of delightful contacts with those most genial folk, the collectors of old silver.

Whether its possession has a mellowing effect upon its owners, or whether the action is in the reverse direction and people of sympathetic and hospitable natures are peculiarly susceptible to the charm of old silver, is a difficult point to determine. My experience assures me, however, that one or the other must be true.

My first acquaintance with early American silver was made through Judge A. T. Clearwater of Kingston, New York. For many years Judge Clearwater has been gathering rare pieces, and though he whimsically describes this habit as his "folly," he has pursued it with such zeal and enthusiasm that his collection, which is now on loan at The Metropolitan Museum of Art, New York, is one of the foremost in the country. His natural hunting-ground has been the Hudson River region, especially New York, Albany, and Kingston, where so many enterprising and wealthy Dutch mer-

[vii]

Acknowledgments

chants settled and where so much of their handsome old plate has been found. However, Judge Clearwater has not limited himself to this locality. Searching with persistence and discrimination, he has secured many rare New England pieces and a suitable number from other places, so that his collection now represents fairly American silver as a whole.

His enthusiasm is infectious. With great good humor he will describe how, after years of waiting, he eventually was able to secure some long-coveted piece, or will tell with what satisfaction he purchased at auction in London and brought back to America some other Colonial piece that had been carried off to England during the American Revolution.

To another distinguished collector of American silver, R. T. H. Halsey, I am equally indebted for wise guidance and stimulating friendship. By combining in himself the rôles of collector, research-worker, writer, and lecturer, he has probably done more than any other one person to contribute to our knowledge of this subject, to bring to light and to identify hundreds of early pieces, and to inspire others with a love for the work of our Colonial silversmiths. One of Mr. Halsey's outstanding characteristics is his great generosity in putting at the disposal of his friends both his time and his knowledge.

H. W. Kent, Secretary of the Metropolitan Museum, because of his keen interest in design has always stressed the decorative elements in American silver. When the catalogue of the Clearwater collection was in preparation, it was he who urged the treatment of the subject from this point of view and arranged to have it ade-

Acknowledgments

quately illustrated. I am happy to make acknowledgment to him here for this inspired direction.

During the last ten years I have had the enjoyable privilege of meeting many collectors of American silver and of seeing their treasures. I cannot pay too high a tribute to their kindness, cordiality, and courtesy. If at times, in pursuing the subject alone, I find myself growing a trifle stale, I have but to meet some one of them to find my enthusiasm running high again. Those to whom I feel especially warm gratitude are Philip Leffingwell Spalding and Hollis French of Boston, William Davis Miller of Providence, Rhode Island, and Harrold E. Gillingham of Philadelphia. To Mr. Gillingham I am particularly indebted for many items of information that he has discovered in his researches and most unselfishly placed at my disposal.

Many other collectors have permitted me to see their silver and to use photographs of it as illustrations in this book, or have otherwise assisted me. I here express my appreciation of their courtesy to Mrs. E. S. Chaffee of Providence, Rhode Island; Hermann F. Clarke of Boston; Mrs. Stanley Cunningham of Milton, Massachusetts; Frederic Ashton de Peyster of New York; H. F. du Pont of Winterthur, Delaware; Francis P. Garvan of New York; Miss Elizabeth S. Gilbert of Brooklyn, New York; Edward Jackson Holmes of Boston; Mr. and Mrs. Roger F. Hooper of Boston; Mr. and Mrs. Charles E. Ingersoll of Penllyn, Pennsylvania; Mr. and Mrs. John C. Jay of New York; Pierre Jay of New York; William A. Jefferies of Boston; Luke Vincent Lockwood of New York; Miss Mary Mills of Charleston, South Carolina; Mrs. Rich-

[ix]

Acknowledgments

ard H. Morgan of Plymouth, Massachusetts; Mrs. Adolpho Carlos Munoz of Chestnut Hill, Pennsylvania; Mrs. Henry Parish of New York; Miss Ella Parsons of Philadelphia; Miss S. H. Pickering of Boston; Dudley L. Pickman of Boston; Foster Pruyn of Albany, New York; Mrs. Lois B. Rantoul of Jamaica Plain, Massachusetts; Charles D. Rupert of Wilmington, Delaware; Mrs. Charles F. Russell of Castine, Maine; Henry Davis Sleeper of Boston; Mrs. Robert Soutter of Brookline, Massachusetts; Dr. Isaac Starr, Jr., of Wilmington, Delaware; Mrs. Nathaniel Thayer of Boston; Charles H. Tyler of Boston; Miss Anne S. Van Cortlandt of Croton on Hudson, New York; Mrs. Miles White, Jr., of Baltimore, Maryland.

I am under a similar debt to the pastors and other officers of many of the early churches, including The First Church, Boston; Old South Church, Boston; St. Mary's Church, Burlington, New Jersey; First Congregational Society and Church, Chelmsford, Massachusetts; First Church of Dorchester, Massachusetts; Newman Congregational Church, East Providence, Rhode Island; Church of the Unity, Neponset, Massachusetts; Trinity Church, Newport, Rhode Island; South Reformed Church, New York; Christ Church, Philadelphia; Congregational Church, West Barnstable, Massachusetts.

For their liberality in contributing information in their special fields I am indebted to E. Alfred Jones of London; to Dr. S. W. Woodhouse, Jr., of Philadelphia; to Dr. J. Hall Pleasants of Baltimore; and to Howard M. Chapin of the Rhode Island Historical Society in Providence. Especial thanks are due to Henry

[x]

Acknowledgments

C. Kirk of Baltimore, Maryland, for his courtesy in showing me how modern silver is made and for his extremely generous assistance in my study of the methods employed by the early silversmiths. The Gorham Company of Providence, Rhode Island, kindly supplied the photographs illustrating the process of raising, from which Plates XL and XLI were made.

The view of a London silversmith's shop of 1707, which is illustrated in Plate XXXIX, is reproduced by kind permission of the Worshipful Company of Goldsmiths of London from "The Plate of the Worshipful Company of Goldsmiths," by J. B. Carrington and G. R. Hughes, Oxford University Press.

To my friend, Hazel de Berard, who made the line drawings which appear throughout the book, I make grateful acknowledgment. Josephine Barnhardt offered the stimulus of her advice and criticism when this was particularly needed. My colleagues at The Metropolitan Museum of Art, especially Ruth Ralston, Frances Little, and Lois L. Comings, have been unfailingly solicitous and helpful. To Louise Burroughs I pay a special tribute for her eager interest in the progress of the work and for much research undertaken in my behalf. Members of the staffs of other museums, to whom I have had occasion to turn for assistance, have extended cordial coöperation. Especially do I appreciate the warm support given me by Kathryn Clark, Assistant in the Department of Decorative Arts in the Museum of Fine Arts, Boston, who has enabled me to secure important illustrations and has supplied valuable data.

Observation and my own experience indicate that

Acknowledgments

back of every writer stands a small group of devoted and long-suffering friends. To mine I owe a deep debt of gratitude for their encouragement.

C. Louise Avery.

New York
July 1930.

FOREWORD

How many people forty years ago had any idea that fine silver was made in the American colonies? Almost none. The general notion was that whatever plate the colonists were fortunate enough to possess they had imported from abroad, chiefly from England. Luckily a few people were curious and began to look into the matter. When in 1888 John H. Buck published his book, "Old Plate," which described not only European but also American silver, so far as he could find record of it, he had accomplished a bit of genuine pioneering. Though it met with an incredulous and somewhat disinterested public, in time the book won such recognition that another edition was issued in 1903.

Meantime, in 1896, in the more popular channels of "Harper's Magazine," another pioneer, the late Professor Theodore S. Woolsey, of Yale University, brought out a brief article descriptive of American silver. He and others like him were learning to recognize our early plate, to appreciate its charm and excellence, and to form their own collections. Among the first to have a collection of importance was R. T. H. Halsey of New York. With his tremendous energy and enthusiasm, he has probably done more than any other individual to discover information about the early American silversmiths and to bring their handiwork to the attention of the public.

[xiii]

Foreword

Enthusiasms are contagious, collectors want to share their hobbies, and so the first exhibitions came about. At the instigation of Mr. Halsey and Francis Hill Bigelow of Cambridge, Massachusetts, an exhibition of old American silver was held at the Museum of Fine Arts in Boston in 1906. Undoubtedly the display of these handsome old pieces, so rich in associations—especially in Boston, where there is great pride of family—did more to spread the knowledge and the love of old silver than a dozen books could have done. Mr. Halsey's introduction to the catalogue, which offered information concerning the early New England silversmiths and their manner of work, gave the silver personality and human appeal. So much interest did the event arouse that Boston held another exhibition in 1911 that, though limited almost entirely to church plate, included more than one thousand items. As an introduction to this catalogue another worthy writer on American silver, George Munson Curtis, supplied a note on Connecticut silversmiths.

Meantime the Colonial Dames of the State of New York had assembled a group of American silver, which was shown at the Metropolitan Museum in New York and at the Jamestown (Virginia) Exposition in 1907. In 1909, in connection with the Hudson-Fulton celebration in New York, nearly three hundred pieces of plate were included in the general exhibition of American art held at the Metropolitan Museum. Two years later at the same museum the Colonial Dames of the State of New York sponsored an exhibition of "Silver Used in New York, New Jersey, and the South." Not only was this notable because it was

Foreword

the first to place particular emphasis on New York styles, but also because there appeared as introduction to the catalogue a note by Mr. Halsey on "Early New York Silversmiths," which was the result of much original research and a valuable contribution to the literature on American silver.

Thanks again to the efforts of the Colonial Dames, in this case the National Society in Rhode Island, in 1911, an interesting display of early plate given to Rhode Island churches prior to 1850 was shown at the Rhode Island School of Design in Providence.

Philadelphia has had a series of exhibitions that have stressed local types. The most significant were those held in 1921 at the Pennsylvania Museum, and in March 1929, when a fine group of ancestral plate made by Philadelphia silversmiths was shown at the Colonial Dames' House.

Though they have less local silver upon which to draw, several of the smaller cities have arranged exhibitions from time to time. Thus the Connecticut Society of the Colonial Dames of America assembled an important group of plate from Connecticut churches for display at the Wadsworth Atheneum in Hartford in 1919, and the Worcester Art Museum showed "Old Silver Owned in Worcester County" in 1913.

The influence of these exhibitions has been tremendous. Quantities of handsome and historic pieces have come to light, and have been carefully studied and described in the exhibition catalogues. Often the fortunate owners have come to take greater interest in their ancestral possessions; in some instances they have discovered that pieces are of Colonial instead of Eng-

lish workmanship, and frequently they have been inspired to share their good fortune with others by leaving their treasures on loan in museums. Americans in
general have gained a deeper respect for the taste and
ability of their early craftsmen, and many, becoming
sensitive to its appeal, have begun to collect this old
silver.

Not only have splendid private collections been
formed, but most of the larger museums now have on
view many rare and historic pieces, which are thus
delighting hosts of visitors. A number of the oldest
Boston churches have lent their communion plate to
the Museum of Fine Arts for an indefinite period, with
the reservation in some instances that the plate be sent
to the churches for the Christmas and Easter services.
The practice of lending or giving to museums such notable pieces cannot be too highly commended, as it en-
sures the preservation of the silver and permits many
to enjoy it.

With the growing interest in the subject a considerable literature has developed. In addition to the
valuable introductions to the catalogues of the museum
exhibitions already mentioned, a number of books have
appeared, each of which in its individual way has made
a definite contribution.

E. Alfred Jones, who has catalogued many historic
and important collections of English plate, was so
impressed by the reports he received of the Boston exhibitions that he came to America to make a study of
Colonial silver, a study that resulted in the publication
by the Colonial Dames in 1913 of a volume on "Old
Silver of American Churches." With its full descrip-

Foreword

tions, splendid illustrations, and informing introduction, this book will long serve as a record of our early communion silver. Unfortunately, since it was issued in a limited and costly edition it cannot enjoy the widest use.

One of the best and most useful books on the whole subject, "Historic Silver of the Colonies and Its Makers," was published by Francis Hill Bigelow in 1917. Mr. Bigelow has done a vast amount of careful research and supplies many interesting genealogical data concerning both the makers and the former owners of the silver he describes. To New Englanders the book will always be a mine of information. To New Yorkers and Philadelphians it may prove disappointing, as the plate of these localities is but meagerly represented.

About this same time the Walpole Society brought out in a limited edition a book of a different sort. This "List of Early American Silversmiths and Their Marks," compiled by a member of the society, Hollis French, was the first publication of its kind, and because of its usefulness has been in great demand. A second book of "American Silversmiths and Their Marks" was issued in 1927 by Stephen G. C. Ensko.

The Metropolitan Museum in New York has had on loan for many years the distinguished collection of American silver belonging to Judge A. T. Clearwater of Kingston, New York. Deeming this collection one of first importance, the museum in 1920 issued a descriptive catalogue, which is preceded by a general historical account of American silver, together with a chapter on the evolution of the more important forms and their decoration.

Foreword

E. Alfred Jones's volume on American church silver was inacessible to all but a few. By the publication in 1928 of a new work, "Old Silver of Europe and America," he has put within the reach of many a brief survey of the wide field indicated by his title.

Several of the most helpful books have been those devoted to silver of a particular locality, such as "Early Silver of Connecticut and Its Makers," by George Munson Curtis, issued by the International Silver Company in 1913; a beautifully printed little volume by William Davis Miller, published in 1928, on "The Silversmiths of Little Rest" (Rhode Island); and the "List of Philadelphia Silversmiths and Allied Artificers from 1682 to 1850," compiled by Maurice Brix in 1920. The late Alfred Coxe Prime carried on extensive research work on Philadelphia and Southern craftsmen. Some of his findings were published by the Pennsylvania Museum in various issues of its "Bulletin," and far more appear in "The Arts and Crafts in Philadelphia, Maryland, and South Carolina," issued in 1929 by the Walpole Society. Data of a similar sort but concerning another locality appear in "The Arts and Crafts in New England, 1704–1775, Gleanings from Boston Newspapers," compiled by George Francis Dow and issued in 1927. Data discovered by Dr. J. Hall Pleasants and the late Howard Sill will be published this fall in a book entitled "Maryland Silversmiths, 1715–1830, with illustrations of their Silver and their Marks and with a Facsimile of the Design Book of William Faris."

In any subject there will always be room for general works of a more or less popular type designed to give

Foreword

the amateur a readable and balanced survey of the whole subject, as well as for works that treat in an intensive way some special aspect of it. To the collector who is out to secure rare and early pieces, and especially to the collector who is primarily interested in silver of one locality, the monograph that makes an exhaustive study of the work of a single silversmith or of a small group of related silversmiths will especially appeal. Such books and monographs can be written only by those who have time to do an endless amount of research, but upon the results of their labors our ultimate knowledge of American silver will rest.

To the average person the specialized work seems too detailed. The present book aims to furnish to those who are more or less unfamiliar with the subject a general survey of the whole field of American silver, presented as impartially as possible. Its divisions have been suggested by Sir Charles James Jackson's incomparable "Illustrated History of English Plate, Ecclesiastical and Secular." To give the student a comprehensive knowledge of the subject, Jackson described English plate by grouping it into chronological periods and discussing the dominant styles in each, and then by dividing it into ecclesiastical and secular plate and tracing the evolution of the various objects under each head. As the bulk of the earliest Colonial silver was produced in localities where little distinction was made between ecclesiastical and secular plate, this division may be disregarded. In the main, Jackson's arrangement functions admirably for American silver, which can readily be divided, on the basis of its style, into

Foreword

chronological periods corresponding to those generally
assigned to American architecture and furniture and,
with some adjustment in dating, to those of English
silver. Unlike English plate, however, American silver falls into rather definite geographic groupings,
dependent upon different national, social, religious, and
economic conditions. These local variations demand
detailed discussion.

The second part of the book contains a chapter descriptive of the early American silversmiths' methods
of work and another chapter that reviews briefly the
course of development of characteristic objects, such
as the beaker, standing cup, tankard, tea-pot. The
emphasis throughout is placed upon the development of
styles in Colonial silver and upon their derivation from
European design, with very little stress upon the historic or sentimental associations of individual pieces.
To make this development clearer, a series of outline
drawings to show characteristic shapes has been added
at the end of the book. Owing to a lack of date-letters
in American silver marks, it is extremely difficult to
judge when a particular style came into or passed out
of fashion. In these drawings the effort has been made
to indicate the approximate period at which a style was
at its height.

Some readers will undoubtedly look for reproduc-
tions of the silversmiths' marks and will criticize the
book for this omission. The primary and sufficient
reason for not including such a list is that the repro-
duction of these marks is extremely expensive and
would at once put the present volume outside the class
of moderate-priced books. Moreover, the compilation

Foreword

of such a list is a subject in itself, requiring exhaustive research into the life and activities of each individual silversmith. The aim of The Century Company in this "Library of American Antiques," to present a general survey of each subject, does not call for this intensive specialization.

Jackson in the preface to his "History of English Plate" reviews some of the causes of delay in the preparation of such a work on silver, mentions the difficulty of securing satisfactory photographs, and concludes with the telling statement, "The task which was to have been completed in 1907 appears four years late. In the meantime, the work has grown from the one volume of about 600 pages, which the original subscribers were promised, to two volumes of 600 pages each." A similar situation prevails in the field of American silver. There is no limit to the possibilities of the subject, to its ramifications, to the lines of research and inquiry that may profitably be pursued. But one cannot go on forever, for sooner or later a completed manuscript must pass into the publisher's hands. If this book does no more than increase interest in American silver and provoke others—aye, provoke them!—to study the subject more intensively, whatever its inadequacies, it will have justified its printing. Like all other human creations, it will inevitably reveal errors. We hope these may, however, be few, and toward them we beg our critics to be as lenient as those of seventeenth-century England, to whom one writer, William Leybourn, author of "The Art of Dialling," thus addressed himself:

Foreword

"Candido Lectori:

Correct (Kind Reader) what thou find'st amiss;
And then it matters not whose Fault it is:
For all men Err, since Adam first transgrest,
The Printer Errs, I Err Much like the rest:
The Faults in this by neither were intended,
But being past, they thus may be amended."

CONTENTS

[xxiii]

Contents

[xxiv]

Contents

ILLUSTRATIONS

[xxvii]

Illustrations

[xxviii]

Illustrations

[xxix]

Illustrations

[xxx]

Illustrations

[xxxi]

Illustrations

[xxxii]

Illustrations

[xxxiii]

Illustrations

[xxxiv]

Illustrations

[XXXV]

Illustrations

[xxxvi]

Illustrations

Illustrations

[xxxviii]

Illustrations

[xxxix]

Illustrations

[xl]

Illustrations

[xli]

Illustrations

[xlii]

FIGURES

[xliii]

Figures

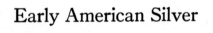

Early American Silver

Early American Silver

CHAPTER I

THE COLONIAL BACKGROUND

A PERSON unfamiliar with American silver who drops into an exhibition that is fairly representative of its range, finds himself much at sea. Here, for instance, is a crude little tea-pot standing all by itself, while farther on is an elaborate service comprising tea-pot, coffee-pot, sugar-bowl, cream-jug, and waste-bowl. It is evident that the single piece is early, and that the group designed *en suite* is a much later development, but what were the conditions that account for this difference and what were the intermediate steps? Or the visitor, seeing tea-pots by Jacob Ten Eyck, obviously a Dutchman, and by Charles Le Roux, a Huguenot, both working in New York, and noticing farther on tankards made by Edward Winslow of Boston and by Philip Syng of Philadelphia, finds himself wondering how such widely different backgrounds and traditions as these men represented affected the style of their silver. If he has a curious mind, a dozen other questions will at once present themselves; he will realize that the subject of American silver has endless ramifications, that to get orderly knowledge out of his present chaotic questioning, he must adopt a serious and logical plan of investigation, but that the

[3]

charm of the silver itself and the fascination of discovering its relationship to Colonial life will carry him just as far as he has opportunity to follow.

Before describing American silver in detail, before even attempting to divide it into chronological periods or into geographical groups, it is wise to take a broad view of the whole Colonial situation. The specific conditions affecting the production of silver in any given locality will be discussed in detail in the chapter devoted to that Colonial group, but these can be better understood if certain generalizations are first made. To understand why, for example, more silver was produced in one region than in another, it is necessary to look rather closely into the social, religious, political, and economic conditions as these affected the rise of local industry and craftsmanship. Silver is obviously not a necessity but a luxury, and will not be produced in any community until more necessary industries have become well established. Its possession presupposes the existence of people of wealth and refined tastes.

The establishment of essential industries in the American colonies and the consequent development of crafts to supply the amenities of life were largely dependent upon such economic considerations as the motives behind emigration to America, the character of the people who settled it, the natural resources of the land, and finally the attitude of the mother-country toward her colonies.

The motives that induced any group of settlers to come to America are an important consideration. Colonists who came primarily because they were disaffected with conditions at home were eager to establish a permanent community in America, and straightway strove to develop those activities and industries which would tend to make it self-supporting and to secure as many comforts and amenities as possible. Other settlements were founded primarily for trade or profit, and were naturally for a longer period provided with only the necessities of existence.

The character and temper of the colonists directly affected the quantity and style of silver they possessed. Those who were almost exclusively concerned with religious matters and more absorbed in contemplation of the future life than in present comforts, were disposed to take little interest in such worldly things as silver. On the other hand, those endowed with wealth and broad culture generally took great delight and pride in its possession and made considerable sacrifice, if necessary, to secure it.

The character of the land and its natural resources were also important factors in determining the industries pursued by the colonists. Communities chiefly engaged in agriculture were slow in developing any industries and crafts other than the most essential. When they had little outside market for their produce, they remained poor and unable to indulge in silver. When they were fortunate in finding a ready market for their crops, they built up credit and, though they might not themselves produce silver, could afford to import it from abroad. When the land offered a diversity of products, suitable for trade and export, when it had navigable rivers and good harbors, there soon developed commerce, local industries, and an increasing amount of specialization. The population in time became composed of rich merchants, artisans, craftsmen, farmers. Naturally it is in such communities that one may expect to find the most extensive production of local silver.

Had the colonies developed freely and spontaneously, conditions might have been quite different from what they actually became. For the present, it is wise to disregard Holland and to consider the colonies as they were controlled by England. The reason that they did not develop more freely is inherent in England's underlying motives in allowing or encouraging the establishment of colonies in America. At the time that the earliest settlements—such as Jamestown, Plymouth, and Massachusetts Bay—were founded, the British Ministry was acutely aware of the fact that England was desperately in need of certain commodities and that unless she could provide herself with them, her future was insecure indeed.[1] The necessity of meeting the Spanish Armada with an enormous fleet had made serious inroads upon her supply of timber. Yet timber she must have, partly to carry on certain of her industries but primarily to build and maintain her merchant marine, without which the little island could not exist and could not carry on her trade against the increasing competition of her Continental rivals. Then too, the close of England's wars with Spain had released many able-bodied seamen, thus augmenting the numbers of her unemployed until they constituted a most serious problem.

[1] Much of the following discussion is based on T. J. Wertenbaker's "The First Americans, 1607–1690," Macmillan, 1927.

[6]

The Colonial Background

Consequently America, with its wealth of natural resources, seemed to offer England the solution of her various perplexities. She hoped to get from the new region the raw materials she needed; to send to the new colonies some of her unemployed, thereby relieving her own situation and at the same time providing labor where it could well serve her ends; and, as the colonies became settled, to establish there a new market for many of her manufactured goods. A consummation devoutly to be wished—but unfortunately a series of unexpected difficulties arose. The high cost of labor, due to the great expense of transportation, and the difficulties encountered in settling the new land delayed the exploitation of its natural resources. When finally established, certain colonies were able to supply in quantity raw materials that England desired, and therefore tended to trade extensively with England, building up a credit with which they purchased English manufactured goods, including silver. As a result, these colonies had little occasion to develop local craftsmanship and remained dependent upon England. Other colonies found it impossible or impracticable to produce in quantity commodities for which England offered a market. Such colonies had scant credit with the mother-country, and were forced to a considerable extent to develop local industries to supply their own need for manufactured goods. Though not finding a ready market in England, their produce was often sufficiently varied and valuable to be keenly desired in other quarters with the result that they created a sturdy independent commerce in spite of England's restrictions upon Colonial trade. European wars, delayed

[7]

peace negotiations, controversial foreign relationships, all afforded the colonists opportunities for irregular or illicit trading. The British Ministry, unable to grasp the situation or unwilling to accept it, blundered on, endeavoring by coercive and restrictive measures to force the colonists to trade exclusively within the British dominions. These curbs cramped the colonists painfully, and not only failed to accomplish England's end but made the colonists aggressive and resourceful, until ultimately they asserted and won their complete independence.

Other aspects of the Colonial trade-situation had a direct bearing upon the local production of silver. All the colonies during the period of their early development, although they exported raw materials to England, had of necessity to import manufactured goods of much more value, so that the balance of trade was against them and their coin went out to England. In consequence, they suffered from a lack of coin for the transaction of local business, and resorted to various expedients to provide a convenient medium of exchange. Much trading was necessarily accomplished by barter. The Indians used wampum, and the colonists soon learned from dealing with them that, though of no intrinsic value, it formed a handy sort of small change. Massachusetts Bay sought relief by establishing in 1652 a mint for coining money for local circulation, which functioned for thirty years. Many colonies undertook at various times to issue paper money or "bills of credit." Often they did not make adequate provision for the redemption of such paper money and consequently it fluctuated in value and sometimes de-

[8]

See pages 17–19

SEVENTEENTH CENTURY ENGLISH STANDING CUPS
Presented to New England Churches

PLATE I

preciated disastrously. There were no banks in the colonies, so that people had the alternative of keeping their savings in paper currency or in coin, often termed "hard money."

The early American silversmith generally received his material in the form of coins brought to him by his customers. As there were no deposits of silver ore in the colonies, this was practically the only way in which the metal was available. When there was little "hard money" in circulation, his trade was inevitably limited. But this situation was offset by the desirability of hoarding savings in this form instead of in unstable paper, and by the further desirability of converting such coin into wrought plate. In the form of plate, silver was not only more useful and far more delightful to behold than a bag of miscellaneous coins but was also more readily identified in case of theft, and was always available for reconversion into money if need arose.

In beginning the study of early American silver, the first and most obvious step is to divide the whole field into chronological periods and thus to consider the development of styles. But the very phrase "Colonial silversmiths" implies that these men had definite traditions back of them, and in order to understand them and their work one must study their backgrounds and the sources from which they drew their inspiration. In other words, to comprehend the sequence of American styles, one must look to Europe, and especially to England and Holland, whence these colonists had emigrated and upon which they remained dependent in a multiplicity of ways.

At once another division becomes necessary. There were many influences at work in American silver and, as already suggested, widely different conditions existed in the various colonies, which directly affected the quantity and the style of the silver there produced. It will be simpler and productive of less digression to make a geographical division and to consider one Colonial group at a time. Of these groups the one in which the chronological development of styles can best be traced is New England. Though Virginia was settled at an earlier date, for reasons that we will not now discuss such evidence as we now have leads us to conclude that silversmiths were not active there until a much later period. New Netherland was settled almost as early as New England, but does not afford as satisfactory an approach because its early silver followed Dutch traditions, thus constituting the only real exception to the prevalence of English styles throughout the colonies. Quantities of fine silver had been fashioned in New England before Penn's "greene country towne" could boast a silversmith. Hence, to trace the history of American styles one may best turn to New England, and especially to its great center Boston, for there the bulk of the early silver was wrought, there a longer and fuller sequence of styles can be traced than in any other single locality, there the English tradition was but little affected by foreign admixtures. Once oriented, one can then turn to New York, Philadelphia, and the South to discover what peculiar set of circumstances in each produced local variations.

CHAPTER II

CHRONOLOGICAL DEVELOPMENT OF MASSACHUSETTS SILVER

The settlers of Plymouth, the first colony established in New England, were Puritans of the stricter sort. Their intense preoccupation with religious concerns and the struggles through which their little community passed precluded the possibility of their enjoying many of the luxuries or amenities of life.

The people who came to Massachusetts Bay were also Puritans and Nonconformists, emigrating to the New World in order that they might live according to their religious convictions. They were also unwilling to conform to the political régime in England. A striking evidence of this, as Lockwood points out,[1] is the fact that 26,000 came to New England between 1629 and 1640, the years in which Charles I refused to summon Parliament. So for religious and political reasons these colonists were eager to establish a permanent home in America and to keep it free of those influences to which they had been particularly opposed in England. The leaders of the Massachusetts Bay Colony were wise enough to secure the transfer of its charter and government from London to America, thus giving them more direct control. When, in 1691, a new charter was granted, its more liberal provisions

[1]L. V. Lockwood. "Colonial Furniture in America," 1913.

[11]

insured a wide measure of popular control in the affairs of the colony. This tendency was increased by the gradual growth of a great middle class.

Not only did large numbers of colonists come to Massachusetts Bay at an early period, especially during the years of the Great Migration, but among them were many folk of wealth, intellect, culture, and enterprise. The community therefore rapidly grew and prospered, particularly when an aggressive merchant class arose to check the domination of the small group of religious leaders who, considering themselves "God's elect," had at first held undisputed sway in both church and state affairs.

The land lent itself to agriculture, but rather grudgingly. [1] Large staple crops raised with unskilled labor were out of the question. However, Massachusetts Bay possessed a variety of resources, including lumber, grain, and fish, of which she straightway availed herself. She did not find it practicable to export these extensively to England, yet of necessity she had to import certain manufactured goods from the mother-country, so that the balance of trade was in the latter's favor. But the colony was independent in spirit and aggressive, and soon began to develop her own industries and to seek other markets for her commodities.

Fortunately there were good harbors, timber, and other naval supplies with which ships could be built, and energetic men to sail them. The first sea-going ship built in New England was launched in 1631. Even though labor was more expensive in the colony

[1]The following discussion summarizes the argument followed by T. J. Wertenbaker in "The First Americans, 1607–1690."

than in England, the materials for ship-building were so plentiful that there was soon no occasion to rely on the mother-country. Her own boats enabled the Bay to conduct an extensive carrying trade.

Massachusetts soon built up an active and varied commerce, not only with her Colonial neighbors but also to some degree with England, and particularly with the West Indies, where the sugar-planters proved most eager for the fish, lumber, live stock, and provisions that Massachusetts either produced or was able to procure and transport. In return for these goods, the West Indies sold the colonists indigo, cotton, and quantities of sugar and molasses. The last two were made into rum in the New England distilleries and used for local consumption, for the Newfoundland fisheries, and for facilitating the African slave-trade. The better grades of fish Massachusetts shipped to the Catholic countries of southern Europe, receiving wines in return. In the course of her trading she picked up some tobacco from Virginia and Maryland and furs from New Netherland and transported them to England to enable her to buy manufactured goods there.

The liberal variety of Massachusetts imports and exports and consequent industries provided employment for numerous types of society, farmers, fishermen, merchants, skilled artisans, and tradesmen. These activities required a high type of labor. Slaves were not sufficiently hardy or intelligent to be used to advantage. Even indented servants, as a class, were not sufficiently skillful to be of great service. The diversity of industry tended to encourage increasing specialization. The rise of a number of prosperous little towns gave an ad-

[13]

ditional impetus to craftsmanship, and in their competition with each other they often sought to induce special craftsmen to settle in their communities. The control that the New England town exerted over land tended to encourage many small holdings rather than large landed estates, which meant the consequent possession of moderate wealth by a number of people.

The development of town life and of a mercantile class, the increasing specialization in industry, the rise of many people with ambition, enterprise, and moderate means, all fostered the development of local industry and craftsmanship. Not only were necessary industries pursued, but also crafts of a highly specialized sort, which contributed things more or less in the nature of luxuries, received substantial support. Among these was the craft of the silversmith. Rich merchants who in the course of their trafficking had acquired quantities of silver coin provided him at the same time with patronage and with the medium of his craft. He also received no inconsiderable amount of orders from prosperous artisans; the donations of silver to New England churches included gifts from men who were blacksmiths, coopers, and the like.

Long before local silversmiths began to ply their trade in Massachusetts, however, many colonists possessed plate. Though the early settlers of Massachusetts Bay were Puritans and Nonconformists, narrow and uncompromising in their religious beliefs and extremely harsh toward any who were unable to agree with them, their prejudices did not alter the fact that many of them had been people of wealth, culture, and social position in England. Naturally they brought

[14]

with them to America many of their household furnishings, to lend to their new homes much of the comfort, dignity, and charm their old homes had known. Wills and inventories bear witness that a considerable amount of silver was thus imported.

Besides the inventories, there is the evidence of the silver itself, actual pieces brought over by the early colonists and still extant. Naturally only handsome pieces or those valued for special associations would have been thus treasured. As a matter of fact, most of this early English plate now extant consists of various forms of cups, and owes its preservation to the fact that it was early presented to New England churches for use in their communion services. The majority of these communion vessels are described and illustrated by E. Alfred Jones in "Old Silver of American Churches," to which the student may profitably refer. In many instances, these pieces were presumably brought to America as domestic drinking-cups and were first used here as such. Quite apart from their historic or sentimental associations and from their interest to us as possible models for the early Colonial silversmiths, they may well claim our attention as splendid examples of English plate.

The English silver brought to America by the early colonists was naturally looked upon as the embodiment of correct London styles, and so afforded the models to which the ambitious Colonial silversmiths turned for inspiration. While a number of notable examples still exist, a far larger number must have perished. To understand the genesis of early Massachusetts silver, it is therefore desirable not merely to describe existent

pieces of imported plate but first to review briefly
those English styles of the Charles I and Commonwealth periods upon which the earliest Colonial silver
was based. Then the important examples that remain
may be described and their significance better appreciated.

I. ENGLISH SILVER OF THE EARLY STUART AND COMMONWEALTH PERIODS

(1603–60)

At the beginning of the seventeenth century English
plate tended to carry a good deal of decoration, the
elements of which were chiefly of Renaissance origin.
As the century advanced, increasing Puritan sentiment
resulted in a preference for plainer and less ostentatious styles. During the Civil War great quantities of
plate were melted down to provide funds for the con-
tending armies, and at its close the Commonwealth
was established and Puritan influences were in the ascendant. Not much silver was wrought during the
Commonwealth period, and what was made was of a
severely plain and substantial type. It comprised standing cups, beakers, tankards, and similar practical objects.

The silver with which the early New England colonists were familiar was chiefly of this sort. Fortunately,
a number of typical English pieces made during these
periods and brought to New England are still in existence. Some of them indeed were too early in style
to have been in fashion when the New England silversmiths began to ply their trade actively, but no account

PLATE II

BEAKER AND STANDING CUP BY HULL AND SANDERSON
BEAKER BY EDWARD WINSLOW

See pages 23, 24, 43

of American silver can properly omit some description of them.

The earliest is an elegantly formed silver-gilt standing cup made in London in 1607 and later presented to the Old South Church in Boston. Its bowl is decorated with a band of fluting, and above this a grape-vine design set against a matted ground and executed by flat-chasing. Flat-chasing, which differs from engraving in that it is accomplished by a tool without a cutting edge so that the lines of the pattern are impressed instead of cut into the surface, was a mode of ornamentation much used in English plate at this period. The cup rests upon a well-shaped baluster stem and slightly domed foot, the latter decorated with flutes and flat-chasing. It is an admirable example of its type and an altogether charming piece.

A no less characteristic method of decoration in English plate of the early seventeenth century is illustrated by a standing cup made in London in 1610 (Plate I, center; height 11⅝″). This cup belonged to Governor John Winthrop (1587–1649), who presented it to the First Church of Boston (founded in 1630). Here the decoration is embossed and chased, covers practically the whole surface, and consists of acanthus borders and of strapwork forming reserves enclosing sea-monsters and dolphins, and bunches of fruit and flowers. The cup stands on a high bell-shaped foot, and the effect of height which this gives was probably increased by a tall steeple cover, which must originally have surmounted the cup and which is now lost. The stem was characteristically enriched by three scroll brackets, two of which are also lost.

[17]

Early American Silver

Next in date is a London cup of 1626 (Plate I, right; height 9″), which depends for its appeal solely upon its grace of outline. The proportions of its deep bowl, slender baluster stem, and slightly spreading foot give it height and distinction. As it is undecorated, it offers a pleasant contrast to the highly ornate cup just described, and it constitutes a notable example of the style of plain standing cups much favored in the time of Charles I. Like the Governor Winthrop cup, it belongs to the First Church of Boston, to which it was presumably presented by Atherton and Elizabeth Hough.

The three cups just described were so early in style that they had relatively little effect upon Colonial silver. Other imported English cups of somewhat later date seem, however, to have made a very definite contribution. For this reason three of the more important have been illustrated in Plate I, so that their influence upon the work of the earliest Boston silversmiths may be demonstrated. All of these English pieces have been described and illustrated by Mr. Jones in his "Old Silver of American Churches" and upon this volume we have drawn in recording the histories of the individual cups.

The earliest of the three to which we now have reference (Plate I, next to right; height 7½″) was made in London in 1631 and is a charming example of a plain baluster-stemmed wine-cup, such as any good Puritan of the period would have approved. It commends itself for its pleasing proportions and for its practicability. The inscription reads: "The Gift of our Revᵈ Pastor Mr. Noah Newman who went to

PLATE III   *See pages 26, 48*

TAZZA BY JOHN CONEY, SPOONS BY HULL AND CONEY

the Church Triumphant Ap^r 16, 1678." The cup was probably brought to America by the Reverend Samuel Newman, first pastor of the Church of Rehoboth (founded 1643; afterward called the Newman Congregational Church of East Providence) and was bequeathed to the church by his son and successor.

A trifle more heavily built but generally similar is the second cup (height 7⅜"), made in London in 1638 (Plate I, next to left). From the initials engraved upon it—W ^{F} P—it appears to have belonged to William Franklin, a Boston blacksmith, and his third wife, Phebe. Another cup of rather similar form was given by Hezekiah Usher, Sr., to the Old South Church, of which he was one of the founders in 1669.

The third example (Plate I, left; height 9⅜"), made a year later, is much more capacious, and altogether broader and bolder in plan. Its wide bowl is decorated with a band of granulation, a style of ornamentation probably derived from Germany and used to a considerable extent on seventeenth-century English plate. It offered a simple method of breaking a plain surface without doing so ostentatiously. Within this band of granulation is enclosed an oval medallion with the pricked initials B ^{T} C for The Boston Church (The First Church of Boston), to which this cup was presented, probably by Jeremy Houchin, who had joined the church in 1640. The stout baluster stem is enriched with a beading and with chased foliage around its lower sections, and both stem and foot are decorated with granulation.

Early American Silver

Massachusetts Bay was more consistently and whole-heartedly in sympathy with Puritan ideas than England, with her mixture of social and religious elements, could ever be. Moreover, the rigorous conditions of early Colonial life imposed restraint upon any impulse toward luxury. In consequence, the early Boston silver tended to be, if such were possible, a little simpler than even the severely plain English plate of the Commonwealth era. But there is not room for much contrast between the two. These Puritan styles remained in favor longer in the colony than in England.

While English plate is conveniently hall-marked with a date-letter that indicates the year in which it was wrought, there is nothing of the sort to establish the exact year in which a piece of Colonial silver was made. Sometimes other records exist that suggest or prove the date of production, but these do not always mean what they imply at first glance. Thus a piece of communion silver may bear an inscription to the effect that it was presented by so-and-so in such a year and later investigation will show that it was made at a convenient time thereafter with funds bequeathed by so-and-so for that purpose. The year in which a piece was given to a church often bears no relation to the year in which it was made, as it may have been owned by the donor long before its presentation to the church. Under these circumstances, in many cases one can only gage the period of a piece by its general style, by the active years of its maker's life, and by piecing together

[20]

such other bits of information as can be discovered concerning it.

It would be extremely difficult, if not impossible, to determine when the first silver was wrought in New England, but one can form a general opinion. The earliest silversmith of whom we thus far have record is John Mansfield (1601–74), who came from London to Boston in 1634. Of his work there is no example known. John Hull (1624–83) came to America when he was still a child. As his father was a blacksmith, he readily turned to work with the anvil and hammer. In his diary Hull writes: "After we here arrived, my father settled at Boston: and after a little keeping at school, I was taken from school to help my father plant corn, which I attended for seven years together; and then by God's good hand, I fell to learning (by the help of my brother), and to practising the trade of a goldsmith, and through God's help, obtained that ability in it, as I was able to get my living by it." This "brother" was presumably his half-brother, Richard Storer, who in 1629 began his apprenticeship in London.[1] Hull was probably the first silversmith to learn his trade in New England. Robert Sanderson (1608–93) was thirty years old when he came to Massachusetts, had learned his craft abroad, and probably thus gained the experience that enabled him to become the "father of American silversmiths." From these facts it is safe to draw the deduction that silver was fashioned in Boston before 1650.

Another circumstance tends to support this theory. At this time there was in circulation in Massachusetts

[1] E. Alfred Jones, from Records of the Goldsmiths' Company.

a varied supply of foreign coin, which had been derived
from trade with England and the West Indies. This
coin included a mixture of Dutch, English, and Spanish money of varying standards of fineness, and also
much base and counterfeit coin, so that business trans-
actions were at best laborious and at the worst the
cause of much confusion and dispute. To facilitate
local trade by providing a uniform and guaranteed
medium of exchange, the General Court of Massachusetts Bay, after trying out other methods, at last in
1652 ordered the establishment of a mint in Boston.
As the Crown had sole right to coin money, this was
a defiance of the royal prerogative, but the colony presumably did not appreciate the magnitude of its offence
and was only striving to alleviate a desperate situation by what appeared to be the only adequate method.
John Hull, who was appointed mint-master, comments
in his diary: "The General Court ordered a mint to
be set up. And they made choice of me for that employment: and I chose my friend, Robert Sanderson, to be
my partner, to which the court consented." This indicates that at this date the reputation of Hull and
Sanderson as silversmiths was already established.
For thirty years thereafter they continued to mint the
famous pine and oak tree shillings and sixpences.

From these circumstances it seems safe to assume
that silver was produced at least as early as 1650 and
probably before. However, the earliest date that can
be affixed to any actual piece is 1659, the date engraved on a beaker made by Hull and Sanderson and
presumably representing the year in which it was presented to the First Church, Boston. Thereafter a series

PLATE IV   *See page 40*

CAUDLE CUPS BY HULL AND SANDERSON AND BY DUMMER

of such presentations occurs, testifying to the activity of Boston silversmiths.

As already noted, English plate of the late Charles I and Commonwealth periods was relatively meager and was chiefly of a utilitarian character and undecorated. It is not surprising, then, to find that the earliest Boston silver extant comprises a few standing cups, beakers, and spoons. These, whatever the actual date at which they were made, quite definitely reflect Puritan styles of the late Charles I and Commonwealth periods, and more specifically show the influence of some of the imported London pieces already described.

One of the earliest, perhaps the earliest, is a beaker made by Hull and Sanderson and apparently presented in 1659 to the First Church of Boston (Plate II; height 3⅞"). It is patterned after similar straight-sided English beakers of the seventeenth century, has no reinforcing molding at its base, and is decorated with a band of granulation similar to that on the English standing cup of 1639 (Plate I, left). It is a fair supposition that Hull and Sanderson derived their decoration directly from this English cup. Other beakers of the same general style are instanced on page 280.

Robert Sanderson (1608–93) and John Hull (1624–83) made most of the earliest Boston silver. Both were members of the First Church, and they undoubtedly were familiar with whatever silver belonged to this church or was commonly used in its services; consequently it is not surprising to find standing cups made by them that show fairly close kinship to such London cups as those of 1638 and 1639 described above (Plate I, two cups at left).

[23]

One of the earliest standing cups made by Hull and Sanderson belongs to the First Church, and bears underneath its base the date "1661." Though in the sharp outline of its bowl and in its domed foot it does not closely resemble either of the two English cups just mentioned, it does follow English styles of the Charles I and Commonwealth periods, and for all we know may have been inspired by some imported London cup that has long since perished.

In a number of other cups made by Hull and Sanderson there appears definite reflection of the shapes of the 1638 and 1639 cups. None of these is an exact copy. It is extremely interesting to see how each Colonial example seems to combine features from the English models to make a satisfying whole. Plate II, center, illustrates one of these cups (height 7¼") by Hull and Sanderson, bearing the inscription: "Capt. Willets' donation to ye Ch: of Rehoboth, 1674." Captain Thomas Willet left to this church (founded 1643; now the Newman Congregational Church of East Providence, Rhode Island) a legacy of £5, with which this cup was purchased. In its general proportions it is quite similar to the London cup of 1638, though the knop of its stem is somewhat more bulbous and intricate, resembling that of the 1639 cup.

Another plain cup of pleasing outline (Plate LI), made by the same two Boston silversmiths, resembles in its general proportions the 1638 cup, but in the beading and suggestion of foliation that ornament its stem it is reminiscent of the more elaborate London cup of 1639. It offers an interesting basis for a comparison of English models and Colonial adaptations.

See pages 39, 341

PLATE V

A RARE EXAMPLE OF A STANDING SALT
BY EDWARD WINSLOW

Though they were inspired by London silverwork, Hull and Sanderson proved themselves possessed of no small amount of technical skill, when with meager equipment they fashioned this piece. Moreover, less sensitive craftsmen might have attempted to copy or adapt another piece and yet have failed to get the nice proportions and good modeling that give distinction. Both this and the preceding cup offer abundant evidence that these craftsmen were artists in their own right. The cup shown in Plate LI bears the inscription "B ^{T} C"—for The Boston Church—and "The Gift of a Freinde T.C." It was presumably the gift of Thomas Clarke, a wealthy Boston merchant who joined the First Church in 1647, became ruling elder in 1673, and whose will was proved in 1682/3.

Several other cups by Hull and Sanderson, which are not illustrated, are of similar form but vary in details, some having broader bowls, others a higher foot. Those which are definitely of small size were presumably designed for domestic use and only because of the scarcity of communion plate were they later devoted to sacramental purposes. Those which are larger and more capacious may quite possibly have been originally intended to serve for communion. Three such large cups came to the First Church, Boston, as the bequest of the Reverend John Oxenbridge, one of its pastors, who died in 1674. "To the Elders and Deacons of the First Church of Boston I give £20 for the use of the Church to be paid after my decease and to continue for their service at the Lords Table." Another cup belongs to the Old South Church in

Boston, and two others to the First Congregational Society at Quincy, Massachusetts.

Two other pieces of Boston silver that follow the traditions of the Commonwealth period are illustrated in Plate III. One of these spoons was made by John Hull and is now owned by Essex Institute in Salem, Massachusetts; the other was made by John Coney (1655–1722) and is in the collection of Hollis French. The bowl in each case is oval; the handle is straight and of rectangular section, and is cut off sharply at the end. Both spoons are severely and uncompromisingly plain and reflect Puritan styles of the Commonwealth period, even though the Hull spoon may have been and the Coney spoon obviously must have been made after the year 1660. They demonstrate the fact that in the early colonies styles tended to last for a much longer period than they did in Europe. The emphasis of the present discussion is upon the evolution of styles, and therefore specific pieces are described under the period to which they belong stylistically, rather than according to the dates at which they may perhaps have been made.

With the exception of these spoons, all of the Boston pieces thus far described owe their survival to the fact that they were presented to the churches to form part of the communion service; they claimed, as it were, the right of sanctuary, whereas other plate of the same period, meeting the greater vicissitudes of domestic use, passed long since into the melting-pot. But as a matter of fact many of these pieces made in the seventeenth century which eventually became communion plate were probably originally designed to serve as domestic drinking-cups and were so used. For this adoption of domestic silver for church use, the New Englanders had ample precedent. In the Catholic Church the form of sacramental vessels was carefully prescribed. Though the Church of England, when it was established, discarded these conventions, it held rather strictly to conventions of its own. The Nonconformist churches expressed their protest against both Catholic and Anglican ritual by declining to accept communion silver of these orthodox types, and supplied their own immediate needs by employing a wide variety of domestic vessels.

The New England churches presumably at first owned little if any communion plate, and it has been suggested by F. H. Bigelow that devout worshipers carried to church for the communion service their own drinking-cups of English or Massachusetts silver. Certain it is that when they felt disposed to make gifts or bequests to their churches, they regarded such silver as the most fitting and acceptable form of donation. Sometimes they did not happen to possess pieces suitable for church use, but left money in order that such pieces might be purchased. In consequence of this custom, the communion services of the early New England churches comprise a delightfully miscellaneous assortment of domestic types and thus, fortunately for us, preserve many handsome examples that would long since have disappeared had they not, by their devotion to a holy purpose, been placed above any considerations of fashion.

Sacramental objects have almost universally been made of gold or silver, so that we entertain this idea

[27]

without conscious effort. It requires a greater stretch of the imagination to appreciate how important a rôle silver and its humbler sister pewter played in the household furnishings of Colonial days. Nowadays inexpensive and serviceable china is readily procurable and for general use is preferred to metal. In the seventeenth century, the European potter was vainly striving to discover the secret of making porcelain like that imported in such quantities from China and so highly prized. In the meantime he was making various sorts of earthenware that were much more fragile than metal, and which, as they were usually crude and often porous, were more readily permeated by food. Consequently silver was extensively used for ceremonious occasions, pewter proved extremely serviceable for ordinary tableware and was the kitchenware in practically all households, and wooden dishes served as a still cheaper type. But as pewter was a comparatively soft metal and easily marred, it was frequently melted down and reshaped. Quantities of it appear in contemporary inventories. Had it been more durable, we might to-day be able to form a much more vivid picture of the equipment of the average seventeenth-century household. As the matter stands, however, we gain perhaps our clearest idea of what the domestic forms of this period were like from the communion plate preserved in the Nonconformist churches.

Massachusetts Silver

III. ENGLISH STYLES OF THE LATE STUART AND WILLIAM AND MARY PERIODS [1]
(1660–97)

Before discussing Massachusetts silver of this period it is important to consider those influences which determined its shape and decoration, the prevailing tendencies in English plate. The constraint which Puritan sentiment imposed during the period of the Commonwealth soon gave way before the returning Stuart court. Charles II came home, as it were, on the crest of a French wave. He brought to England many things French—courtiers, craftsmen, fashions, and a taste for luxurious living. The desire for extravagant display and sumptuous appointments resulted in an extraordinary use of silver, not only for such things as had been customarily made before but also for great garnitures, elaborate toilet-services, and even for furniture encased in silver. This widespread production of plate would not have been possible except for the sudden influx into Europe of silver from the Spanish possessions in South America, especially between 1670 and 1685.

The shapes that the late Stuart silversmiths fashioned were bold and handsome—great platters, wine-coolers, vases, boxes for comfits, imposing candlesticks, tankards and flagons of vigorous outline, swelling caudle-cups. Of the forms that found more or less reflection in American silver, we may briefly sketch the styles.

---

[1] The discussion of English styles is based on C. J. Jackson, "An Illustrated History of English Plate," 1911.

Early American Silver

One of the most popular and characteristic objects in the late Stuart plate was the two-handled cup. Of bulbous form, contracted toward the mouth, it was admirably adapted for caudle and the other hot spiced drinks of curdled wine that the great draughty halls and cold bedchambers of seventeenth-century England made so welcome. The fashion of making these full-bodied two-handled cups of thin silver and decorating them with repoussé designs in bold relief had come into England from Holland during the last years of the Commonwealth period. Doubtless the exuberance of their ornament accorded well with the taste of the restored Stuarts. Sometimes these cups were given a formal treatment of panels enclosing conventionalized floral motives; sometimes they were embossed with freely modeled sprays of flowers or foliage, and running animals. At first produced as display pieces, they soon proved themselves effective for use also.

As the period progressed, however, both the form and the ornamentation of the caudle-cup became more chaste. Its swelling gourd shape was lost and it became more straight-sided and more simply decorated. The latter type in England is sometimes termed a posset-cup or porringer, a term which must not be confused with the shallow bowl with a pierced handle that is called a porringer in American silver. English posset-cups sometimes had scroll-shaped brackets on their covers, which served to support the latter when inverted, and which remind one of similar scrolled projections on the standing salts.

Another familiar object in seventeenth-century plate that passes out of fashion with the close of the century

[30]

is the great or standing salt. It is easy to appreciate how such an imposing piece served as an object of ceremony. At this time it was usually spool-shaped, of circular, square, or octagonal section, and topped by scrolled projections to support a napkin over the salt-well. Those characteristic of the late Stuart and William and Mary periods are tall and usually ornamented with embossing or with borders of gadrooning.

In addition to the standing salt there were coming into more general use small trencher-salts to be set at the individual place at table. The former gave place to the latter style as salt became more easily procurable and as more modern ideas of convenience and delicacy began to obtain.

Tankards were extremely popular in all those countries where beer was extensively drunk. Those made in England at this period had a straight, slightly tapering body; a flat lid with an ornamental thumb-piece by which it could be raised conveniently; a proportionately heavy handle; and either a flaring skirt or, somewhat later, a molded base. As the years passed, tankards tended to gain in height and slenderness.

Flagons were attenuated tankards. Some authorities distinguish between the two primarily on the basis of use, flagons being generally for sacramental and tankards for secular purposes, while others make a distinction on the basis of height and general proportions. The general decorative details of both are much the same at any given period.

English standing cups of the late Stuart period followed a variety of shapes. Some have a trumpet-shaped base, but the majority have a well-turned baluster stem, and this is the type generally copied in New England.

A candlestick suggesting Gothic colonettes was formed by clustered columns with wide square, or occasionally circular, base and projecting flanges to catch the dripping wax. This type was popular from about 1660 to 1670, after which it was succeeded by other columnar candlesticks, especially those in the form of a simple Doric column. Many of those made in the last quarter of the seventeenth century were enriched with gadrooned borders. The baluster stems of standing cups of the Restoration period presumably inspired the production of candlesticks with a baluster shaft, which appeared during the last twenty years of the century, anticipating their greater vogue in the earlier eighteenth century.

Boxes for comfits or sweetmeats were made in considerable numbers and make handsome pieces of plate. They are frequently in the form of a rather shallow oval box with bulbous sides, set on scroll feet and completed by a domed cover. The sides are often beaten out into a series of bosses interrupted by acanthus leaves or other ornament.

Tea, coffee, and chocolate during this period became so well established as popular beverages that silver pots for them were wrought in some numbers. The earliest appear to have been of so-called lantern shape, that is, the pot was in the form of a truncated cone topped by a tall conical lid. Occasionally tea-pots were made of more or less globular form, in imitation of Chinese porcelain models.

Spoons during this period showed a very definite

See pages 41, 42, 63

PLATE VI

BEAKER, STANDING CUP, AND CAUDLE CUP BY DUMMER

SHOWING A FLUTED SURBASE

development from the Commonwealth types with oval
bowl and straight stem of rectangular section into
more modern styles with a bowl that was beginning to
become slightly narrowed at its tip and a stem that
was flattened out and widened at its end.

It is important to remember that the purely utilitarian plate made in England in the time of Charles II
and William and Mary was wrought in plain and substantial forms. This type naturally commended itself
to New England taste. But a great deal of London
plate of this period was intended primarily for display and so was elaborately ornamented. While such
ornamental plate found little favor in New England at
this time, some of the more characteristic modes of
decoration did find reflection in the work of contemporary Massachusetts silversmiths, and for this
reason it seems pertinent to describe them in some
detail.

As much late Stuart plate was designed for display,
and consequently would not be subjected to rough
wear, it could be made of thin silver. This thin silver
lent itself admirably to *embossing*, by which means
elaborate and bold patterns could be hammered out
from the inside of the piece to stand in high and bold
relief upon its outer surface. Holland presumably
created the vogue for this style of silverwork and supplied many of the elements of design in which it
found expression. Freely rendered floral decoration,
animals coursing amidst foliage, friezes of acanthus
and palm leaves, were the themes often repeated. Such
embossed or repoussé decoration occurs on caudle-cups,
on vases, on flagons and tankards, sometimes covering

most of the surface of the piece, sometimes confined to limited areas.

Another favorite method of enrichment during the seventeenth century was *flat-chasing*, which Jackson has defined as a type of "surface decoration composed of flat lines incised, or rather depressed, with a mallet and chisel without a cutting edge; and differing from engraving in that the latter is executed with a sharp-edged graver which, in being used, actually cuts away a part of the metal worked upon." Flat-chasing was continued in late Stuart times and was often employed to depict stiff flower-sprays, set off in compartments, a simple and formal arrangement suggestive of Dutch gardens.

With flat-chased designs there was frequently combined a *matting* or *granulation* of the ground wrought by the repeated stamping of a small cup-shaped tool. This granulated ground was a favorite mode of decoration in Germany and the Scandinavian countries and to a lesser degree in Holland, and was considerably used in English silver from the sixteenth century on. We found it occurring in bands around the bowl and on the stem and foot of the London standing-cup of 1639 (Plate I), which was presented to the First Church of Boston. It was continued to some extent in the late Stuart period but was too simple and quiet a mode of ornamentation to commend itself highly to the spirit of the Restoration.

Often featured in late Stuart plate is a simple but effective type of decoration known as *cut-card work*. By cutting out of a plain sheet of silver the desired ornament, as one might cut it out of cardboard, and applying the cut-out to the object to be ornamented, the silversmith had achieved a satisfying result. Lids of tankards, the point of attachment of handles, spouts, and the like were often so decorated.

In the last quarter of the seventeenth century, and more particularly during the last decade of it, there came into favor the use of *flutings*, often alternately concave and convex, with matted scallops and other simple devices surmounting the flutes. This was especially attractive around the bases of cups, tankards, ewers, and other more or less bowl-shaped pieces.

Cast ornaments, such as fruit and flower-shaped finials, caryatid handles, thumb-pieces and feet in the form of lions, show evidence of great sculptural skill on the part of the silversmith. The details themselves make charming designs.

At this period, when the ornamentation tended to be bold and plastic in character, comparatively little resort was made to more delicate methods of decoration, such as *engraving*. The latter is reserved almost entirely for coats of arms and other marks of ownership but is excellently done.

Other modes of decoration also occur on English plate of this period but do not claim our attention here, as they do not often reappear on American silver.

IV. MASSACHUSETTS SILVER INSPIRED BY RESTORATION AND WILLIAM III STYLES

(ABOUT 1660–1710)

During the Commonwealth period, English styles were exceedingly conservative and plain, so that there

[35]

was little contrast between England and Colonial plate. With the Restoration, English silver was made in great quantity and in a great variety of forms, including most elaborate articles, and was usually richly decorated. By this time, too, Colonial silver was made in quantity, and there are left to-day pieces of sufficient number and variety to make comparison possible. Much of this Colonial silver was used as communion plate and owes its preservation, as did that of the earlier epoch, to its presentation to the churches, but a good deal is wholly domestic.

By this time the colony of Massachusetts Bay was thoroughly established. Its merchants were engaged in a profitable trade with the other colonies, England, and the West Indies, and were well able to afford silver. Moreover, they were glad to encourage local craftsmen. It was customary for those who had a surplus supply of coin to take it in a bag to the silversmith, and the latter, as his bills prove, charged only for the fashioning and the engraving.

London naturally was the arbiter of styles and what she decreed was deemed the height of fashion. Buying in London then was considered even more an evidence of luxury than is buying in London, Paris or New York to-day. In its turn, Boston was the chief town of New England, and so those who could not afford to secure London goods, or who preferred to patronize American craftsmen, elected to buy in the Colonial metropolis. Much silver made in Boston, or in other thriving towns, is on this account to be found in outlying districts.

Communication between England and America was

slow and difficult, consequently a style usually flourished in London some time before it was adopted in the colonies, and was more quickly superseded there by a new fashion. The Colonial silversmith, with his more limited custom and more conservative patrons, tended to cling tenaciously to the old until the new had become thoroughly established. This situation was even more pronounced in the smaller towns and country districts than it was in the more progressive centers, such as Boston.

The conditions which caused this slower progression of styles in the colonies also account for their simpler and more rugged character. In London a luxury-loving court, a large and established aristocracy, and a well-organized craft gild combined to foster extensive production and a consequent desire for rapid changes of fashion. The more original silversmiths competed among themselves to devise novel and arresting designs. In the colonies, on the other hand, the rigorous conditions of living, especially in the early days, militated against sharp class-distinctions, set a limit upon luxuries and leisure, and made elaborate furnishings seem out of keeping against the austere background. Consequently, Colonial silver follows chiefly the simpler and more vigorous English fashions, seldom becomes extravagant in form or in detail, serves utilitarian rather than purely ornamental ends. With the plainer English silver the Colonial compares very favorably, evidencing as fine a sense of proportion and as much technical skill. It is hardly fair to compare early American silver with more elaborate English work. The Colonial silversmiths were capable, sensitive, and some-

times prolific craftsmen; the demands of their patrons
and the extent of their patronage did not tend to
develop versatility and imagination to the degree that
was displayed by some of the greatest English craftsmen, but on the other hand the Colonial silversmiths
did not produce the riotous combinations of meaningless ornament of which the English were sometimes
guilty.

Of the English styles that flowered under Charles
II there appear subdued but definite reflections in Boston silver. In a community so strongly Puritan in
sentiment as Massachusetts Bay, extravagance and
ostentation were not merely considered in bad taste
but held to be sinful, and consequently one does not
expect to find anything comparable to the silver furniture or great ornamental vases that were made in
England. On the other hand, there were in the colony
a sufficient number of prosperous and worldly people
who affected silver, or who appreciated its charm, to
give the local silversmiths an extensive and varied
patronage. The silver made in Boston at this period,
that is, from about 1660 to 1710, is extremely interesting because the designs were ambitious and force-
ful, but were not strained by a too great desire for
novelty and elaboration.

As evidence of the increasing amenities of Colonial
life at this time there appears a wide variety of objects
in native silverwork. In addition to the standing cups,
beakers, and spoons of the preceding epoch, there are
now fashioned tankards, caudle-cups, mugs, standing
and trencher-salts, candlesticks, porringers, plates,
tazze, boxes for sweetmeats, etc. These pieces are richer

Massachusetts Silver

in their contrasts of surface and in the resulting play
of light and shade than the severely plain forms developed under Queen Anne, and less mannered than
the rococo. The simple embossed patterns, fluting, and
finely executed cast ornaments represent the highest
and boldest development of the silversmith's craft.
Under such puissant men as Hull and Sanderson,
Dummer, Coney, Dwight, Allen, Edwards, and Winslow—to mention the more prolific and versatile—
Colonial silver reached perhaps its highest development.

Symbolic of hospitality and imposing in its form,
the standing salt may well merit first notice. Its outlines are commandingly presented by three examples
by Edward Winslow (1669–1753) (Plate V), Allen
and Edwards, and Jeremiah Dummer, from the collections of Messrs. Spalding, Hayward, and Tyler
respectively. Of the three, that by Allen and Edwards has the somewhat compressed feeling which
seems to mark silver made by these two men, whereas
the salt by Winslow is rather more delicate in scale.
This spool or reel-shaped salt finds its prototype in
English plate of its period. The four scrolled projections on the top are designed to support a napkin over
the salt-well. The borders of gadrooning are one of
the most characteristic features in the decoration of
silver at this time; presumably they were at the height
of their popularity in New England about 1700.

In addition to these great salts we also find occasional examples of trencher-salts made at the end of
the seventeenth or beginning of the eighteenth century.
The Museum of Fine Arts in Boston owns one of these

[39]

early circular salts decorated with a border of gad-rooning, the work of John Coney (1655–1722). The form of this rare piece is similar to that of a number made by New York silversmiths, such as Ten Eyck (Plate LX) and Van der Spiegel. Though small, these are extremely pleasing bits of silverwork.

The caudle-cups in which hot spiced drinks were served seem to have been almost as popular in Massachusetts Bay as they were in England, for a large number have survived. Many were used as communion cups in the Nonconformist churches. Their fearlessly rounded sides imply vigor and skill in the hands that raised them from a flat sheet of silver. Many were left plain. Dummer made a large number of this sort, including four given to the First Church of Christ in Farmington, Connecticut; another by David Jesse (1670–1705) is in the same church. Possibly the simpler silver made a special appeal to people living in the more rural communities.

The bowls of other caudle-cups were decorated. Some, following English models of the late Commonwealth and early Restoration periods, were divided into panels or compartments, in each of which was set a formal flower, usually executed by flat-chasing. A cup by Hull and Sanderson in the collection of Philip Leffingwell Spalding is decorated in this manner with tulips (Plate IV A). This decoration was superseded by a freer style, which consisted of embossing the bowl of the caudle-cup with a naturalistic rendering of flowers and leaves (Plate IV B) or with a running frieze of animals amidst foliage.

Toward the end of the period we are considering,

See page 44

PLATE VII

TANKARD MADE BY JEREMIAH DUMMER
WITH CUT-CARD DECORATION

borders of fluting were coming into use and occasionally appear as a surbase for two-handled cups. Plate VI (right) shows a small two-handled cup, the lower portion of which is girdled by a band of flutes, alternately concave and convex. Its proportions are the same as those of the bowl of the standing cup shown next to it, and the assumption is that the silversmith, Dummer, made several of these little bowls and then, by the addition of a stem and foot or of two handles, transformed them into standing cups or into caudle-cups. This particular caudle-cup bears the initials—I ^{F} L—of John and Lydia (Fletcher) Fisk, who were married in 1666. It now belongs to the First Congregational Society of Chelmsford, Massachusetts.

Standing cups, when well proportioned, are among the most delightful shapes wrought by the silversmiths. A number made toward the end of this period are peculiarly satisfying, because the most popular style of ornament at this time, a border of fluting, gracefully emphasizes the outlines of the cup and its foot. They form an interesting contrast to the plain, slender cups described earlier, which owed their appeal entirely to grace of line. The later styles are usually of more ample outlines and derive much of their interest from the variety of their plain and embossed surfaces. John Edwards (1671–1746) made one such cup, which was later presented to the Christ Church Parish in South Carolina. Jeremiah Dummer (1645–1718) made a great number in this style, as he seems to have had a particular fondness for broad and capacious forms, and for ornament that emphasized full curves.

The frontispiece represents one of these cups made by Dummer. It is one of a pair, both engraved with the Stoughton arms, and inscribed: "Ex dono Hon^bls Guliel: Stoughton Armig^ris Anno 1701." A more recent inscription reads "The Gift of Gov. William Stoughton to the Church in Dorchester 1701." They were the result of a legacy of £12 left to the First Church of Dorchester by Stoughton, who died in 1701. He left to the First Parish Congregational Church at Milton, Massachusetts, in which town he had owned four hundred acres of land, a similar legacy of £6, with which a similar cup by Dummer was purchased. According to E. Alfred Jones, William Stoughton graduated from Harvard College in 1650, was incorporated as a member of New College, Oxford, in 1652, ejected (*rege reduce*) in 1660, after which he returned to New England, where he served as lieutenant-governor of Massachusetts.

Another cup (Plate VI) also illustrates Dummer's broad modeling and a pleasant contrast of plain and fluted surfaces. It bears the inscription: "The Gift of James Everill to the first Church in Boston 1705." E. Alfred Jones tells us that Everill was a shoemaker of Boston who, with his wife, joined the First Church in 1634. By the terms of his will, dated December 1682, and proved in February 1683, he bequeathed £5 for the use of the church, with which fund this standing cup was presumably procured. As many similar bequests evidence, this was a common custom in New England in Colonial times.

Of the beakers made at this period, some are relatively low and broad, without any reinforcing molding at the base, continuing the general shape that had been in favor earlier. Typical examples measure about 3⅞" in height and about 3⅝" in diameter at the lip. Of this style is one by Edward Winslow (1669–1753) (Plate II, right; height 3⅞"), which now belongs to the Congregational Church in West Barnstable, Massachusetts. It is inscribed: "The Gift of Mary Haughton to B.C." (Barnstable Church), and was made to carry out the following provision in her will, proved April 1693: "I give and bequeath unto ye Church of Christ in Barnstable five pounds to be converted in to a piece of plate for ye use of ye Church."

Other beakers of much the same general proportions are distinguished by having a molding at the base. The majority are plain. Toward the end of the seventeenth century beakers tend to become rather more slender and often considerably taller. Though they vary greatly in height and width, as a group they are usually readily distinguishable from the earlier style. They mark a transition to the new styles of the eighteenth century.

Another innovation that appears late in this period is the beaker with sides curving slightly inward just above the base, which is usually in the form of a ring foot. This style in the eighteenth century became exaggerated into the so-called bell-shaped beaker.

The communion services of many of the old New England churches include not only these standing cups, caudle-cups, and beakers just described, but also a considerable number of tankards which, though in most instances designed originally for domestic use, seem to have proved quite satisfactory for communion cups. They follow the style of English tankards of this period, the most distinguishing feature of which is their flat lids. The majority of seventeenth-century Boston tankards are relatively small, averaging perhaps 5½" to 6¼" in height. The very low lid, the narrow base moldings, the long tongue reinforcing the junction of handle and body, the double-cupped thumb-piece, which are characteristic of the earliest examples, all appear in the tankard by Dummer illustrated in Plate LIII A and described fully on page 298.

Another early tankard, also by Jeremiah Dummer (1645–1718), now the property of Philip L. Spalding, is illustrated in Plate VII (height 6¼"). It, too, is a typical example of the period, as shown by its flat lid with split-scroll thumb-piece, by the long tongue at the upper junction of the handle and body, by the simple base moldings. The hinge of the cover is not given any decorative treatment. Two thirds of the way down the handle is a tube or loop applied presumably to facilitate holding the tankard. This loop is more frequently found in conjunction with a vertical grooving of the handle, as illustrated in Plate LIII. Mr. Spalding's tankard is particularly interesting because it is decorated on the cover near the thumb-piece, and on the body at the lower attachment of the handle, with applied cut-card ornaments. This type of decoration occurs fairly often in Massachusetts silver of the late seventeenth and the early eighteenth century, following English plate of about 1660–90.

The body of the early Boston tankards was customarily left plain but in exceptional instances it received enrichment. A most unusual, perhaps unique, tankard by Timothy Dwight (1654–91) has an embossed frieze of acanthus leaves above its molded base (height 6″). Embossed borders of acanthus and palm leaves occur quite frequently in English plate from about 1670 to 1695, but are rare indeed in American silver. The Dwight tankard belonged at one time to William and Elizabeth (Edwards) Cheever (married in 1749) and eventually passed to one of their descendants, a member of the Shattuck family.

Fluting, which occasionally appears round the lower part of the body of English tankards, was apparently not so used in New England, but does occur on the lids of some Boston tankards, where it was employed to emphasize the rise. Examples occur in the work of Jeremiah Dummer (1645–1718), Henry Hurst (1665–1717), and John Coney (1655–1722), which probably date from the late seventeenth or the early eighteenth century. They are more or less transitional between the period we are discussing and the one that follows.

In tankards the thumb-piece, intended for the practical purpose of raising the lid, was always made a decorative feature. Often English models were copied, as in the double-cupped (Plate LIII, left), and various scroll designs. Also reminiscent of English design, and comparable also to the Scandinavian, is the finely modeled lion thumb-piece found on the Timothy Dwight tankard mentioned above. More peculiarly American is the eagle thumb-piece found on a tankard by Coney, belonging to Mrs. W. Wanton Dunnell, and the sun-and-dolphin thumb-piece (Plate LIII, right) which is more fully discussed on page 301 and occurs in the work of a number of New England silversmiths of the late seventeenth and the early eighteenth century.

The tip of the handle also afforded the silversmith an opportunity to exercise his fancy. The simpler methods of terminating the handle, seen in early examples, are illustrated in Plates VII and LIII. Often shield-shaped ornaments occur.

Unquestionably most of these tankards were designed originally to serve as cups for beer, as the secular character of their decoration would imply. Mr. Jones reports about twenty that may safely be dated before 1730 which were given to the old Colonial churches, a considerable number to testify to the early acceptance of tankards as communion cups.

Although at this period in England a number of flagons were made, they did not commend themselves to use in the Puritan churches of New England, presumably because they savored too much of the Established Church. By the early eighteenth century this prejudice wore off and flagons made by Colonial silversmiths appear.

We do not need the evidence of contemporary inventories to prove the popularity of the porringer in New England households, for quantities of examples have come down to us to-day. They must have been considered quite indispensable for serving children's food, broth, or cereals. They were often presented to a bridal pair and were usually marked with the initials of the two owners' first names and the surname, as for

example T ^{B} M for Thomas and Mary Barton.

Though most of the English bowls of this form are described as barber-surgeons' bowls, it seems incredible that others should not have served for domestic purposes in England, as they were so extensively used in the latter manner in New England. Perhaps the English bowls of this sort that were used for food, as they were of simple form and not decorated, were discarded when they became battered or misshapen and so have long since disappeared and become forgotten. In New England they must have been more highly treasured, perhaps for their sentimental associations, perhaps because the New England menu made them particularly serviceable. Some of these early Colonial porringers are small, suggesting a close relationship to their English forebears, but the majority average about five inches across the bowl. The pierced designs of their handles are simple, such as the crudest tools might execute, but are pleasing because their very simplicity accords with the plainness of the bowl and with the practical purpose for which the whole was designed. The piercing was done to prevent the handle from becoming too hot if the contents of the bowl were heated.

It is a matter for profound regret that more early American silver candlesticks do not now exist, for those which have been preserved are among the most sumptuous pieces of plate wrought by the early Colonial craftsmen. An especially imposing stick, measuring 10¾″ in height, is illustrated in Plate LXI. It now belongs to William A. Jeffries and is one of a pair. It consists of a square shaft simulating a cluster of columns, with wide nozzle and drip-pan, and a square base, a form that is a direct reflection of English styles of the Charles II period.

Such columnar candlesticks gradually gave place to those of baluster form, which were fully established in the eighteenth century. A stick that belongs to the interval of transition between the two types is that by Coney in Plate IX, left. Its wide base and flange and its gadrooned borders suggest English styles of the late seventeenth century. Its shaft is a baluster that shows interesting similarity to the stems of the two English cups shown in Plate I. The other candlestick in Plate IX is a fully developed baluster form, and though by the same silversmith as that just described, it belongs stylistically to the period of the eighteenth century.

As charming as they are rare are the plates and tazze made at this period. Many of the latter, made in the late seventeenth and the early eighteenth century, like that by Allen and Edwards illustrated in the center of Plate XLVII, are bordered by gadrooning. Extremely interesting is the plate by Coney shown in Plate III. The margin of this plate is engraved in a free but careful manner with sprays of carnations, sunflowers, and tulips, with three cherub heads. Crossed feather-sprays, very like the feather mantling found in representations of coats of arms of the same general period, enclose the initials C E R, presumably those of the original owners. These floral designs are suggestively like those found in Indian printed cottons, sufficiently similar to suggest that the latter may quite indirectly have afforded inspiration to silversmiths.

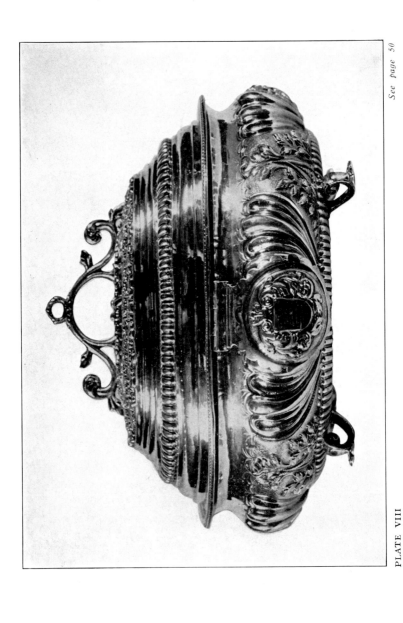

PLATE VIII

SWEETMEAT-BOX MADE BY EDWARD WINSLOW

See page 50

Massachusetts Silver

A tazza bearing the mark of Timothy Dwight
(1654–91) has a wide margin similar to this plate by
Coney and is also similarly engraved with a running
border design. In addition to the flowers mentioned
above, the tazza decoration includes a lion, a unicorn,
an elephant, and a stag. This engraved design encloses block initials, but underneath these may be
faintly seen other pricked initials. It seems probable
that Dwight, who made the tazza, originally left it
undecorated except for these pricked initials, and that
later, when the tazza passed into the hands of new
owners, Thomas and Mary Barton, married in 1710,
they had their own initials cut to obscure those of their
predecessors and had the engraved design added. If
this is the case, the engraving was probably not done
by Dwight. In general character the design is much
like that on the Coney plate but differs in the manner
in which the detail is rendered and the precision with
which it is engraved.

An object which suggests that life in New England
was not all frugality and asceticism is the silver box
made to hold comfits or sweetmeats. These boxes are
now extremely rare, and being among the more ambitiously designed pieces of early Colonial silver are
highly esteemed. One which may properly be assigned
to the period we are discussing is the work of John
Coney (1655–1722) and belongs to the Museum of
Fine Arts in Boston, to which it was presented by Mrs.
J. B. Churchill. It is inscribed: "Grandmother Norton
to Anna Quincy." Its general form and decorative
features are quite similar to a London piece of 1676,
illustrated by Jackson in his "History of English

[49]

Plate" and at that time in the collection of Lord Llangattock. Another box by Coney belongs to Charles H. Tyler.

Of three sweetmeat-boxes by Edward Winslow (1669–1753), one belongs to Philip L. Spalding, another to Miss S. H. Pickering (Plate VIII), and the third is illustrated by Jackson and was formerly in his collection. It is inscribed: "Ex dono Sarah Middlecott N. England 10 Mch. 1702," and was given by Sarah Middlecott to her son Edward, then resident in England. The example illustrated in Plate VIII suggests the general design of all three of these Winslow boxes. Its bowl is divided into four sections of erect acanthus leaves and groups of spiral flutes, alternately concave and convex. Its high domed cover has borders of gadrooning and acanthus ornament and a wire handle in the form of a coiled serpent.

Another unusual piece of New England silver fashioned about this time is the gracious little inkstand made by John Coney (Plate L) with extremely well-modeled lion feet. Interesting to compare with these is the lion thumb-piece on the tankard by Timothy Dwight already mentioned.

Spoons of this period were generally made with flat stems, which widen out at the tip into trifid or wavy ends. The bowls usually have a grooved tongue or rat-tail, often bordered by scroll ornaments (Plate LXIII, upper left).

Summarizing briefly the forms of decoration most favored in the seventeenth century and the beginning of the eighteenth century in New England, we find that they followed the fashions of the late Stuart and

Massachusetts Silver

William and Mary periods in English silver. The embossed designs, which are the most characteristic kind of decoration in late Stuart plate, occur most frequently in Colonial silver on caudle-cups, where freely drawn designs of flowers or of animals and foliage appear (Plates IV and LII). Borders of acanthus leaves were favored in English plate from about 1670 to 1695. They appear very rarely in American silver; one example has been noted in the tankard by Timothy Dwight and another, a beaker, is illustrated in Plate L. That they occur so infrequently is possibly due to the fact that Colonial silversmiths were just getting into their stride and attempting real enrichment of their silver, or perhaps popular taste was only beginning to demand more ornate treatments, by the time these acanthus borders were slipping out of fashion, to be succeeded by the borders of fluting that were adopted with such enthusiasm in Massachusetts.

Bands of fluting afforded a means of breaking a broad expanse of plain surface and yet were essentially simple. They must have come into fashion in New England about the end of the seventeenth century and continued in favor for some time in the eighteenth. Jeremiah Dummer, if we can judge by extant pieces, followed this treatment more than did any other American silversmith. It was suitable for the bowls of standing cups, caudle and other two-handled cups, for the lids of tankards, the shafts of candlesticks, and the bases of many objects. One reason for its appeal is that it is a mode of decoration eminently proper to silver and one that emphasizes its charm.

Another simple mode of decoration current in England from about 1660 to 1690 was cut-card work. This too was frequently used by the New England silversmiths, especially to ornament the point of attachment of a tankard handle or thumb-piece, as illustrated in the example by Dummer shown in Plate VII.

In the designs that they modeled and cast to serve as thumb-pieces or to ornament the tips of tankard handles, the Colonial silversmiths of the late seventeenth and the early eighteenth century exhibited their skill in the field bordering on sculpture and came off with much credit. As in English plate, the lion was favored; witness the feet on the Coney inkstand (Plate L), which probably dates from the early eighteenth century, or the lion thumb-piece on the tankard by Timothy Dwight (1654–91) already described. Probably during the period under discussion the eagle and the sun-and-dolphin thumb-pieces (Figures 2 and 4) were coming into vogue.

The decoration of English and also of Massachusetts silver at this period was chiefly of a bold character, which could be seen at some distance, and lighter treatments, such as those accomplished usually by engraving, occur but rarely. Engraving, however, was employed in the form of coats of arms and is executed with skill and taste. Its primary purpose, in this case, is not decoration but the indication of ownership.

As a number of important silversmiths have been mentioned and numerous examples of their work have been illustrated, it may be well to pause here long enough to give these men more recognition. They were pioneers, and their achievements, which are distinguished in any case, seem especially notable when we realize that they were accomplished under many adverse conditions and probably with relatively meager tools and equipment.

Of John Mansfield, who came to Boston in 1634, we have scant record and know of no example of his handiwork. Of John Hull (1624–83) a great deal is known, owing to the facts that he kept a most informing diary which has been preserved[1] and that he figured largely in public affairs as wealthy merchant, mint-master, and holder of various other public offices. He left a large estate. His statement that "I fell to learning (by the help of my brother), and to practising the trade of a goldsmith" suggests that he learned his trade from his half-brother Richard Storer, who had begun his apprenticeship in London in 1629.

Hull's partner, Robert Sanderson (1608–93), was less in the public eye, but may have been the quiet practical craftsman of the firm. Sanderson had come to New England in 1638 from London, where he had previously practised silversmithing, and reached Boston by way of Watertown. Together Hull and Sanderson produced the bulk of the earliest Boston silver, much of which is still in existence. Because it was wrought chiefly during the third quarter of the seventeenth century, it was made under strong Puritan influences and is correspondingly plain. Though Hull did not die until 1683, at which time Sanderson was already seventy-five years of age, they did not do much if any work in the spirit of the Restoration. So far as we know it, their work consisted chiefly of

[1] Published by the Massachusetts Historical Society.

beakers, standing cups, caudle-cups, an occasional tankard or spoon—the objects for which there was apparently earliest demand. Considering the limitations under which these men labored, their work implies great dexterity and a fine sense of craftsmanship.

Next in date is Jeremiah Dummer (1645–1718), an able and vigorous personality, as is evidenced by his silver. Much of his knowledge he may have gained from Hull, from whom he learned his trade. Hull's diary under date of 1659 states: "I received into my house Jeremie Dummer and Samuel Paddy, to serve me as apprentices eight years. The Lord make me faithful in discharge of this new trust commited to me, and let his blessing be to me and them!" Dummer printed and probably also engraved the plates for the first paper money of Connecticut, 1709–13, showing his skill with engraving tools. We have already dwelt at some length upon his penchant for making stout forms in silver, especially standing cups, caudle-cups, and beakers, and upon his choice of fluting as a favorite mode of decoration. Dummer was an important man in his community, belonged to the First Church and to the Ancient and Honourable Artillery Company, was selectman, county treasurer, justice of the peace, judge of one of the inferior courts, and a member of the Council of Safety. His son William Dummer became lieutenant-governor of Massachusetts.

The next outstanding personality among Boston silversmiths at this period is John Coney (1655–1722). Apparently Coney had come as a child from Boston in England to Boston in Massachusetts, where he may have learned his trade from his brother-in-law, Jere-

miah Dummer. He enjoyed the distinction of having
engraved the plates for the first paper money made in
the colonies, that issued by Massachusetts Bay in
1690. (He passed on the knowledge of his craft to
another notable silversmith, Apollos Rivoire, a Huguenot refugee who anglicized his name to Paul Revere
and became father of the more famous son of the same
name). On his death, the Coney estate amounted to
£4,000. An entertaining way of gaging his skill, pro-
ductivity, and versatility is to stand in front of a case
of his silver exhibited at the Museum of Fine Arts in
Boston. From these and other examples scattered
through numerous public and private collections, we
find that Coney made a wide variety of pieces, including beakers, tankards, caudle-cups, candlesticks,
spoons, forks, mugs, casters, tea-pots, chocolate-pots,
braziers, salts, porringers, boxes for sweetmeats, tazze.
These do not all date prior to 1710, the date we have
selected as the approximate end of this period, but as
Coney died in 1722, his work is all necessarily quite
early. The list indicates what a number of domestic
pieces Coney turned out. Perhaps he catered to people who wished silver chiefly for their homes, and this
may account for the fact that his silver tends toward
lighter effects than does that of Dummer. He was
an able modeler, as the lion feet of the inkstand
(Plate L) and the eagle thumb-piece on his tankard,
now owned by Mrs. W. Wanton Dunnell, demonstrate. He also accomplished clever engraving, as in
the plate in Mr. Pickman's collection (Plate III).

Among the abler New England silversmiths of
the seventeenth century should be mentioned Timothy

Dwight (1654–91), who in his short life developed marked skill. Hull, in his diary, speaks of Timothy Dwight and Daniel Quincy as living with him, and it is possible that they served an apprenticeship to him. Dwight was the maker of the tankard with the acanthus surbase and well-modeled lion thumb-piece already mentioned, now the property of a member of the Shattuck family. He also made the tazza described on page 49.

Another silversmith who came into prominence during this period, though much of his work falls in the succeeding period, is Edward Winslow (1669–1753). He is one of the greatest of early Boston silversmiths. From the superior quality of his work it has been presumed that he served part of his apprenticeship abroad. On his paternal side he was grandson of John Winslow and Mary Chilton, and on the maternal side he was great-grandson of Mistress Anne Hutchinson, that indomitable lady who so seriously disturbed the equanimity of the Puritan Fathers. That her descendant Edward inherited her energy is demonstrated by the list of public offices which he held. He served as constable of Boston, 1699; tithing-man, 1703; surveyor, 1705; overseer of the poor, 1711, 1712; selectman, 1714, declining reëlection in 1715. He was captain of militia; major of the Boston regiment, 1729, and colonel, 1733; second sergeant of the Artillery Company, 1702, lieutenant, 1711, captain, 1714 and 1729; sheriff of Suffolk County, 1728–1743; judge of the Inferior Court of Common Pleas from 1743 until his death. Two of his sons were lost in 1745 in the ill-fated Louisburg Expedition. Of Winslow's silver

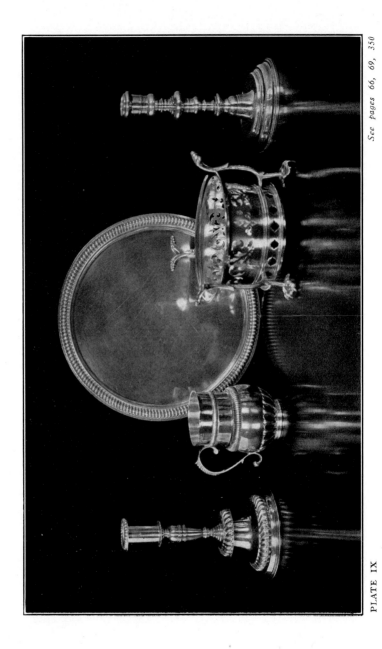

PLATE IX

SILVER MADE BY JOHN CONEY

See pages 66, 69, 350

we shall have occasion to speak more in detail later as one example after another is illustrated.

Though we find work by John Allen (1671–1760) and John Edwards (1671–1746) done independently, more often we find work they did in partnership. Plate XLVII shows a number of fine examples, of which the central piece, a tazza, is a splendid production of this period. They also made a number of handsome standing cups, which demonstrate the small size but rather simple sturdiness that characterize their handiwork. Mr. Hayward of Philadelphia owns a standing salt by Allen and Edwards that in comparison with those by Winslow and Dummer bears out this characterization.

David Jesse (1670–1705), though born in Hartford, Connecticut, lived in Boston and became a distinguished silversmith. Of his work we have already mentioned a beaker with strapwork decoration.

V. ENGLISH SILVER OF THE HIGH-STANDARD PERIOD
(1697–1720)

Changes in fashion usually spring from a complexity of causes. Doubtless after the ostentatious and exuberant ornamentation of Restoration plate, a desire for a greater restraint was natural. The return of Charles II in 1660 had ushered in a period of gaiety and riotousness after the long era of Civil War and Puritan repression. The coming of William and Mary in 1689 and the reign of Anne (1702–14) found England relatively settled and tranquil. These conditions

[57]

may well be reflected in the arts of the different periods.

But a situation also existed that directly affected silver, and which made the increasing simplicity in this field even more pronounced than in that of furniture, for example. This arose from the widespread use of silver for wrought plate and the resultant scarcity of it for the coinage of the realm. The situation became so acute that at length the Government took action, and in 1697 a law was passed requiring that wrought plate made thereafter should be of a higher standard than that employed in the mint, that it should contain 11 oz. 10 dwt. of pure silver in every 12 oz. or a pound Troy, and be hall-marked with the figure of Britannia—from the latter fact it derived the name of the Britannia standard. The sterling or coinage standard was 11 oz. 2 dwt.

The silversmiths promptly reacted to the new regulation, for the greater fineness meant greater softness in the metal, and the highly embossed plate they had been producing in thin silver would in the new metal soon show marks of wear and so was no longer practicable. They therefore turned their skill to fashioning plate of a more substantial and heavier sort, relying upon the shape and upon the more firmly executed types of decoration to give it distinction. Under Queen Anne even greater simplicity was developed, many objects appearing with little or no ornamentation.

So far as shapes are concerned, there is a gradual transition during the reign of William and Mary from those of late Stuart type to the plainer and definitely

new shapes under Queen Anne. With the early eighteenth century we see the use of many baluster forms,
appearing as candlesticks, casters, the stems of standing
cups, and the like, and of allied bulbous shapes forming the bodies of mugs, spout-cups, tea-pots, cream-
jugs, and so on. Some are full and squat, like the tea-
pot of pear shape. Other forms reflect the popularity
of Oriental porcelain and the adoption of Chinese
shapes in European art. For example, the little
globular tea-pots begin to appear, though their greatest vogue comes later. The tankard and the flagon
gain in slenderness and height during this period, the
former adding to its distinction by the doming of its
lid.

Octagonal shapes enjoyed a great vogue in the first
quarter of the eighteenth century; their various surfaces offered an opportunity for the play of light and
shade and thus served in lieu of decoration. The fashion did not long survive the reign of George I.

As with the shapes, so with the ornamentation there
was a gradual transition. Prior to the extreme plainness seen in silver of the reign of Queen Anne, there
was an interval when the silversmiths were adjusting
themselves to the high standard for plate. Instead of
making plate of very thin sheets and embossing it with
elaborate designs, which in the soft metal would very
soon show signs of wear, they chose the more deeply
impressed types of decoration that could be effected
in heavier metal and which would not be so readily
marred. There had come into vogue at the end of the
preceding period, and still remained much in favor,
the bands of *spiral gadrooning* or of *fluting*, alternately

concave and convex. When the latter was used, the boldness of the top line of fluting was softened by a mat border and by simple punched devices.

Allied to these embossed flutes but developed a little later and even more in harmony with the plain styles of the new period was the use of *flat flutes*, which were hammered into the surface of the piece. The effect was rather hard and brilliant and the variety of the surface lent interest. The rows of flutes were usually rounded at the ends and bordered by matting and a scalloped border with simple punched dots or flowers.

From the plain cut-card work of the preceding period is evolved the new *pierced cut-card work*, which under the new standard afforded a satisfactory and durable mode of decoration. The designs were cut, as before, out of a sheet of flat silver, but before they were applied to the object they were pierced.

Where the posset-cups of Queen Anne's time were girdled by spiral fluting, those of her successor's reign were further decorated by a *cartouche* that interrupted the band of flutes and served as an enclosure for initials or a coat of arms.

Under the new standard for silver, the use of objects such as caudle-cups or beakers without any reinforcement at the base was presumably discontinued, as in the soft metal they would straightway have become battered. Reinforcing moldings enjoyed an extensive use because of their practicability.

Though usually very simple in design, the pierced borders of kettle-stands, braziers, etc., and the tops of casters are quite charming, and would in themselves offer an interesting study in design.

Massachusetts Silver

At the period under discussion cast ornaments were often splendidly executed, with much of the sculptor's skill. Lions served to uphold tankards or crouched upon the lid to serve as thumb-pieces. Excellently modeled figures were used as handles on ewers and other display pieces.

As at the end of the preceding period, it may be noted that on plate of this period engraving rarely appears as decoration *per se*, but in the guise of badges of ownership, in beautifully executed coats of arms with their decorative enframements, it is widely current. There is an exquisitely rendered detail and a flow and sweep of line in these that proclaim the skill of their engravers.

VI. MASSACHUSETTS SILVER INSPIRED BY ENGLISH STYLES OF THE HIGH-STANDARD PERIOD

(ABOUT 1700–35)

Although there were no regulations in Ireland and Scotland to raise the standard of plate made there to correspond with the Britannia standard in England, yet their silversmiths quickly responded to the changes in fashion. So, too, in the American colonies there was no requirement for a change in the quality of metal used, but there was a reflection of the current styles of England.

Fashions do not switch on and off with the immediacy of an electric light. The old merges imperceptibly into the new even in a community where there is great stress laid upon style. In English plate, all pieces made in the large towns were hall-marked with a date-letter, by means of which the exact year of production can be determined. Even here we find occasional instances of the use of a style much later than the time of its real vogue. In provincial communities fashions were followed for a much longer interval, and in the absence of a date-letter or other record of the date of production, the assigning of a piece to a particular period is often quite arbitrary. For example, in the styles of the William and Mary period previously described, and also in the High Standard period now under discussion, there were generally used such types of ornament as the borders of fluting. The earlier were usually simple and straight; the later were spiral and usually accompanied by a band of laureling above. But many examples are neither definitely early nor definitely late, and we are forced, therefore, to make a somewhat arbitrary division.

In New England silver the period of the late seventeenth and the early eighteenth century marks a gradual transition from the rather ambitious designs based upon English plate of the Restoration and William III periods to the very plain styles characteristic of the reign of Queen Anne. In the early eighteenth century some of the shapes previously wrought continue, generally with certain modifications and with more height and slenderness. There also appear shapes that are quite new.

Beakers continue more or less as before, of varying height and diameter, the majority being straight-sided and plain, with a molding at the base. A number are bell-shaped, and some of these have a border of fluting at the base, occasionally accompanied by a fillet of laureling above. A beaker of this sort is illustrated in Plate VI, made by Jeremiah Dummer (1645–1718). Its base is enriched by a border of straight flutes, alternately concave and convex. The inscription upon it reads: "The gifft of E B" (Edward Boylston, who died in 1729). It formerly belonged to the Brattle Street Church and is now the property of the Museum of Fine Arts, Boston. Typically, beakers are without handles, but many were either made with or subsequently provided with one or two handles, doubtless because they were thus more convenient for use as communion cups.

Of plain bell-shaped beakers fitted with two handles, that made by John Dixwell (1680–1725), now the property of Philip Leffingwell Spalding, is not only a characteristic example but also one peculiarly rich in associations (Plate XI B). It is inscribed: "The gift of Sarah Knight to the Chh of Christ in Norwich, Apr 20, 1722." Sarah Kemble (1666–1727), daughter of a Charlestown and Boston merchant, married Richard Knight. A woman of great spirit and enterprise, she taught school, kept a shop, and conducted a considerable business in real estate. Apparently in connection with the settlement of an estate, she found it necessary to journey from Boston to New York on horseback in the year 1704. Her journal of the trip is one of the most entertaining records of the time. Incidentally, later editors of her journal have mused over the fact that her journey from Boston to New York took a fortnight. One editor in 1858 notes that "at present we are usually

[63]

whirled over the ground in about eight hours," and another, in 1865, further comments: "One may venture to think that the speed of travel will never be carried to a much greater degree than it has now reached." Madame Knight, some years after her famous adventure, moved to Norwich, Connecticut, joining the church to which later she presented the beaker.

The bulbous caudle-cups of the preceding period have now given place to two-handled cups of straighter form set upon a distinct foot. One with characteristic decoration consisting of a surbase of spiral flutes and a fillet of gadrooning below the lip (Plate XI A) was made by William Cowell (1682–1736). It has notched handles and a reeded ring foot. This cup was the gift of Ebenezer Withington to the First Church of Dorchester, Massachusetts, and now belongs to the Neponset Church of the Unity. This style seems to have been particularly favored by Cowell; similar cups belong to the churches in Farmington and Stratford, Connecticut.

Two-handled cups of imposing size are among the handsomest pieces of this period. Harvard University owns one made by John Coney, the gift of Governor William Stoughton. Another splendid example was made by Edward Winslow (Plate XXXVIII) and now belongs to Mrs. Lois B. Rantoul. Excellent use is here made of the bands of fluting and narrow borders of gadrooning, which give to both cup and cover charming variations of surface and play of light.

Probably for the first fifteen years of the eighteenth century the flat-topped tankard continued in undisputed sway. Like those described in the preceding

PLATE X

See pages 67, 72

EARLY NEW ENGLAND PORRINGERS
CHOCOLATE-POT MADE BY JOHN CONEY

period, it was characterized by a flat lid in two stages, a plain tapering body, and simple base moldings. The majority of early-eighteenth-century thumb-pieces are either of sun-and-dolphin design (Figure 2) or of scroll form. Shield, oval, or cherub-head tips terminate the handle.

About 1715 to 1730 a change took place, and the flat-topped tankard yielded place to one of more slen-

FIGURE 1   FIGURE 2   FIGURE 3

FIGURES 1-3. Tankard Thumb-Piece and Handle-Tips

der and tapering form, usually girdled by a molding placed about one third of the way up from the base, with domed cover topped by a finial. A transitional stage is represented by the tankard shown in Plate LIII, right, made by John Dixwell. This has a low domed lid without a finial, and no molding around the body, but compared with its predecessors of the seventeenth century is considerably taller and more tapering. The majority of Massachusetts tankards made after 1725 have a tapering body girdled by a mid-band, a domed lid with turned finial, an erect scroll thumb-piece, an applied molded drop on the handle (Figure 26), and a cast mask ornamenting the end of the handle (Figures 1, 3).

[65]

By this period flagons had ceased to be looked upon with disfavor by the Puritans of Massachusetts, for between 1711 and 1713 five handsome examples were presented to Boston churches, the work of John Noyes, Nathaniel Morse, Peter Oliver, John Edwards, and Edward Winslow. Their general form is illustrated by the one made by Noyes, in Plate LV, with its flat-topped lid, simply turned finial, double-cupped thumb-piece, and convex base. Like the tankard, the flagon gained in height and slenderness as the century advanced; its lid became domed and surmounted by a more elaborate finial and its base became higher.

Mugs that served as lesser tankards remained popular throughout the eighteenth century. Many of those made in the early part of the century are straight-sided and tapering, much like the tankard, though smaller and without a lid. Frequently bands of molding around the body give these early mugs a sturdy look and serve in lieu of other decoration.

At the end of the seventeenth or in the early eighteenth century another shape began its development. Starting with a slight incurve just above the base, these mugs were made with increasingly bulbous sides. Contemporary records frequently describe them as "cans."

Quite a common style of small cup was that with straight sides tapering inward to the base and with a simple strap handle. John Dixwell made a number in this form. More unusual is the cup with borders of gadrooning illustrated in Plate IX, one of a pair made by John Coney. That illustrated belongs to Dudley L. Pickman.

[66]

Massachusetts Silver

Porringers are made in increasing numbers during this period. Some have simple geometric piercings of circles, quatrefoils, and hearts; others are of the type known as "keyhole," so called because of the resemblance of the central opening to a keyhole. This style became by far the most popular in the eighteenth century. Three characteristic types are illustrated in Plate X. That at the left is a keyhole pattern made by John Dixwell (1680–1725), that at the center has geometrical piercings and was made by Jeremiah Dummer (1645–1718), and that at the right has what is termed a crown cresting and bears the mark of William Cowell (1682–1736). Other styles are illustrated by Figures 28 and 29.

The illustrations of earlier Boston silver have shown a relatively large number of standing cups; by the eighteenth century these were no longer in favor for domestic use and were made quite exclusively for communion. The deep, rather straight-sided bowl with outcurving lip, the baluster stem, and the high domed foot that are characteristic of the first half of the eighteenth century, are illustrated by two cups (Plate XLVII) made by John Edwards (1671–1746). That shown at the right is engraved with the Hall arms and was presented, probably by Hugh Hall, to the church in Lynde Street, Boston. The standing cup on the left is inscribed: "The Legacy of Stephen Minott, Esq. to the Church in Brattle Street, 1732." Both now belong to the Museum of Fine Arts.

There are few adjuncts to the table or sideboard that have greater decorative value and charm than candlesticks. One could wish they were not so rare

[67]

in American silver. That by Coney shown at the right of Plate IX is one of a pair belonging to Dudley L. Pickman, and is a delightful example of the early-eighteenth-century baluster style. Another pair of baluster candlesticks was made by John Burt (1691–1745). They are of octagonal outline, or what some of the old records called "eight-square." The Burt candlesticks were given to Nicholas Sever, a tutor at Harvard College, by his students in 1724 and now belong to the university.

Trencher-salts for use at the individual's place at table come increasingly into popularity with the progress of the eighteenth century. The circular salt decorated with borders of gadrooning, such as the one by Coney belonging to the Museum of Fine Arts, dates probably from the end of the seventeenth or the beginning of the eighteenth century. This style is superseded by plainer and usually somewhat smaller salts, of oval, circular, or octagonal plan.

The earliest Colonial casters probably date from the early eighteenth century, and are straight-sided and cylindrical, with flaring or spreading base, and pierced cover secured by what is known as a bayonet fastening. The form is analogous to English casters of the late seventeenth and the early eighteenth century and is represented by an example made by John Coney (1655–1722), now in the Spalding collection (Plate XII, center). A trifle later in general style, although actual examples may have been made contemporaneously, is that of baluster form, of which the pair by Coney, also shown in Plate XII, are early examples. It is rare indeed to find a pair of casters dating from

[68]

Massachusetts Silver

this early period, although originally they were often
made in sets of two or three. Those belonging to Mr.
Spalding formerly belonged to the Gibb family.

Braziers or chafing-dishes, which were made in some
numbers during the eighteenth century, generally consist of a shallow bowl with pierced and removable
bottom plate and a shallow compartment beneath,
which had pierced sides. The brazier was supported
by three scroll feet, and a corresponding number of
scroll brackets above its rim served to hold the tea-pot,
plate, or other object that the brazier was to keep hot.
An early brazier without a handle, one of a pair, is
illustrated in Plate IX, and is now in the collection
of Dudley L. Pickman. The feet are in the form of
claws and originally rested upon wooden balls. Many
braziers are equipped with a straight, turned wooden
handle that must have increased their usefulness.

Tazze, which consist usually of a circular plate with
more or less defined rim and trumpet-shaped foot, were
made in New England in considerable numbers in the
late seventeenth and the early eighteenth century. An
early style was described on page 49, one made by
Timothy Dwight (1654–91) and engraved with a
border of flowers and animals. Slightly later in style
are those tazze with gadrooned borders, such as that
shown in Plate XLVII, made by Allen and Edwards,
and engraved with the Cotton arms. The manner in
which these arms are represented would suggest that
the tazza is an early example of its style. It now belongs to Mrs. Richard H. Morgan. Another of generally similar type was made by John Coney, and like
the little cup shown to the left of it in the illustration

(Plate IX), it once belonged to Mary Willoughby
of Salem, born in 1676. Like the other pieces shown
in this group, this tazza has now descended to Dudley L. Pickman. A not dissimilar tazza with gadrooned border made by Jeremiah Dummer belongs to
Mrs. Ernest W. Bowditch. Mr. Pickman also owns
a tazza made by Jeffrey Lang (1707–58), which is
plain and of somewhat later date than the preceding.
While these examples were in domestic use, others of
similar style were sometimes included among communion plate.

A superb evidence of the refinements and of the hospitality possible in some Colonial households at this
period is the large punch-bowl illustrated in Plate XII.
The general form of its hemispherical bowl, high
domed foot, and scalloped rim, originally removable,
follows closely the outlines of English pieces of the
Queen Anne period. The type is known as a Monteith, after a "fantastical Scot" by this name, who, it
is reputed, wore a cloak with a scalloped border. Here,
as in many another instance, when one stops to admire
a particularly delightful piece of Colonial silver, one
discovers it to be the handiwork of John Coney. As
Coney was an able engraver on copper, it is a fair
supposition that he himself executed the Livingston
arms, with their handsome ornamental framework,
which are engraved upon this punch-bowl (see line
drawing, Figure 23). Above, in one of the scallops
of the rim, is a graceful cipher. This bowl, one of the
largest and handsomest pieces of Colonial plate known,
now belongs to a descendant of its former owners,
Mrs. Henry Parish.

[70]

Massachusetts Silver

From the beginning of the eighteenth century on, there appears an abundance of domestic silver, and not only is it of a useful sort but also it implies increasingly lavish and constant hospitality. One of the best evidences is the occurrence of tea-pots, chocolate-pots, and coffee-pots. These beverages at the present time seem essentials of everyday living, but in the early eighteenth century they were distinct luxuries. In consequence, the tea-pots are generally considerably smaller than those of a century later; and presumably they were sometimes used interchangeably for tea or coffee.

The ambitiously designed chocolate-pot (Plate XIII, left), belonging to Judge A. T. Clearwater, illustrates an early style. In England the earliest known examples of tea or coffee pots have the form of a truncated cone with a conical lid, sometimes described as lantern-shaped. From these rather primitive shapes there soon developed pots of more graceful outline, which still maintained the straight tapering sides but modified the lid to one of domed form. From these in turn sprang pots with a slight incurve just above the base like this one by Winslow. To add to the charm of its surface by contrasting cleverly plain and broken surfaces, Winslow has fluted the curve of the lid and the lower part of the body, and enriched the edge of the cover and foot with bands of gadrooning. Furthermore, he has added incident to the cover by a border of pierced cut-card work and has broken the severity of the long slender spout by a graceful little cut-card floral ornament. The thumb-piece is a simple interrupted scroll, similar to those on late-

[71]

seventeenth-century English tankards. So that the thick chocolate might be stirred in the course of its preparation without chilling it unnecessarily, a small hole was left in the cover, which is closed by the finial, and the latter is secured by a chain to the handle. It was customary to remove the finial occasionally and insert a stick to stir the chocolate. Many French coffee-pots have their handles at right angles to their spouts and the early English and American pots occasionally show the same arrangement. The Winslow chocolate-pot is engraved with the arms of the Hutchinsons, a family that gained distinction from its insurgent ancestress, Mistress Anne, and from a quieter but none the less eminent member, Governor William Hutchinson.

Another early and extremely interesting chocolate-pot was made by John Coney (Plate X) and was recently presented by Edward Jackson Holmes to the Museum of Fine Arts. It is of what may best be described as gallipot shape, a shape probably derived originally from Oriental porcelain and used occasionally by English silversmiths. The use of this form in Colonial silver is extremely rare, this Coney piece being the only known instance of its employment for a chocolate-pot. A similar shape occurs in a spout cup belonging to the Worcester Art Museum and made by John Edwards. Like the Winslow chocolate-pot, this Coney pot has a removable finial and corresponding hole in its cover, and the latter is separate and insetting, an early type. Coney, like Winslow, has made his spout long, slender, and curving, and has ornamented it with beading by way of breaking the sur-

PLATE XI

(Left) TWO-HANDLED CUP BY WILLIAM COWELL

(Right) BEAKER MADE BY JOHN DIXWELL, GIVEN BY MADAME KNIGHT
TO THE CHURCH IN NORWICH, CONNECTICUT

face. At the lower attachment of the handle he has added a graceful bit of cut-card work. The Coney chocolate-pot is inscribed: "The gift of Wm Stoughton Esquire to Mrs Sarah Tailer [1]701." Probably it was made to carry out the following provision in Governor Stoughton's will, proved in 1701: "Unto my Niece Mrs. Sarah Tailer I give as a particular remembrance of me twelve pounds to buy a piece of plate." Mrs. Tailer's husband, William, was nephew and chief heir of Governor Stoughton.[1]

A later type of chocolate-pot, developing out of the style of the one by Winslow described above, is represented in Plate XIII, right. This example has attained a fully developed pear outline, has a domed lid of moderate height, a spreading molded base, and a swan-neck spout with cut-card ornamentation at its junction with the body. In all these features, it is typical of the period. Again it represents the work of that most able silversmith, John Coney (1655–1722) and is now the property of Mrs. Robert Soutter.

Corresponding to the pear-shaped chocolate-pot just described is the pear-shaped tea-pot, of which style there is an excellent example, also by Coney, in the collection of Judge A. T. Clearwater. Tea-pots of this period were probably accompanied by little pear-shaped creamers on a simple base and by bowl-shaped sugar-dishes with saucer-shaped covers. An example of the latter type made by a New York silversmith is illustrated in Plate LVIII, left.

As indicated by the numerous illustrations drawn

[1] "A Silver Chocolate Pot," by Edwin J. Hipkiss, "Bulletin of the Museum of Fine Arts," Boston, Vol. XXVIII, No. 4.

from their work, Coney and Winslow were the outstanding exponents of the styles of this period. There were also active at this period many other silversmiths scarcely less able. In the front rank stand John Burt (1691–1745), John Allen (1671–1760), William Cowell (1682–1736), John Dixwell (1680–1725), John Noyes (1674–1749), George Hanners (1696–1740), Moody Russell (1694–1761), and Andrew Tyler (1692–1741).

VII. ENGLISH SILVER OF THE ROCOCO PERIOD
(ABOUT 1720–65)

English silver of the time of Queen Anne had been very plain, largely as a result of the regulation in force from 1697 to 1720 requiring plate to be of a higher standard than sterling and hence of a quality too soft to make elaborate ornamentation practical. Although the high standard was not enforced after 1720, for a few years the making of silver proceeded much as before. There was, however, evidence of a coming change of taste, which by 1725 was assured. The new rococo styles followed fashions then prevailing in Europe and especially in France. They were given a tremendous impetus in England by the great numbers of Huguenots who had fled from France, because of the religious persecution that followed the revocation of the Edict of Nantes in 1685. These refugees included many skilled silversmiths who had been thrown out of employment at home, because their patrons had been impoverished by the heavy taxes incident to Louis XIV's wars and the building of his palace at Versailles.

Massachusetts Silver

These sensitive and able craftsmen who settled in England added great luster to the annals of her silver-smiths. Among them were such illustrious men as Pierre Platel, Paul Lamerie, Grégoire Massé, and Lewis Mettayer.

The word rococo was probably derived from *rocaille*, the French term for the rockwork that, in combination with shell forms, is so characteristic a feature of the decoration. This style, which reached its highest development in France under Louis XIV and his successor, gradually spread over most of north-western Europe. Deriving its inspiration from rock and shell forms, it wholly abandoned the straight line and rectangular compositions, and chose instead curved and scrolled outlines both for shapes and for ornamentation. Scrolls, rockwork, shells, naturalistic flower and leaf motives, masks, escutcheons, and diapered and reticulated reserves were combined with the utmost ingenuity. The effects thus achieved were light, dainty, and fanciful when cleverly handled, but they easily slipped into the heavy and the grotesque. The style at its best in France was refined and sumptuous, but eventually it degenerated into overwrought and meaningless ornament.

In English silver the rococo style began to develop during the reign of George I and rose to its height in the second quarter of the eighteenth century. By about 1760 it had passed its prime and had become so heavy and ornate that people welcomed a return to simplicity and purity of form as expressed in classic styles. During the rococo period, English silver was made in shapes built up by curved lines. Globular, pear-shaped, and, later, objects of inverted-pear shape had extensive use. There was a tendency to make things taller, more definitely shapely, and more slender, which resulted in lighter effects and greater elegance. Handles were in the form of double scrolls, spouts were curved and often elaborately modeled with scrolled ornaments. The feet of such pieces as creamers, salts, and sauce-boats were often of shell or scroll outline or were modeled in the form of animal hooves, lion's paw, claw and ball, or spade form, and may be compared to the feet of chairs and tables of the same period.

The ornamentation of this period was accomplished by embossing, flat-chasing, engraving, and the application of cast decoration. Frequently all these methods were combined in the enrichment of a single piece; indeed the embossed or applied ornament at times completely obscured the outline of the original piece. As the period advanced and the rococo style reached fuller development, the arrangement became increasingly asymmetrical. The outline of the shield and the disposal of the ornament around it in the elaborately engraved coats of arms often afford a definite index of date.

VIII. ROCOCO INFLUENCES IN MASSACHUSETTS SILVER (ABOUT 1730–75)

Colonial silversmiths during this period were in close touch with England and quickly responsive to changes in style. However, the fundamental desire for utility and simplicity kept them from following the

[76]

more extravagant and ornate designs of their London confrères. Rococo influences in American silver are chiefly manifested in the shapes employed, in a tendency toward greater refinement and richness of effect, and in the adoption of a moderate amount of rococo motives in decoration.

Tankards and flagons continue in their established forms but become taller, more tapering, and more shapely. Their height is increased by a high domed cover and elaborately molded finial. The latter often occurs in an urn-and-flame pattern similar to the ornaments on the pediments of highboys of the period.

Mugs also assume more sophisticated outlines. That made by Paul Revere (1735–1818) (Plate XLVI), belonging to R. T. H. Halsey, has pronounced curves. Its handle, which does not show in the illustration, is in the form of a double scroll with acanthus-leaf ornament to serve as thumb-rest. The engraved cartouche enclosing the inscription, though restrained, is essentially in rococo style. This inscription reads: "Stephano Scales, HARVARDINATES A.D. MDCCLXVIII. Conscripti Biennio sub ejus Tutelia per acto Hoc Poculum, Grati Animi Monimentum DONANT." Bulbous forms also find expression in the bell-shaped beaker on a spreading foot, which was quite extensively made at this period.

By far the most popular style of tea-pot during this interval was that of globular outline, which though extremely simple is almost invariably charming. An example by Jacob Hurd (1702–58), now the property of the Museum of Fine Arts in Boston, is illustrated in Plate LVI. The arms engraved on its side have been

[77]

tentatively assigned to the Andrews family. The inscription on the base: "E. Storer 1756" indicates that this tea-pot belonged to Ebenezer Storer, Jr., grandson of the silversmith John Edwards.[1] It was presented to the museum by his descendants, Francis S. and William S. Eaton.

It is interesting to compare the tea-pot just described with that shown in Plate XIV A, which is the work of Jacob Hurd's son Nathaniel (1729–77). The earlier example is simple and globular; the later shows more consciousness of form, more refinement of modeling. Nathaniel made other tea-pots much like this in style and proved himself a silversmith of no mean order. But his reputation rests primarily upon his ability as a copperplate engraver. He executed quantities of bookplates. Stauffer[2] quotes his advertisement in the "Boston Gazette" for April 28, 1760: Nathaniel Hurd "continues to do all sorts of Goldsmith's Work, Likewise engraves in Gold, Silver, Copper, Brass, and Steel in the neatest Manner, and at reasonable Rates." Stauffer also quotes a bill which suggests the variety of tasks that Hurd undertook:

BOSTON, June 16, 1773.

Thos. Fayerweather Esq., to Nat. Hurd, Dr.

To taking out Crest from Salts & putting in New	£1.4
To Mend'g Sauce pan & can	12
To Large Crest on Sauce pan	12
To taking out Arms from Coffee pott and y'r arms in	2.5
O. tenor	£4.13

[1] F. H. Bigelow, "Historic Silver of the Colonies and Its Makers," 1917.

[2] D. M. Stauffer, "American Engravers on Copper and Steel," 1907.

Considering Nathaniel's proficiency in engraving, there is no doubt that the Gibbs arms that appear on this tea-pot were executed by him. The piece now belongs to Hollis French.

While tea-pots are quite common, kettles are extremely rare. Mrs. Stanley Cunningham owns the example illustrated in Plate XLIV, which in its general contours is much like the tea-pots just described. Its duck-neck spout suggests a relatively early period. The kettle once belonged to James Russell Lowell, grandfather of the present owner. That it has been continuously in the family is proved by the Lowell arms engraved upon its side. The ornamental design enclosing the arms is in the style of the early rococo period and is similar in character to numerous other heraldic designs found on silver made by Jacob Hurd. While such engraving may have been executed by his son Nathaniel, it seems equally possible that the father may also have been proficient in this art and may have actually cut the arms on the silver that he fashioned. Even before Nathaniel's birth, Samuel Sewall noted in his diary, under date of June 2, 1725: "Gave my daughter Cooper for her Son Samuel a Silver Spoon weighing one ounce and 12 pw^t. Mr. Hurd engraved on the back side of it . . . S C."

Shortly before the Revolutionary War and for some years thereafter, tea-pots were made with more undulating outlines than those already illustrated, and these we shall describe, for want of a better appellation, as of inverted-pear shape. The general shape is illustrated in Plate XLIII, a pot made by Moulinar of New York.

[79]

English potters, and also Chinese potters who were executing orders for the European market at this period, made many little tea-pots of circular form with straight sides, flat base, and straight spout. The shape occurs very frequently in those Chinese porcelain tea-pots sometimes described as "Chinese Lowestoft." The shape was extremely popular with Philadelphia silver-smiths, but apparently did not make a strong appeal to Bostonians. Practically the only Massachusetts examples of this general style are two made by Paul Revere, one now in the collection of Mrs. Nathaniel Thayer, the other in the Garvan collection.

There are two chief types of chocolate and coffee pots at this period. One is straight-sided and tapering, the other is a sort of attenuated pear shape. The decorative features of both are much the same. The earlier examples have lower and more simply modeled lids, simple goose-neck spouts, and little elaboration. The examples of later date are more pretentious, have higher lids and more elaborate finials, scrolled spouts and handle-supports, and higher bases. The Museum of Fine Arts owns a rare example of a pear-shaped coffee-pot supported by three scroll legs on shell feet. The majority of pots have circular domed bases. Toward the end of the period taller coffee-pots appear, corresponding in general style to the tea-pots of inverted-pear shape.

The commonest style of creamer during this period is that with pear-shaped body and either circular base or more often three scrolled feet. The lip is broad and cut in scroll outline. The sugar-bowl by this time has developed from the early bowl form into one of

PLATE XII *See pages 68, 269, 338*

CASTERS AND PUNCH-BOWL BY JOHN CONEY

rather more gracious outline and has a domed lid with ornamental finial.

Sauce-boats are much like the contemporary creamer but lower and much elongated. Their underslung appearance is relieved by the upstanding scroll that serves as handle. A very stocky little example is that shown in Plate XIV, made by Daniel Parker (1726–85), now in the collection of Philip Leffingwell Spalding. More rarely the sauce-boat is set on an oval base, instead of upon three feet.

Scrolls and curves make up the outline of the three-legged salt of the rococo period. The feet may be claw and ball, hoof, spade, or shell shaped, and their junction with the circular bowl is often elaborated into shell or scroll ornament, all characteristic details of the period.

The baluster caster becomes somewhat taller and more elegant than before but for the most part keeps a rather simple outline. Existent candlesticks of the period are rare; they are generally of baluster type with more or less rococo decoration. Porringers continue as before, the keyhole pattern being the one most favored.

One charming article of silver at this period is the tray, which conforms to prevailing fashions by its curved and scrolled outlines; by its feet, which follow the same shapes as those of creamers, salts, and sauce-boats; and by the flat-chased and engraved designs that ornament its surface. Paul Revere (1735–1818) made the tray (Plate XLIX) that, according to tradition, was presented to Lucretia Chandler, daughter of Judge John Chandler, the "Honest Tory," upon her marriage in 1761 to Colonel John Murray. The tray is engraved with the Chandler arms in rococo style and has a scalloped margin interrupted by shell ornaments. It was presented by Henry Davis Sleeper to the Museum of Fine Arts in Boston.

Perfectly simple in its form but betraying the influence of the rococo in the engraved arms on its rim, an alms-basin made by Samuel Minott (1732–1803) identifies itself with this period. It bears the Hancock arms and was the gift of Thomas Hancock to the Brattle Street Church, Boston. It is now in the collection of Judge A. T. Clearwater. (Plate XLIX).

Especially in the use of ornament, Massachusetts silver of the rococo period is much more restrained and conservative than is the English plate of the same epoch. It may be claimed that this was due to a lack of imagination, but more probably it was the result of a deeply ingrained desire for simplicity and a dislike of ostentation. The decoration that appears at this time is based essentially upon rococo styles and employs scrolls, shells, rockwork, palmettes, flower-sprays, masks, and escutcheons of fantastic outline. These features occur in the scroll decoration on spouts and handles; in the feet of creamers, trays, salts, and sauce-boats; in the ornaments applied to the bowls of spoons; in the molded borders of trays; and more especially in the engraved and flat-chased ornamentation applied around the tops of tea-pots and in the coats of arms that are so widely employed. In many of the pieces illustrated these rococo elements may be distinguished.

[82]

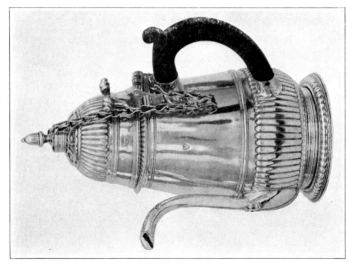

See pages 71, 72

PLATE XIII   EARLY CHOCOLATE-POTS MADE BY EDWARD WINSLOW AND JOHN CONEY

Massachusetts Silver

THE CLASSIC REVIVAL (ABOUT 1765–1800)

Excavations begun at Herculaneum in 1738 and at Pompeii in 1755 were carried on for a period of years, and resulted in the discovery of Greek and Roman art of such extraordinary quality and in such great quantity that the art of Europe was quite transformed. Not only were descriptions of the treasures unearthed in these two cities widely published, but other records of classic styles were also eagerly sought out and carefully studied. So completely did the restraint and dignity of the antique capture the popular imagination that the elaborate designs of the rococo period, which had passed their prime and had already degenerated into a conglomeration of meaningless ornament, were speedily discarded, and new styles, based upon classical models and marked by great simplicity and balance, sprang suddenly into favor. The architects instigated the movement and other craftsmen followed after. In England the leading exponents of the classic revival were the brothers Adam, who designed buildings and interiors and furniture, all in the same spirit and with intelligent organization. The impulse was spread by other cabinet-makers and designers, such as Hepplewhite and Sheraton.

The silversmiths were soon affected by this movement, and modeled their new creations, to greater or less extent, upon classical prototypes. They made wide use of certain classic shapes, preëminently the urn,

[83]

and they discarded the full bulbous shapes of the rococo era. In some objects, such as candlesticks, columnar shapes were followed. Elsewhere, forms were built up of straight upright lines, such as could readily be fashioned from sheet silver. The silver as a whole expressed slenderness, delicacy, lightness, and brilliance, and it harmonized perfectly with the interiors designed by the Adam brothers and with the slender and elegant furniture of Sheraton and Hepplewhite.

Silver of this period affords a striking contrast to that of the rococo period that preceded it. To rococo curves are now opposed straight structural lines and rectangular compositions. Instead of the asymmetrical, heavy, exuberant ornament of the earlier period there is now the restrained use of classic elements in a balanced arrangement. These classic motives consist chiefly of slender columns, friezes, drapery, pendent husks, acanthus foliage, laurel-leaves, swags, masks, rosettes, and medallions. As in the furniture the effect of lightness was achieved by inlays of various light-colored woods, so in silver a similar effect was produced by executing the ornament by that style of engraving known as bright-cutting. The designs were lightly cut into the surface of the silver in such a way as to offer a highly reflective surface. The whole effect is formal, delicate, and brilliant.

X. MASSACHUSETTS SILVER OF CLASSIC STYLES
(ABOUT 1770–1810)

Comparatively little silver was produced in America during the time of the Revolution, but in the period immediately succeeding, when the new republic was quite proud and self-conscious, much silver, especially in the form of tea-services, was fashioned, and lent brilliance to the homes of energetic merchants of Boston, Salem, Newburyport, and other thriving cities.

One shape is carried over from the rococo period, the tall coffee-pot of inverted-pear form. Though not at all in the classic spirit, it seems to have retained its popularity for some time after the close of the American Revolution. A handsome example by Paul Revere (1735–1818) indicates its general outline and decorative details (Plate XV). This coffee-pot, now owned by Mrs. Nathaniel Thayer, was made for Paul Dudley Sargent in 1781. In Revere's ledger the charge for it is recorded in detail:

For making	39 oz. 3	£12.
For engraving arms		1.4.0

The weight of the silver is scratched on the base— 39 oz. 3; the present weight of the piece with its wooden handle is 40 oz. 5 dwt.

The American silversmith of this period, like his English brother, sought to produce light, elegant, formal effects and placed his emphasis on straight, upright structural lines, no doubt inspired by the classic column. His most characteristic shapes are based either upon this form or upon the urn. He found it practicable to create many of his shapes with sheet silver, rolled thin, cut and bent around into the desired outline, and seamed. Flutes were a favorite mode of ornament and were made wide, shallow, and concave because thus they contributed to the effect of lightness and delicacy. The shallow gouges in the surface, made by the type of engraving known as bright-cutting, lent brilliance to the surface and at the same time did not weaken the thin metal.

People at this period felt expansive and hospitable and entertained extensively. Tea-drinking became more general than ever before, and so all the pieces in the service, which was now designed *en suite*, were more capacious. The most imposing of the group was the tall urn for hot water. That by Paul Revere (Plate XVI, center), belonging to Mrs. Charles F. Russell, is a distinguished example. Shallow upright flutes lend variety and play of light to its deep vase-shaped body. It is topped by a reel-shaped cover and well-modeled finial and stands on a square base with ball-and-claw feet. Bright-cut borders and pendent festoons brighten its surfaces.

Other typical Revere pieces, the property of Judge A. T. Clearwater, are illustrated in Plate XLII. While Philadelphia at this period developed a great vogue for coffee and tea pots of tall vase shape, corresponding more or less to the form of the Revere urn just described, in Boston the preference seems to have been given to the low, oval, straight-sided little tea-pot. Judge Clearwater's piece is a delightful illustration. Revere has taken a strip of sheet silver, bent it around into oval form and seamed up the side. To this he has added a flat base and top, a slightly domed and hinged lid, and a straight spout. To keep the heat of the tea-pot from marring the mahogany tea-table, an oval stand on four legs is supplied. Its fluted outline

PLATE XIV

See pages 78, 81

TEA-POT BY NATHANIEL HURD
SAUCE-BOAT BY DANIEL PARKER

corresponds to the shallow flutes on the tea-pot, and both pieces are lightly engraved with pendent drapery and tassels. The vase-shaped sugar-bowl is closely akin in its form to the hot-water urn. The helmet creamer seeks greater height by its high-arched strap handle. All of these pieces can be matched again and again in the work of Revere and other silversmiths working at this period.

Classic inspiration is likewise evident in the shapes and in the extreme simplicity of the two cups shown in Plate XVI. The standing cup is the work of Joseph Foster (1760–1839) of Boston and is one of a set of six originally belonging to the Brattle Street Church. This cup and another of the set now belong to Judge A. T. Clearwater. The same collector owns the two-handled cup by Joseph Loring (1743–1815), which, with three similar cups, also formerly belonged to the Brattle Street Church.

Paul Revere was Boston's most notable silversmith during the period just before and after the Revolution. He was a versatile and highly productive crafts-man, working as copperplate engraver, wood-carver, cannon and bell founder, as well as silversmith. He was an ardent and active patriot. Assuredly one does not wish to disparage Revere, but in justice to other Colonial silversmiths, a readjustment of values is called for. Every one is familiar from childhood with Revere's name and exploits. This familiarity, contrary to the old adage, has not bred contempt, but has occasioned a tremendous demand for his silverwork. Examples, when up for sale, bring three and four times the prices brought by comparable pieces made by other Colonial silversmiths. This is paying a very high price for sentiment. Looked at dispassionately and without bias, Revere's silver is of varying quality, some of it quite distinguished, some of it only average. Incidentally, because of the inflated state of the market, there has come forward more than one piece supposedly bearing his mark that is not his handiwork. It is most commendable in Mrs. Nathaniel Thayer, who is a descendant of Revere, to form a collection of his work, and she has done him great credit by her selection. Henry Davis Sleeper also chose to collect silver by Revere and has presented an interesting group of it to the Museum of Fine Arts in Boston. But the average collector may well turn his attention to earlier styles and to other puissant Colonial silversmiths—to John Coney, for example, who was as productive as Revere himself, who was an extremely versatile silversmith, and a magnificent craftsman. It is a matter of taste whether one prefers the work of the late seventeenth and the early eighteenth century, when shapes were vigorously modeled, even though sometimes a trifle tentative, or silver made in the brilliant and sophisticated manner of the late eighteenth century with its chaste pseudo-classicism. If one is seeking technical skill and satisfying design, if one looks for the most mellow and gracious effects that can be produced in silver, one may well turn to the earlier styles and make every effort to obtain some characteristic piece by Hull and Sanderson, by Dummer, by Jacob Hurd, by Josiah Austin, by Edward Winslow, by William Cowell, by John Dixwell, or by their worthy contemporaries.

PLATE XV   *See page 85*

COFFEE-POT BY PAUL REVERE
Made for Paul Dudley Sargent in 1781

Massachusetts Silver

The title "Early American Silver" implies that some limit is set upon the period to be discussed. We have chosen to close our study with the classic revival of the late eighteenth century and to omit the styles of the early nineteenth century, which become not only very diverse but heavy, cumbersome, and lacking in artistic interest.

CHAPTER III

RHODE ISLAND SILVER

THE character of the early Rhode Island settlers differed essentially from that of the early Massachusetts Bay colonists. The controlling group in the Bay was determined to set up a civic government that should support and protect its church. Any religious dissension was promptly and drastically checked by both church and civil authorities. Among those whose liberal views the Massachusetts Bay leaders could not tolerate were Roger Williams, Captain John Clarke, and William Coddington. Expelled in heartless manner, they sought refuge in Rhode Island, where, with their followers and those refugees of other faiths who sought a haven with them, they built up a colony "distinguished in Puritan New England for its religious toleration and democratic government." In the colony itself, however, three broad groups stand out, groups determined partly by geographic conditions, partly by other circumstances. These are Providence Plantations, situated at the head of Narragansett Bay; Aquidneck, the island at the mouth of the bay on which were located Portsmouth and Newport; and the South or King's County, the Narragansett country situated on the mainland west of the bay. Each of these sections had a distinctive development.

Providence was settled first. Here Roger Williams,

Rhode Island Silver

William Harris, and their fellows came in 1636, after
their expulsion from Massachusetts Bay. The latter
colony ostracized them so completely that she would
not even sell them necessary supplies and equipment.
Land they had in plenty, but it did not at first give
them products sufficiently in excess of their own needs
for them to export goods elsewhere. Moreover, their
settlement, considering the early difficulties of transport, was too remote from the sea to make commerce
feasible. Lacking credit and the means of developing other industries, they were forced to live almost
entirely by agriculture. Roger Williams will live in
history for his concept of "soul liberty," and for his
generous and courageous dealings with the Indians.
He lacked, however, a genius for statecraft and political organization. His people were highly individualis-
tic, loth to commit themselves to any sort of government that might curtail their liberties. Because of these
economic and political handicaps, the colony of Providence Plantations developed slowly. For a considerable
period, its inhabitants were forced to content themselves with little more than the necessities of life. Wills
and inventories of estates prove the possession of earthenware and wooden dishes but omit silver plate and
carved furniture, luxuries these folk could not afford.
Not until the late seventeenth century does plate
occur in such records.

By contrast, the island of Aquidneck enjoyed a
decided advantage. John Clarke and William Coddington were men of a liberal culture and had occupied important offices in Massachusetts Bay before
their expulsion. They and their followers had a far

greater aptitude for political organization than had Roger Williams and his colonists. Moreover, many of the settlers of Portsmouth (founded 1638) and of Newport (founded 1639) possessed wealth and culture and were able to establish comfortable homes for themselves. The island itself was fertile and afforded opportunities for stock-raising as well as agriculture. It was immediately adjacent to the sea, so that commerce inevitably developed early.

The considerable influx of Jews and Quakers proves not only that the colony was an asylum for religious refugees but also that it early gave promise of its commercial growth. Many Jews immigrated to Newport from Portugal and Holland, especially in 1655 and 1658. While the religious toleration attracted them, they would not have settled in such numbers had the town not offered prospects of commercial expansion. By their wealth and initiative, they gave a tremendous impetus to the town's wide trade and mercantile development. Similarly the thrift and business acumen of the Quakers were a great influence toward sound business policies.

Newport, because of its nearness to the sea and good harbor, was destined to become an important trading-port and to serve the back country as a means of export for its agricultural and other produce and of import for other supplies it required. Newport's earliest commerce was with her colonial neighbors, but this soon extended to include England and the West Indies. The abundant timber and other naval stores of the region afforded the means of ship-building, and the independent and resourceful Rhode Islanders soon ceased to rely upon England for ships and built their own. Newport must have begun this industry very early; at Providence it began actively in 1711 under the direction of Nathaniel Browne.

The commodities most available for trade were fish, timber, cattle, horses, wool, agricultural produce. Relatively few of these found a good market in England, and as various manufactured goods must be imported from England, the Rhode Islanders found their credit there small. They were therefore forced to market their raw materials where the returns would be more adequate. Daring and ingenious, the colonists developed an extensive circular commerce. The best fish they shipped to the Catholic countries of Europe, to be exchanged for wines; inferior grades they shipped to the West Indies as food for negro slaves. Wool from their many sheep they sent to France to be exchanged for linen. Horses, cattle, and dairy products went to the West Indies, to be traded for sugar and indigo. Some furs, sugar, and lumber were shipped to England; with the credit thus gained, cloth, ironware, and other necessary goods were purchased, some of which eventually found a Massachusetts or Connecticut market. The more active trade of Newport also created a market for Providence, so that the latter in time received a sufficient stimulus to engage extensively in commerce. In the long run, the fact that Providence was located on the mainland, in direct communication with the back country, instead of being on an island as Newport was, proved an important advantage, contributing to her eventual superiority over the island town.

The third great division of the Rhode Island colony

was the South or King's County, where fertile land and salt-marshes made a country admirably suited for stock-farming and dairying on an extensive scale. These Narragansett planters came in the course of time to own large estates, some of them five, six, or even ten miles square, while smaller landowners averaged three hundred acres. Here they raised corn, some tobacco, cattle, sheep, and horses, many of which they exported with gratifying profit, chiefly by way of Newport. The Narragansett pacer was bred for speed and endurance and was tremendously popular among the West Indian planters. The Narragansett planters themselves took great pride in their horses, bringing them out for races on the smooth, hard beaches and sometimes offering as prize a silver tankard.

Whereas in most of New England the various industries required more hardy or more skilled labor than the negro, in Narragansett stock-farming could be most advantageously carried on with slave-labor. Consequently Newport merchants engaged extensively in the slave-trade. They obtained sugar and molasses in the West Indies, brought it to the New England distilleries, where it was made into rum, and in turn shipped it to Africa to facilitate the purchase of slaves. One Rhode Island merchant wrote to his brother in the West Indies: "If you cannot sell all your slaves to your mind, bring some home. I believe they will sell well. Get molasses or sugar. Make despatch for that is the life of trade." To another correspondent he wrote: "My Gineman is arrived. You may have A slave, if you cum or sand Befoar they air Gon."[1] Senti-

[1] Quoted by W. B. Weeden, "Early Rhode Island," 1910.

ment in New England was not against slavery for a long period, although, except in Narragansett, the conditions of industry did not make their employment generally profitable.

The extensive use of slavery in the Narragansett lands made possible the rise of a wealthy, cultured society, by releasing it from constant and menial tasks. Sons and daughters of the planters were generally educated by private tutors and were sometimes sent abroad to complete their education. Leisure and wealth made possible great refinements of life and encouraged an expansive hospitality. Madame Knight in her travels through this country comments upon the lack of good taverns and inns; the lack was the direct consequence of the hospitable nature of the people, who entertained guests so easily and so graciously in their own homes. Their sports and festivals were also conducted on a lavish scale and included fox-hunting, racing, and long-continued Christmas festivities. As James Truslow Adams, in "Provincial Society," has summarized this situation in Narragansett: "Here a society grew up which was an anomaly in New England and which was much more akin, in its creation of large landed estates with troops of Negro slaves, to the planter type of the South."

As in New York and in Charleston, South Carolina, so in Newport, piracy and privateering were direct or indirect sources of wealth. The profits were so rich as to tempt Colonial merchants and at times even public officials to connive with the pirates. England's wars with France and Spain also provided valuable prizes for Colonial privateers. Through both these types of enterprise the colonists were able to derive very considerable revenue, much of which came to them in the convenient form of coin that was readily convertible into silver plate.

The general scarcity of legal tender in the early colonies was a continuous source of difficulty. Some suggestion of this is revealed in a quotation from W. B. Weeden's "Early Rhode Island." "George Ireish bought a famous Narragansett . . . horse at fifty-five silver Spanish milled dollars. The transaction reveals a curious course of trade and indirect balancing of values. 'I am to take 1 hoggshead of molasses, 1 barrell of Sugar at £70 old Tenor per Hundred, the Molasses at the value of 36/ old Tenor, a Doller being considered at the Value of Eight Pounds old Tenor the Remainder in Tea at ye Rate of eight Pounds old Ten^r, and in Indigo at the Rate of Twelve Pounds, old Tenor; to have one half of ye remainder in Tea, & the other in Indigo.' " Small wonder that the colonists endeavored to find some means of securing money for local trading. The frequent issues of paper currency in Rhode Island were designed to facilitate and increase trade and commerce and it is to be presumed that they actually had this result. But as proper provision was not made for its redemption, the money proved highly unstable.

Presumably because of their close intercourse with England, Newport and King's County were the home of many people of the Anglican Church. Trinity Church in Newport was founded in 1698 and St. Paul's in Narragansett in 1707. Both were strongholds of Anglicanism. Elsewhere throughout the colony were

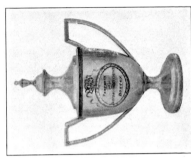

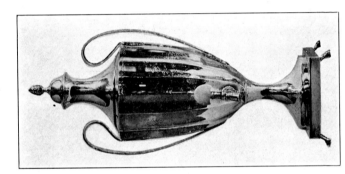

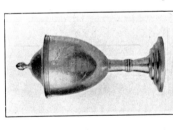

See pages 86—87

PLATE XVI

STANDING-CUP BY JOSEPH FOSTER, TEA URN BY PAUL REVERE,
AND TWO-HANDLED CUP BY JOSEPH LORING

Rhode Island Silver

many Jews, Quakers, and people of various Protestant sects. The liberal religious attitude of the early settlers had been continued by these other groups, and their diversity, coupled with the Quakers' strong opposition to an established church, accounts for the lack of religious organization throughout the colony, and the relative scarcity of churches. Inasmuch as long-established churches tended to accumulate communion plate, thus preserving much old silver for posterity, the opposite tendency in Rhode Island worked against the preservation of its early silver.

The various economic, social, and religious conditions just described [1] interacted to affect the possession and production of silver plate in Rhode Island. The wills and inventories of the property of deceased persons offer direct evidence concerning the plate owned in different sections at different periods. Providence, settled by relatively poor people and slow in developing her industries, commerce, and consequent wealth, evidences no silver plate until the late seventeenth century. One of the earliest inventories to mention plate, according to the "Early Records of the Town of Providence," is that of Stephen Arnold of Pawtuxet, taken in 1699, which in an estate of £495.11.1 included plate worth £17. Mrs. Freelove Crawford, whose estate totaled £947.1 in 1712, and who evidently kept a shop, owned bonds and mortgage deeds to the amount of £642.12, had a share in two sloops, and owned a "silver Tankerd, salt seller, porrengers and tispoones" worth £21.5.5. In an estate of the value of £1556 in

---

[1] For fuller treatment, see W. B. Weeden, "Early Rhode Island," 1910, from which much of the foregoing material has been drawn.

1707, Gideon Crawford owned plate worth £15.11.
In other inventories, dating from 1697 on, occur entries of various "silver Buttons," "Silver Dram Cupp,"
etc.

The citizens of Portsmouth and especially those of
Newport owned silver plate at an early period. Thus
in 1767 a Portsmouth inventory shows plate. In the
same year Peleg Sanford,[1] a Newport merchant, writes:
"Cozen I pray sent my wine cupp from Mr. Hull"
(John Hull, Boston silversmith). From these inventories it becomes clear that the early tableware was of
earthenware, wood, and pewter. As wealth and refinement increased, there was a continually increasing
amount of silver and relatively less value was represented in the coarser materials. King's County residents also owned considerable plate. By about 1730–
35, William Gardner of Boston Neck had "Rought
plate" valued at £92.8 and pewter at £13.7.[2] The
majority of inventories show spoons. George Hazard,
living near Point Judith, in 1738 had a "tankard
worth £30; two porringers, salt cellar, and 11 spoons
at £49.10," and pewter to the value of £8.18. His
possession of five punch-bowls, valued at £1.15, and
glasses suggests the extensive entertainment he offered
guests. In 1751 William Robinson, a Quaker and governor of the colony, left a personal estate of £21,573.5,
including silver plate "in the bowfatt" of the "Great

[1] "The Letter Book of Peleg Sanford of Newport, Merchant
(later Governor of Rhode Island), 1666–1668," Rhode Island Historical Society, 1928.

[2] This and the succeeding inventories here noted are taken from
W. B. Weeden, "Early Rhode Island," 1910, who in turn has quoted
chiefly from the South Kingston manuscript probate records.

Rhode Island Silver

Room" valued at £374.8, which, according to Weeden, was "the largest so far recorded." By this time Providence too was becoming affluent, for John Mawney in 1754 had plate to the value of £911.8.3. The items themselves are of interest: "1 silver tankard, 1 do. teapot, 2 large 'canns,' 13 large spoons, 1 silver . . . , 12 tea spoons, 7 porringers, 1 sugar dish and cover, 2 pepper boxes, 1 cream pot, 2 salts, 1 pair tea tongs, 1 small bowl, 1 small spoon strainer, altogether weighing 214 oz. 9 dwt." at 85 shillings per ounce. Quakers, whose religious tenets did not permit them to indulge in personal finery, were nevertheless free to own a lavish amount of plate.

These wills and inventories do not in any way indicate whether the silver plate owned by the deceased person was of European or of domestic production. It is reasonable to suppose that at first well-to-do Rhode Islanders depended chiefly upon English or Massachusetts silversmiths for their plate. The close intercourse between Newport and England would have facilitated the importation of London silver, except for the fact that the balance of trade was generally in the wrong direction.

It is interesting to consider the plate presented to the early Rhode Island churches as an index to the sources of supply of silver in the colony. Rather meager evidence, to be sure, but perhaps it is the best available. Among the earliest churches established was the Church of Rehoboth, founded in 1643, and subsequently known as the Newman Congregational Church of East Providence. Its pastor, the Reverend Noah Newman, in 1678 bequeathed to it the English standing cup made in

[99]

1631 that is illustrated in Plate I (next to right). Presumably this cup had been brought to America by his father, the Reverend Samuel Newman, first pastor of this church. In 1674 a beaker made by Hull and Sanderson of Boston was presented to the church, and later another beaker by Hull (1624–83) found its place there also. Still later donations to the church represent the work of Hurd and of Boyer, Boston silversmiths, and also that of Jonathan Otis and of Thomas Arnold of Newport. The First Congregational Church of Bristol, Rhode Island, founded in 1680, had three beakers by John Coney and Knight Leverett of Boston, which were presented in 1693 and 1718, and in addition three beakers made by Samuel Vernon of Newport, which were presented in 1723. The United Congregational Church of Newport, founded in 1720, owns quite an array of silver made by Newport silversmiths, including Samuel Vernon, Daniel Russell, and Thomas Arnold. The pieces comprise two tankards, six beakers, and a cup. The plate of these churches suggests the general course of events. The earliest silver was that brought over from London, probably by incoming colonists. Somewhat later it became possible to procure well-wrought pieces from Boston, and with the eighteenth century Rhode Island craftsmen proved themselves able to compete with the already well-established vogue of Boston silver.

The Anglican churches of Rhode Island, like those elsewhere in the colonies, owned some English plate. That still in existence is so meager that we are forced to look for some explanation. It seems highly probable that these Anglican churches of Rhode Island may have possessed a considerable amount of English plate and that much of it was carried back to London by returning Royalists during the American Revolution. The Royalist rector of King's Chapel in Boston took to England, at this period, communion plate of such quantity that its estimated weight was 2800 ounces.[1] Similarly, much silver owned in Newport must have gone out of the country at the time of the British evacuation of the city. It is pathetic to find that the English plate presented to the early Rhode Island churches now comprises only a chalice and a paten made in London in 1706 and presented by Queen Anne to St. Paul's in Wickford (founded in 1707) and another London chalice and paten, made in 1702, and given to Trinity Church in Newport (founded in 1698) by the Society for the Propagation of the Gospel in Foreign Parts.

Both these and two other Anglican churches of Rhode Island—St. Michael's Church in Bristol (founded 1718) and King's (later St. John's) Church in Providence—received gifts and bequests of communion plate from Nathaniel Kay, his Majesty's collector of customs in Newport. Prior to his death in 1734, Kay had lived for a considerable period in the colonies. According to his epitaph in Trinity Church graveyard, Newport, "He, after an exemplary life of Faith & Charity, did by his last will, at his death, found and largely endow two Charity Schools in Newport & Bristol within his collection." Kay was a Royalist and an Anglican, and would supposedly have felt a natural preference for English silver. He could, had

[1] J. H. Buck, "Old Plate," 1903.

[101]

he so wished, have made provision that his bequests should be in the form of English plate. It is interesting, therefore, to discover that his gifts and bequests, so far as they are now extant, were the work of Colonial and chiefly of Newport silversmiths. The pieces include six flagons, two made by James Clarke and two by Benjamin Brenton of Newport and one by a silversmith whose initials are I.R.; a chalice by I.R.; a baptismal basin by Daniel Russell (Plate XIX), and a beaker by Doane of Providence. This seems a further bit of evidence to show that by the eighteenth century Rhode Island silversmiths were building up an enviable reputation and catering extensively to local patrons.

Newport, a wealthy seaport, naturally was the first town in the colony to support a considerable number of craftsmen. One of the earliest of her silversmiths was Arnold Collins (married in 1690, died in 1735), who made the Rhode Island seal, Anchor and Hope, in 1690. He was the maker of an early type of beaker (height 4⅝″), which was bequeathed in 1711 by Joseph Church to the United Congregational Church in Little Compton, Rhode Island. A particularly charming caster by Collins, inscribed with the initials of Daniel and Anstis Updike (married in 1720), now belongs to Edsel Ford.

One of the ablest and most productive of Rhode Island silversmiths was Samuel Vernon (1683–1737) of Newport. An impressive quantity of his silver is still in existence to prove his skill. He made a beaker that was presented in 1707 to the church in Groton, Connecticut, and three others that were given in 1723

Rhode Island Silver

to the First Congregational Church in Bristol, Rhode Island. An early type of straight-sided cup belongs to Philip L. Spalding, three porringers to the Metropolitan Museum, and a fourth to Judge A. T. Clearwater. Vernon's early tankards, such as those in the collections of Judge Clearwater and of Mrs. Robert L. Montgomery, have a plain tapering body and a lid that is stepped but has a flat central section. He also made tankards with a rather similar lid to which he added a finial, like the one in the illustration (Plate XVII), now the property of the Worcester Art Museum, formerly that of Josiah Salisbury. This piece has a finely modeled sun-and-dolphin thumb-piece, vertical grooves down the handle terminated by a loop, a cast handle-tip in the shape of a child's head, and an applied cut-out border above the base moldings. This border is a most unusual feature in Rhode Island or indeed in New England. It seems to be a variant of those cut-out borders of foliation found in Dutch silver and so frequently employed by silversmiths of Dutch extraction working in New York. Whether Vernon drew his inspiration from Dutch or New York models it is impossible to determine. Another tankard by Vernon, belonging to the Metropolitan Museum, also has a finial, and a well-wrought eagle thumb-piece (reproduced in Figure 4). Major Gist Blair of Washington owns a tea-pot by Vernon that represents an early type of pear-shaped pot.

Little is known of another Newport craftsman, Daniel Russell, beyond the fact that he made good silver, including beakers presented to the United Congregational Church in Newport and the United Congregational Church in Little Compton, Rhode Island. He has already been mentioned among the silversmiths commissioned to carry out the terms of the bequest of Nathaniel Kay in 1734. The baptismal basin (Plate

FIGURE 4. Eagle Thumb-piece by Samuel Vernon

XIX) that he made for Trinity Church in Newport bears the legend: "Legatum Nathanaelis Kay Armigeri, in usum Ecclesiae Anglicanae, in novoportu, in Insula De Rhode Island Anno Salutis 1734." The basin is of unusual form, oval, with sides sloping inward to the molded foot, and has two loop handles. Its weight is 52 oz. 12 dwt.

James Clarke of Newport likewise was employed to make silver bequeathed by Kay. He made the splendid flagons thus donated to St. John's (King's) Church in Providence and to St. Paul's in Wickford. To Clarke are also attributed a porringer now in the collection of Mrs. Horace B. Hare and a tankard with a coin at the end of the handle, now in the collection of Edwin P. Casey.

Newport also claimed among her clever craftsmen Benjamin Brenton (1695–1749), who made the flagons bequeathed by Nathaniel Kay to St. Michael's

PLATE XVII

See page 103

TANKARD BY SAMUEL VERNON

With Sun and Dolphin Thumb-Piece and
Decorative Border at Base

Rhode Island Silver

Church in Bristol and to Trinity Church in Newport;
John Tanner (1713–85); John Coddington (1690–
1743); Thomas Arnold (1739–1828); Daniel Rogers
(1753–92); and Jonathan Otis (1723–91), who removed in 1778, during the Revolution, to Middletown, Connecticut. They appear to have worked chiefly
for Rhode Island customers, although at times their
silver traveled farther afield, as in the case of the Vernon beaker bequeathed in 1707 to the Groton church.
Undoubtedly a large quantity is still in private possession and has never come to public notice.

Westward across Narragansett Bay was the land of
the Narragansett planters, wealthy, given to entertaining lavishly, broadened by travel and wide commercial associations. Though one would not expect to
find many silversmiths in a region quite exclusively
devoted to agriculture and stock-farming, evidently
here the demand for plate was sufficient to support
local craftsmanship. William Davis Miller has written a short monograph on six "Silversmiths of Little
Rest" (later known as Kingston), in which he chronicles what he can learn of the lives of Samuel Casey
(about 1724–70+) and his brother Gideon (born
about 1726), John Waite (1742–1817) and his
brother William (1730–1826), Joseph Perkins (1749–
89), and Nathaniel Helme (1761–89). Silver made by
these men, with the exception of Casey, is now quite
rare, although it is highly probable that in the course
of time, with more widely disseminated knowledge of
Colonial plate, numerous other examples of their work
will be brought to light and identified.

Drama and near-tragedy make of Casey a most

romantic figure. His grandfather Thomas, tradition states, was the only man to escape from the Irish Massacre in Ulster County, Ireland, in October 1641. For a time he made his home in England but later in Newport, Rhode Island. The grandson Samuel was born about 1724, probably in Newport, became a freeman in Exeter in 1745, and moved to the vicinity of Little Rest about 1750. He and his brother Gideon worked in partnership as silversmiths, 1753–63, when Gideon moved to Warwick. The following year, "the very valuable Dwelling-House of Mr. Samuel Casey . . . unhappily took Fire, and was entirely consumed with a great Quantity of rich Furniture. The whole Loss, 'tis said, amounts to near Five Thousand Pounds, Lawful Money." [1] Despite this serious misfortune, Casey soon after occupied as his residence and shop the finely situated Helme House. Whether he sought to live on too ambitious a scale, whether the patronage he found in Little Rest proved too meager to absorb his energies or provide him with sufficient income, or whether he was simply tempted to acquire "hard money" as rapidly as possible, we do not know. Whatever the occasion, Casey undertook to counterfeit some of the Portuguese and Spanish coins then widely current in the colonies. Other men were also involved in the undertaking, but the work was carried on in Casey's garret and may well have been directed by him, as his silver abundantly proves his skill in manipulating and engraving metal. Finally apprehended and brought to trial, he was sentenced

[1] Quoted by W. D. Miller from the "Providence Gazette," September 29, 1764.

to hang, but on the night before the day of execution, "a considerable Number of People riotously assembled in King's County, and with their Faces black'd proceeded to his Majesty's Goal there, the outer Door of which they broke open with Iron Bars and Pick-Axes; then they violently entered the Goal, broke every Lock therein and set at Liberty sundry Criminals, lately convicted of Money-making, one of whom [Samuel Casey] was under Sentence of Death." [1] With his release from prison, Casey disappears from record; the cloud overhanging him was heavy indeed.

So far as we now know their work, Casey was by all means the leading silversmith in Narragansett, was at least the equal of any in Newport, and can well hold his own with many of the Boston craftsmen. The quantity and quality of his work prove that he enjoyed fairly extensive and well-deserved patronage. He made a considerable number of tankards with plain tapering bodies, domed lids with finials, and handles usually tipped with an ornament representing a grotesque mask (Figure 5). This ornament was much used by Casey; it appears also in the work of Homes, Minott, and Revere of Boston. Handsome tankards of this style made by Casey now belong to Judge A. T. Clearwater and to Francis P. Garvan, and still another, engraved with the Morris arms, was recently sold at Sotheby's in London. Charming little three-legged creamers are in the collections of Hollis French, Edwin P. Casey, and Judge Clearwater.

FIGURE 5. Grotesque Mask used by Samuel Casey

[1] *Ibid.,* November 10, 1770.

[107]

Various other pieces by Casey, including beakers, por-ringers, and tea-pots, are still extant. One of Casey's most successful achievements is the tea-pot illustrated in Plate XVIII, the property of Mrs. E. S. Chaffee.

FIGURE 6. Engraved Design on Casey Tea-pot

The engraved design around the top of this piece is reproduced in Figure 6 and it is quite as ambitious and as nicely executed as any found in Colonial silver tea-pots of this period. Another tea-pot by Casey of very similar outline and also well engraved is the property of the Newport Historical Society and is illustrated in its "Bulletin," Vol. XXI, page 13.

There are extant at least five examples of the work

Rhode Island Silver

of John Waite (1742–1817) of Wickford and South
Kingstown, Rhode Island, who learned his trade from
Samuel Casey. These pieces are all of a simple, unam-
bitious type, but are well designed and wrought. The
one illustrated (Plate XIX) is a three-legged creamer
belonging to William Davis Miller. Waite enjoyed
the distinction of engraving the escutcheons and devices for Rhode Island bills of credit issued in 1776,
"the first emission of paper money in Rhode Island
in which the term 'dollar' was used and in which the
'State of Rhode Island and Providence Plantations'
replaced the former term 'Colony of Rhode Island.' " [1]
An example of one of these bills is illustrated by W.
D. Miller. Waite worked as locksmith as well as silversmith, presumably because in his locality he did not
have sufficient patronage to enable him to live by one
trade alone.

A caster (Plate XIX) made by Nathaniel Helme
(1761–89) and now the property of Miss Elizabeth
Gilbert recalls the work of another King's County
silversmith. Mr. Miller has summarized the few known
facts concerning him. Through his mother Helme was
descended from Gabriel Bernon, one of the original
Huguenot settlers of North Kingstown, a fact that implies a distinct artistic heritage. Wealth and intellec-
tual gifts also came to him from his father, Judge
James Helme of Tower Hill, for many years chief
justice of the Supreme Court of the Colony of Rhode
Island. The inventory of his estate taken after his
death in South Kingstown in 1789, quoted by W. D.
Miller, reveals an interesting equipment of tools.

[1] W. D. Miller, "Silversmiths of Little Rest."

40½	Pewter Patterns
29	Spoon Leads & other Lead
9	pr. brass flasks or Goldsmiths Cast'g forms
1	pr. wooded Cas'g Screws 1 Lamp & 2 blow Pipes
1	Box with Handle on the Top Containing a Number of Clock and Watch Tools
1	Wood Stand or rack with a Number of Old Files & Engravers
1	Gold Smiths Skillet & 2 Ingot Moulds
10	Gold smiths Hammer 1 Soup Spoon punch & 1 Square bottom Tumbler punch
1	Tin Gold Pan
1	Box Containing Spoon & button punches
1	Button Stamp
2	Drawing Irons some large plate Tools
3	pr. Gold Smith Tongs
	Old Steel Chaps & Tongues
1	black Lead pot & abt 1 Doz crucibles
1	round Box of Buckle Tools
1	pr. Gold Smiths Bellows & frame for do
1	Gold smiths Forging Anvil
1	Book Cyphers
1	Hand Laith & Blocks
1	old Tin Box Jewellers & Beed Tools

Newport and Narragansett in the fifty years preceding the Revolution supported a highly cultured, well-to-do, and progressive society. Rhode Island cabinet-makers of the period produced pieces that in the excellence of their workmanship and the refinement of their design compare with the best of Philadelphia cabinet-making, than which nothing finer was produced in the colonies. There is not a very large quantity of Rhode Island silver now publicly known and

Rhode Island Silver

available for study, yet what has appeared indicates craftsmanship in this field of a high order. Practically all of it dates from the eighteenth century and is rather strictly based upon English models. Unfortunately, the British occupation of Newport during the American Revolution proved highly disastrous. Many wealthy residents moved to Providence and others, who were pro-British, left the town when the British evacuated it. Its commerce was badly shot to pieces and its precedence was lost. After the Revolution, Providence came to the fore, growing in population, in wealth, in the extent of its commerce. Rochefoucauld, who visited Rhode Island at this period, estimated that in 1795 the trade of Providence was four or five times greater than that of Newport. This priority accounts for the relative increase of silversmiths in Providence.

CHAPTER IV

CONNECTICUT SILVER

As those who are familiar with her rocky pastures can appreciate, Connecticut lent herself none too amiably to agriculture; nevertheless this was of necessity the chief industry of the colony. The general lack of good harbors hindered the development of an active independent commerce and she was forced to rely to a considerable degree upon her more fortunate neighbors for the shipment of supplies. Much of her produce was shipped through Newport, which had built up a thriving trade and was eager for agricultural goods which she could use in her circular commercial enterprises. In return Connecticut received by way of Newport or Boston various manufactured wares.

The general pursuit of agriculture gave rise to a large number of small independent farmers who had relatively little capital outside of their real estate. Occasional men in the colony were able to acquire fortunes and to possess silver plate. According to the "Public Records of Connecticut," "Ephraim Huit of Wyndsor in Conectecotte" in 1644 owned, according to the inventory of his estate, silver plate which comprised "2 Bec Bowls, 2 wyne bouls, 1 salt, 1 trencher, salt seller, 4 siluer spoons, 13 spoons giuen to children, hauing their names on them, & 1 silver dishe." The-

PLATE XVIII

TEA-POT BY SAMUEL CASEY

Connecticut Silver

ophilus Eaton, a London merchant, emigrated to Boston in 1637 and a year later was one of the founders of New Haven. Subsequently he became first governor of Connecticut and its wealthiest citizen. The inventory of his estate, taken at the time of his death in 1657, is most interesting in the variety and quantity of goods enumerated. He possessed silver plate valued at £107.11. The possession of great wealth was exceptional, however, among Connecticut colonists.

When a man was able to afford a handsome piece of plate, he frequently sent his order to a silversmith in the great town of Boston in preference to giving it to a less experienced craftsman in his own small town. This accounts for the large number of examples of Massachusetts and Rhode Island silverwork found among the communion plate of the early Connecticut churches. But in the course of time the local silversmiths did a fair amount of business, chiefly among their fellow-townsmen, and numerous examples of Connecticut silver are still in existence to indicate its generally simple character and sturdy workmanship. An excellent record of it is given by George Munson Curtis in "Early Silver of Connecticut and its Makers," from which much of the following information has been derived.

The earliest silversmith of whom Curtis finds record is Job Prince (1680–1703) of Milford, but no example of his work is at present known. A mug and porringer by René Grignon, a Huguenot silversmith who settled in Norwich about 1708, remain to indicate his simple forthright craftsmanship. At his death in 1715 he willed his tools to Daniel Deshon (1697–

1781), an apprentice, who afterwards became a silver-smith of New London.

A silversmith of unusual interest is Cornelius Kier-stede. Dutch by descent, he was baptized in New York in 1675, became a freeman there in 1698, and about 1722 moved to New Haven. Though still living in 1753, he was then old and infirm. His work, which will be further described in the chapter on New York silver, was inspired by Continental design, but is strongly individual and considerably more ambitious in character than is that of most of his contemporaries. He brought with him to New Haven certain New York styles but evidently modified them to suit his English patrons in the Connecticut town. The First Congregational Church of Milford has a baptismal basin and beaker made by Kierstede which are sub-stantial and plain in design. The beaker has an applied border at the base with scalloped margin, suggestive of the borders on New York silver. Trinity Church, New Haven, owns a tankard and the Congregational Church of North Haven a caudle-cup bearing Kierstede's mark. Yale University owns an elaborately decorated bowl (Plate XXI A) which is more fully described on page 137.

Peter Quintard, of Huguenot descent, was born in New York in 1700, began his apprenticeship about 1724, became a freeman in 1731, was mentioned in the New York Gazette in 1735 as "Goldsmith, living near the new Dutch Church in the City of New York," and in 1737 moved to South Norwalk, where he died in 1762. A number of rather simple but well-wrought pieces bearing his mark remain, including a caudle-cup

Connecticut Silver

belonging to the Congregational Church of Stamford and a tankard in the Metropolitan Museum, New York.

Connecticut also claims John Potwine, born in Boston in 1698. There he lived and practised his trade until 1737, about which date he went to Hartford. Three beakers made by him belong to the Durham Congregational Church and two to the church in South Windsor.

Timothy Bontecou (1693–1784), a Huguenot by descent, was born in New York but studied his craft in France, and was working in New Haven as early as 1735. New Haven at that time was the richest town in the colony and naturally became its chief center of silversmithing. Hartford seems to have held second place and Middletown and New London ranked after.

Other Connecticut silversmiths of note are Captain Robert Fairchild (1703–94); Ebenezer Chittenden (1726–1812); his apprentice, Abel Buel (1742–about 1825), who became distinguished for his inventions as well as for his silversmithing; Jonathan Otis (1723–91) who lived in Newport, Rhode Island, but removed from there during the British occupation to Middletown, Connecticut; Billious Ward (1729–77) and Samuel Parmele (1737–1803) of Guilford; John Gardiner (1734–76) and Pygan Adams (1712–76) of New London. The last was the maker of the handsome coffee-pot illustrated (Plate XX B), which is now in the Clearwater collection. According to an entertaining tradition, this piece was owned during the Revolution by a New London family from whose house it was taken by a British officer, at the time the town was captured by the British troops, and carried to England. About a century later, it came up for auction in London and was sold, finding its way back to America shortly thereafter as part of Judge Clearwater's collection. Its shape and the decoration of its spout are quite like contemporary English coffee-pots. Its maker by his skill and taste fashioned a delightful piece.

CHAPTER V

NEW YORK SILVER

THE colony of New Netherland was originally established by the Dutch West India Company as a center for what they foresaw would become a profitable fur-trade. But Holland at this period was enjoying newly won freedom from Spanish domination, and her people, however much they might engage in exploration or in commerce with distant lands, were content to make Holland their home. Yet, as was proved in numerous ventures, trading-posts in the New World could not, by themselves, long survive. Their success was only assured when colonists came in sufficient numbers to promote agriculture and other necessary industries. Consequently, in 1629 the Dutch West India Company instituted the patroon system, as a means of inducing colonists to come to New Netherland and give it stability. Any member of the company bringing in fifty settlers was allowed to buy from the Indians an extensive tract of land and was granted semi-feudal control over his tenants. Because the system was a reversion to old customs and was in no way adapted to the peculiar conditions existing in New Netherland, only one of the patroonships thus established was really successful. This one exception was Rensselaerwyck.

[117]

Early American Silver

Until the middle of the seventeenth century colonization went on rather slowly, as neither proper encouragement nor support was offered by the West India Company. In 1650 it changed its policy and endeavored to induce not only Hollanders but also people of neighboring countries to settle in New Netherland. This proved a considerable stimulus to immigration, and with the wiser administration of the colony the number of its inhabitants materially increased. As its population comprised an assortment of freemen, farmers, traders, and artisans, it bore promise of still greater advancement. By 1664 the population of the province is estimated to have been about eight thousand, of which number about thirty-four hundred resided in New Amsterdam.[1]

In 1664 New Netherland, despite the wrath of its peppery little governor, Stuyvesant, passed rather quietly into English possession. Long before this date the English had begun to filter into the province, and by 1700 it is estimated that the two nationalities were about equally represented. Because the new inhabitants were of a different nationality and supported a different church, the Dutch were slow to mingle with them, and Dutch institutions and traditions, toward which the English were inclined to be tolerant, persisted for a long time.

During the period of Dutch rule, the chief industries of the province had been the fur-trade and, to a less degree, the cultivation and export of tobacco. Though these proved profitable, the general commercial situation was much like that in all the other colonies. The

[1] Figures given by George W. Schuyler in "Colonial New York"

value of raw materials exported was much more than counterbalanced by the many costly manufactured articles imported. As a consequence, there was an outflow of specie, resulting in a lack of sufficient coin for local trade. This condition worked great hardship and, as everywhere else, the colonists sought means of ameliorating their unfortunate situation.

The early records of New Netherland continually refer to such measures. Much of the local trade was accomplished by barter—so many hundredweight of tobacco might be exchanged for a quantity of peltries reckoned of equal value. The Indians were accustomed to use seawan, which consisted of white beads made from periwinkle-shells (wampum) and black or purple beads made from the colored portions of clam-shells (suckanhock). The Dutch colonists found in their dealings with the Indians that the latter were rarely willing to consummate a deal unless, in addition to other commodities, a certain amount of seawan was given to them. Once they had discovered how convenient it was as a sort of small change, the Dutch began to employ it among themselves, and for many years, although of no intrinsic value, it passed as legal tender. Beaver-skins were valuable in themselves and were the most important article of trade for a considerable period, so that they came to represent a unit of value, and the value of other things was often reckoned in terms of so many "beavers." Under such conditions, implying a great dearth of silver coin in New Netherland, there can have been relatively little opportunity for the encouragement of local silversmiths.

About the time the English came into possession of

the colony, various circumstances combined to bring it more prosperity. The cultivation of tobacco, which had previously been pursued quite extensively, was now largely discontinued, and the fur-trade, the chief source of the early colony's wealth, was becoming less important. But the flour and bread industry, which had developed more recently, was producing much revenue. In consequence of the Bolting Acts, which were passed in 1678 and 1680, and which decreed that only in New York should flour be inspected and only there should it be bolted and packed for export, the town entered upon a new period of prosperity and established a market for its flour and other bread-stuffs, which enriched it tremendously. The era of prosperity thus begun was not seriously interrupted when the monopoly was broken in 1694. The beavers, the four flour-barrels, and the windmill sails in the coat of arms of New York, designed in 1686, symbolize the sources of its early wealth.

New York merchants in the late seventeenth century also grew rich through other channels. The colonists were remote from Europe and communication was slow, so that they were often long in doubt as to the precise relationship between their mother-country and other European states. Under conditions of war they were permitted to engage in privateering, and when in doubt they seem usually to have interpreted the situation in the manner most favorable to their own interests. Since the Portuguese had discovered a sea-route to the Orient around the Cape of Good Hope, the richest trade of the world had been carried on in these waters. The treasure-ships, laden with the

PLATE XIX

See pages 104, 109

CASTER BY NATHANIEL HELME, CREAMER BY JOHN WAITE,
AND BAPTISMAL BASIN BY DANIEL RUSSELL

wealth of the Indies, naturally roused the cupidity of bold and restless seamen, who were confident that they could enjoy more adventure and greater profits by preying on this commerce than they could by engaging in lawful trade. Especially along the coast of Madagascar, the seas were infested with pirates, and many a ship was overpowered and plundered.

The pirates, seeking a market for their rich cargoes, often had the temerity to land at various points along the Colonial seaboard and especially at Newport, New York, and Charleston, where under cover of an active commerce and with the connivance of merchants and sometimes also of officials on shore they could bring in their goods for quick sale. Conditions at New York, more or less typical of the practice in general, are entertainingly and vividly set forth in the correspondence between Governor Bellomont and the Lords of Trade in London. Bellomont's predecessor in office, Colonel Fletcher, if he had not himself shared in the profits of such unlawful trade had at least permitted it to go on unchecked, for the benefit of some of his friends who were influential merchants. Bellomont was shocked at "the continued groth of Piracy" and sought to contrive "some thorow and effectual remedy." In a letter of bitter complaint addressed to the Lords of Trade, in 1698, he writes: "This city hath been a nest of Pirates, and I already find that several of their ships have their owners and were fitted from this Port, and have Commissions to act as privateers, from the late Governor here. There is a great trade between this port and Madagascar, from whence great quantities of East India goods are brought, which are certainly purchased from Pirates. I find that this practice is set up in order that the spoils taken by the Pirates (set out from this Citty) may be brought in hither in merchant ships, whose owners are likewise owners and interested in the Pirates ships. . . . I know 'tis a thing sometimes practised to take the Governors passe for one port or place and sail to another. And that trick was served me last summer at New Yorke by Baldridge and Taylor who fitted out a Briganteen, and took my passe for Antegoa, but I was told their designe was for Madagascar or Guinea; when the briganteen was at Sea, whether with or without the privity of the forementioned Owners I cannot tell, she turn'd pirate and went to Newfoundland and robb'd ships."

The profits were so great that the merchants boldly opposed the Governor's efforts to check piracy. "When any seizure is made here the merchants are ready to rise in rebellion, and so little have they been used to that in Colonel Fletcher's government that they look on it as a violence done them when we seize unlaw- full goods in their warehouses and shops. 'Tis almost incredible what a vast quantity of East India goods whould have been brought into this port, had there not been a change in the Government. Two men in this town had for their share £12000 each, which were brought from Madagascar and got there with the bar- ter with pirates, and some of those pirates had Colonel Fletcher's commission. Besides there came home to the mouth of this port 8 or 9 pirate ships since my coming to this government, which would have brought in a vast quantity of those goods, and by the confession of the merchants in the town they would have brought in a £100000 in gold and silver, and this inrages them to the last degree that they have miss'd of all this treasure and rich pennyworths of East India goods and now they drink Colonel Fletcher's health with the greatest devotion imaginable. . . . 'Tis the most beneficiall trade that to Madagascar with the pirates, that was ever heard of, and I beleive there's more to be got that way than by turning pirates and robbing. I am told this Shelly [Captain Giles Shelley, a New York ship-owner and merchant] sold rum which cost but 2^s per gallon at New York, for 50 shill^{gs} and £3 p^r gallon at Madagascar, and a pipe of Madera Wine which cost him £19 he sold there for £300. Strong liquors and gun powder and ball are the commodities that go off there, to the best advantage."

Unquestionably this rich traffic with the pirates not only brought fortunes to many enterprising New York merchants but also poured into the city the silver coin that, when converted into plate, was a magnificent evidence of their wealth. Tradition offers us one delightful and vivid instance of this close relationship. Captain Giles Shelley who, Bellomont complained, had come "lately from Madagascar with 50 or 60 Pirates" and "so flushed them at New Yorke with Arabian Gold and East India goods, that they set the government at defiance," had set out for Madagascar in his ship, the *Nassau*, financed by a group of New York merchants. The trade he carried on there was so eminently successful that it is reputed to have profited the merchants £30,000. Bellomont himself comments: "Had there been a man of War at Yorke,

Shelly and his Pirates in all Probability had been taken and £50000 in money belonging to them." This voyage is commemorated by a silver tankard made by a New York silversmith, Garrett Onclebagh, which bears on its lid a representation of Shelley's ship, the *Nassau*. His coat of arms is engraved on the body of the tankard. The story runs that the merchants who had financed Shelley's voyage presented this token to him upon his return. The tankard now belongs to Judge A. T. Clearwater of Kingston, New York.

When Shelley and his associates returned from their voyages with sudden and amazing wealth, and with the exotic merchandise of the East, they must have inspired in the citizens a desire for display and for colorful gear. The houses of the New York patroons and burghers of the period were a reflection of those of their contemporaries in Holland. In the Old World the Dutch had a strong feeling for their homes, which they strove to make comfortable and to fill with all the things they prized most. They had a tremendous admiration for Oriental porcelain, as is proved by the quantities of it that they imported and by the zeal with which, in their delft ware, they strove to imitate it. The Dutch painters loved to depict the interiors of these homes, furnished with massive cabinets and cupboards that served for the storage and display of those things which the owner cherished—his Oriental porcelain, Venetian glass, his native pottery, pewter, and silverware. The inventories of the period indicate that wealthy folk had surprising quantities of Oriental and other goods. Similar records show that the more prosperous Dutch residents of New York in the late seven-

teenth century lived with much the same degree of
comfort and a comparable richness and variety of
household furnishings.

The fruits of foreign trade, legitimate and otherwise, served to satisfy, both directly and indirectly,
the taste for handsome furnishings. Not only were
coveted articles thus imported but also much silver
coin, which enabled the local silversmiths to add their
rich contribution toward the embellishment of New
York homes. As early as 1643 there is record of one
"Jeuriaen Blanck, goutsmidt." Though given this
designation in the early records, it is impossible to
determine whether or not he plied his craft here. Increasing references to goldsmiths and silversmiths occur thereafter, until in the last quarter of the seventeenth and in the early eighteenth century there were
many following this trade in New York. Much of
their handiwork is still in existence.

Among these early New York silversmiths were a
considerable number of Huguenots, who were extremely sensitive and clever craftsmen. Presumably
because persecution had driven them from France, they
did not endeavor to follow distinctive French styles,
but chose rather to adopt the types favored in the
locality in which they had sought refuge and a new
home. The best known of these Huguenot smiths working in early New York was Bartholomew Le Roux
(died 1713). He was extremely active in the contro-
versy centering around Leisler and Milbourne, and was
a member of the popular faction that urged defensive
measures against a possible French and papist inva-
sion. His son Charles later followed the same craft,

winning such distinction that he was made official silversmith of the city.

The great majority of New York silversmiths at this period were of Dutch descent and the traditions of their mother-country were remarkably strong. Unlike the Huguenots, they were not conscious of any sense of estrangement from their native land, so that one would naturally anticipate that men like Ahasuerus Hendricks, Jacob and Hendrik Boelen, Jacobus Van der Spiegel, Koenraet and Jacob Ten Eyck, Peter Van Dyck, and Bartholomew Schaats would produce silver no less sturdily Dutch than their names. They were, indeed, a conservative group, and especially in communion plate held quite closely to Dutch types. These baptismal basins and communion beakers will be described in detail later.

But successful colonists were necessarily capable of adapting themselves to new conditions and environment. Consequently it is not surprising to find that gradually English influences show in New York silver. It was not, however, a sudden conquest, but rather a gradual infiltration. Had it been the former, such popular English styles as the caudle-cup, which was extensively used in both England and New England from the time of the late Commonwealth to the early eighteenth century, would assuredly have been adopted. Yet no caudle-cup bearing the mark of a New York silversmith has ever come to the attention of the writer. Presumably the Dutch did not care for such drinks as caudle, or they preferred to imbibe their liquors from open, two-handled bowls like the *brandewijnkom* they had used in Holland. On the other hand,

these Dutch silversmiths and their patrons did adopt
such English forms as particularly commended themselves, the preëminent example being the tankard.
Tankards were made in England and in Germany and
the Scandinavian countries; we have it on good author-
ity that they were not made in Holland. Yet the Dutch
in New York seem to have appreciated the practicality
of these great covered cups and straightway made
them, after the English model, in great numbers. But
even then, though they adopted the English shape,
they employed modes of decoration more Continental
than English, and gave the whole creation a character
that was neither Continental nor English but distinctively New York. It is a striking instance of what
occurred over and over again in Colonial life. Instead
of merely endeavoring to copy European customs or
styles or institutions, the colonists had the practical
good sense and judgment to carry over only what
pleased them or seemed expedient or what would work
satisfactorily under the peculiar conditions of life in
America, and the result was that they evolved something that still shows its sources of inspiration but
which is nonetheless a distinct entity.

This selectiveness is illustrated in New York silver
as a group. It shows, first of all, Dutch ancestry. This
is evidenced partly by the persistence of certain shapes
of Dutch origin; partly by the wide and continued use
of embossed, engraved, and cast ornamentation; and
partly by a characteristic massiveness and vigor. But
from the late seventeenth century on, there is combined with these elements an increasing evidence of
English influence, which shows partly in the adoption

of some English shapes and details of decoration and partly in a gradual lightening of the general proportions, a greater variety of form, and a more sparing use of ornament. Despite this tendency, New York silver retained its general air of solidity, as compared with plate made in New England and Philadelphia, until much after the middle of the eighteenth century.

By virtue of this commingling of strong Dutch traditions with later English influences, New York silverwork shows a highly distinctive character. It is most interesting to contrast that made from, let us say, about 1675 to 1750 with silver made in Boston at the same period. The New York silver is distinctly more generous in its proportions and more massive. It is not merely a question of over-all measurements, for the silver is also thick in section. The average thickness of a New York tankard drum is appreciably greater than that typical of New England. So, too, a New York beaker is thick-walled and finished at its base with a stout torus molding, whereas the contemporary New England beaker either has a flat base with no reinforcement at all or has a rather delicately molded applied band. New York bowls, when plain, are usually quite heavy. Alms-basins are sturdily made and finished with a bold molding at the rim. Of course, if a piece was to be embossed, a favorite mode of decoration with the Dutch, it was made of relatively thin silver, yet even then a heavy molding or the bold scale of the ornament will often proclaim its origin.

Naturally shapes designed for strength and usefulness are apt to be simple and relatively conservative in style. But New York silver shows a much greater

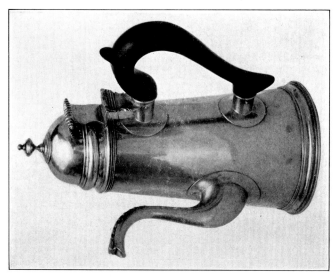

See pages 115, 322-23

PLATE XX

COFFEE-POTS BY A NEW YORK SILVERSMITH AND

New York Silver

conservatism than New England, probably largely due to the fact that much less silver was produced in the south than in the north, but perhaps also because the Dutch in New York under English rule had less contact with Holland and so clung more tenaciously to their old styles instead of refreshing them by new importations and new inspiration. This conservatism, whatever its cause, is expressed in the persistence of certain forms and in a lack of variety. Beakers, for example, tend to be of the same general proportions and height as compared to the tall and thin, short and stout, and middle-sized beakers found in New England. New York tankards are always capacious and almost invariably, prior to about 1735, are fitted with a corkscrew thumb-piece. Nor is there a wide range in the kinds of objects made. Beakers, tankards, baptismal basins, bowls, tea-pots, mugs, small wine-cups, porringers—these are the things most generally met with. This list might be contrasted with the assortment of things made by one Boston silversmith, John Coney, as given on page 55.

A further striking difference between early Boston and New York plate lies in the decoration, that of the former being almost entirely of direct English inspiration, while that of the latter was Continental with a later admixture of some English. This will be described in detail later.

In discussing the forms made in New York, it is wise to begin with the beaker, which is probably the most characteristic of all. In Holland the beaker had long been established as a domestic drinking-cup and after the Reformation was adopted in the Protestant churches as a communion cup. Both facts assured its popularity among the Dutch of New York. The great majority of the early New York-made beakers existent are communion cups preserved in the Dutch churches of the New World, and side by side with them are imported beakers made in Haarlem and Amsterdam.

The latter show clearly enough the genesis of the Colonial styles. Beautifully illustrated and carefully described by F. Alfred Jones in his volume, "Old Silver of American Churches," these beakers are sufficiently rare and interesting for us to look at them in detail. Of those made in Holland, there are the following:

		Property of
1.	Amsterdam, 1637 height 6-7/8″	First Church, Boston.
2.	Haarlem, 1643 height 7-5/8″	Old South Church, Boston.
3.	Haarlem, 1638 height 7-1/4″	Collegiate Church, New York.
4.	Haarlem, 1645 height 7-1/16″	Collegiate Church, New York.
5.	Haarlem, 1655 height 6-3/4″	First Reformed Church, Tarrytown, N. Y.
6.	Haarlem, 1660 height 7-1/8″	First Reformed Church, Albany, N. Y.
7.	Dutch, about 1700 height, beaker, 7-3/4″; beaker and cover, 11-1/4″ St. Mary's Church, Burlington, N. J. (Plate XXII)	

The height of these Dutch beakers varies from 6¾″ to 7⅝″. All have some sort of stout molding at the base and are heavily wrought. All are decorated with engraved strapwork and pendent flower-sprays, while four include in their design symbolic figures in medallions. These figures, often rather crudely drawn, usually represent Faith, Hope, and Charity. Thus in one medallion Hope gaily disports herself with an anchor and a bird, while in a second a less cheerful figure raises the cross of Faith. The third medallion portrays Charity as an expansive matron leading one child by the hand and carrying another, while back of her rises the stepped gable of a typical Dutch house. The Dutch beakers found in Colonial churches are quite representative of seventeenth-century Dutch silverwork and reflect the simple childlike attitude of those folk who used them.

The beaker belonging to St. Mary's Church, Burlington, New Jersey (7 in the list above) is chosen for illustration (Plate XXII), partly because it is elaborately engraved with interlacing strapwork and foliate scrolls, with a cipher or reversed monogram, with a cherub's head and wings, and with symbolic birds and reptiles, and partly because it is an example of the use in Dutch plate of an applied band of foliation at the base. Such borders enjoyed wide favor among New York silversmiths; it is therefore particularly interesting to find a Dutch original. An unusual feature of this beaker is its cover with crown finial. The beaker is marked with the cipher **T B R**. It is traditionally supposed to have been the gift of Colonel Robert Quary.

When E. Alfred Jones made his study of the old silver of American churches, he found, in addition to the seven Dutch beakers noted above, thirteen beakers

made by New York silversmiths and now belonging
to Dutch churches in the vicinity of New York. In
height they range from 6½″ to 7½″. Like the beakers
imported from Holland, just described, these too are
vigorously wrought and all are engraved after the
Dutch manner, ten of the thirteen having symbolic
figures of Faith, Hope, and Charity in medallions.
The accompanying sketch is reproduced from the
Jacob Boelen beaker, which was originally given to
the Reformed Church of Kingston, New York, and
which now belongs to Judge A. T. Clearwater (7 in
the list below). It represents a typical engraved design, the figure in this sketch symbolizing Charity.

LIST OF COMMUNION BEAKERS MADE BY
EARLY NEW YORK SILVERSMITHS

1. Ahasuerus Hendricks. Made 1678, copy of Haarlem,
   1660, beaker (6 in list above); height 7-1/8″. Property
   of First Reformed Church, Albany, New York.
2. Henricus Boelen. Made 1731. Height 6-1/2″. Property
   of Reformed Church, Bergen, New Jersey.
3. Henricus Boelen. Mate to preceding.
4. Henricus Boelen. Height 6-3/4″. Property of Reformed
   Church, Flatlands, New York.
5. Jacob Boelen. Made 1707. Height 6-7/8″. Property of
   New Utrecht Reformed Church, Brooklyn, New York.
6. Jacob Boelen. Mate to preceding.
7. Jacob Boelen. Made 1683. Height 7-1/4″ (see sketch).
   Property of Judge A. T. Clearwater; formerly property
   of Reformed Church, Kingston, New York.
8. Benjamin Wynkoop. Made 1711. Height 7-1/4″. Copy
   of the preceding beaker. Same collection.

New York Silver

9. Garrett Onclebagh. Made 1697. Height 7-1/8″. Property of Reformed Church, Flatbush, New York.
10. Garrett Onclebagh. Mate to preceding.
11. Unknown, probably Jacob Boelen. About 1700. Height 6-1/2″. Property of First Reformed Church, Tarrytown, New York.
12. Unknown, mark V H. Height 7-1/2″. Property of Collegiate Church, New York.
13. Unknown, mark V H. Mate to preceding.

Outside of this group of thirteen sacramental beakers, very few of these cups have come to light.

FIGURE 7. Engraved Design on Jacob Boelen Beaker

Presumably many more were made solely for domestic use but have long since been melted down and reshaped into more modern forms. Two or three of the same general type as those just described, but intended for secular use, deserve attention. One by Jacob Boelen (Plate XXIII; height 6½″) decorated with simple strapwork and scrolled flower-sprays but without symbolic figures, appeared unexpectedly a few years ago, so tarnished that it was at first mistaken for pewter. It is now in the collection of Francis P. Garvan. Like the Dutch beaker in Plate XXII, this Boelen piece is decorated at its base with a heavy molding and above this is an applied leaf border.

Another beaker in Mr. Garvan's collection is considerably smaller than those just mentioned (height $4\frac{11}{16}″$) and its engraved ornament of scrolls, pendent fruit, and grotesques seems too large in scale for the piece and cramped within its confines. The beaker is inscribed "1686" and is marked with the stamp $C_B V$, presumed to be that of Carol Van Brugh, son of Johannes Van Brugh and Cathrina Roelofse, and grandson of the widely known Anneke Jans. Carol Van Brugh, whose name appears in a 1677 New York tax-list with the designation "Silversmith," was plying his trade there in the last quarter of the century. In 1693 he made a gold cup that was presented to Governor Fletcher. Until quite recently his work had not come to general notice, although several examples are extant.

Singularly enough, another of these early domestic beakers is also by Carol Van Brugh and also has rather unusual decoration. It is a piece with a most interesting history, for it is inscribed "Robbert Sandersen 1685" and the tradition is that it was presented by friendly Mohawks to their friend, Robert Sanders, interpreter and commission merchant, who lived in the vicinity of Albany and Schenectady. It is still owned by a member of his family, J. Glen Sanders. Around its lip are engraved interlacing straps enclosing flower-sprays and below are three medallions—thus far it follows the usual formula for New York beakers. But the medallions enclose symbols not thus far found else-where in silver, geese for Holland, a beaver for New York, and a pot of flowers—perhaps with reference to the Sanders family. Just above the base are other groups of symbols, and the base itself is characteris-tically strengthened by a torus molding with a stamped border above, finished with a scalloped margin.[1]

The custom of making tall communion beakers per-sisted, as evidenced by one made probably in the sec-ond quarter of the eighteenth century by Adrian Bancker (1703—about 1761), which is 7″ high. Its heavy torus base molding is also reminiscent of earlier beakers. On the other hand, it is quite possible that English taste has moved the silversmith to leave its surface plain and to make it rather more tapering than were the earlier examples. Originally given to the Rochester Church in Accord, New York, it now be-longs to Judge A. T. Clearwater.

Frederick Philipse and his wife, "the right honor-able, God-fearing, very wise and prudent my lady Catharine Philipse" (daughter of Oloff Stevenson van Cortlandt), in 1699 built the little gray stone church that is still to be seen at Sleepy Hollow, on the Al-bany Post Road north of Tarrytown. To it they gave

[1] Illustrated and described by Anna W. McNeil in "Antiques," Vol. XV, p. 388–90. Height 8 inches.

two beakers, one made in Haarlem in 1655, the other probably by Jacob Boelen of New York about 1700 (see lists above), and a baptismal basin, also by Boelen. The last in its general form was not unlike that illustrated in Plate XXVIII. Both demonstrate that the early baptismal basins, like the early beakers, quite closely followed Dutch models both in form and in decorative treatment. The baptismal basin (Plate XXVIII) made by Jacobus Van der Spiegel (working 1685–1705) has a deep bowl-shaped center and a wide margin inscribed with a verse composed by Domine Selyns, interpreting the meaning of baptism. The congregation of the South Reformed Church of New York (to which the basin still belongs) contributed 63 Holland guilders toward its purchase in 1694. This basin is now generously lent by the church to the Metropolitan Museum, New York. Another baptismal basin, made by Adrian Bancker, belongs to the Collegiate Church, New York. To this church also belong almsbasins by Jacob and Henricus Boelen.

Passing from ecclesiastical plate to that designed primarily for domestic use, we find a charming group of bowl-shaped cups ranging in size from the tiny cups, just large enough to contain a dram of wine to consecrate a marriage, to the great handsome bowls intended doubtless for display or for ceremonial rather than for ordinary use. Most of these shapes are directly derived from Dutch silver, from such forms, for example, as the *brandewijnkom*, and are characteristically ornamented with bold repoussé and flat-chased flower-motives in panels around their sides. The smaller cups are usually flat-bottomed and are simply

PLATE XXI   *See page 137*

BOWLS BY CORNELIUS KIERSTEDE AND BENJAMIN WYNKOOP
WITH CHARACTERISTIC EMBOSSED FLORAL DESIGNS

finished with twisted wire handles or with flat handles
of scroll outline. Their sides may be left plain or
given just a touch of ornament, such as simple panel-
ing or a suggestion of floral forms. The more imposing
bowls, however, are set up on a foot-rim and often furnished with cast handles of caryatid form, and their
sides are effectively embossed with tulips and other
flowers in compartments, as orderly as a Dutch garden. One of the most impressive of these bowls was
made by Benjamin Wynkoop and now belongs to the
New York Historical Society (Plate XXI B). Another bowl by Wynkoop of very similar design is in a
private collection. A third, with caryatid handles and
flowers in panels around the sides, bears a **B R** stamp
assigned to Bartholomew Le Roux and is inscribed
with the initials I ^W S—those of Joseph and Sarah
Wardel of Trenton, New Jersey. This is now in the
Francis P. Garvan collection. Yet another of these
great bowls exists, bearing the mark of Cornelius Kierstede, who worked as silversmith in New York until
1722, when he moved to New Haven. The bowl
(Plate XXI A) is without handles and is decorated
with conventionalized flower-forms in panels. It was
presented in 1745 by his students to Thomas Darling,
a tutor at Yale College, to which the bowl was later
bequeathed by a descendant, Miss Helen Darling.

There are also plain bowls of heavy silver made for
practical use, such as those by Jacob Boelen and Cornelius Wynkoop in the Garvan collection. Though
devoid of ornament, such bowls have a most pleasing
appearance, the slight hammer-marks producing just

enough variation in surface to give the silver character and interest.

As the beaker was the accepted form of communion cup, so the tankard was the most popular form of domestic drinking-vessel, if one can judge by the large number of examples remaining to-day. Quantities of beer were drunk even in Puritan New England, where scarcely a contract was consummated without the consumption of generous draughts. The numbers and proportions of the New York tankards give ample proof that the Dutch were a social folk. It is said that in 1646 New Netherland averaged one beer-shop to every four houses. The "strong liquors" and other drinks that the inhabitants imbibed included Spanish, Rhenish, and French wines, brandy, gin, perry, rum, cider, and ale, some of which they imported and some of which they brewed. For beer and ale the capacious tankard was well adapted; for wines and cordials smaller cups served.

As already suggested, the shape of the New York tankard was presumably derived from the English tankard of the second half of the seventeenth century, which it resembles more closely than it does any Continental model. Whatever its exact derivation, the New York tankard, practically throughout its history, followed the same general outline—a large, straight-sided, slightly tapering body firmly strengthened by moldings at its base; a handle of corresponding size, often so ornamented as to give a firm grip; and a flat-topped cover in two stages. New England and Pennsylvania might in the course of time follow the fashion of doming the lids of their tankards, and Boston might go further and almost invariably add a finial, and a mid-band around the body, but New York sat in the midst of these changes and was practically unaffected by them. The only radical variation from this typical form was the occasional adoption after 1750 of the bulbous shape, corresponding to some English pieces made at about the same period.

The characteristic features of the early New York tankards are illustrated by the three examples at the left of Plate XXIV, by those in Plate LIV, and by the accompanying sketches showing decorative details. (We shall for the time being disregard the piece at the extreme right of Plate XXIV, which represents a later development and which will eventually be discussed from that point of view). The largest tankard in the group in Plate XXIV, that at the extreme left, measures 7⅞″ with its lid lowered. Its ample proportions are increased by the fact that it is almost straight-sided instead of tapering. The great tankard illustrated in Plate LIV, left, fashioned by the same silver-smith, Jacobus Van der Spiegel, is of the same size. The others illustrated, even if not quite so massive, are still far more capacious and heavier in appearance than are those characteristic of either New England or Philadelphia.

The thumb-pieces in these early New York tankards are practically always of the so-called corkscrew type, which appears to have been peculiar to this locality. The lids, though sometimes plain, are more often looked upon as a worthy place for decoration. Sometimes this is merely a circle of foliation (see Plate XXIV), sometimes the circle encloses a cipher or reversed monogram. Occasionally much more elaborately engraved designs appear, such as that shown in the

FIGURE 8. "Corkscrew" Thumb-piece

sketch. This particular one is reproduced from the tankard by Wynkoop (Plate **XXIV**) in the collection of Foster Pruyn, but similar designs occur on tankards

FIGURE 9. Engraved Design on Wynkoop **Tankard** Lid

by Jacobus Van der Spiegel and by a silversmith whose initials were P. V. B., which fact suggests that it may have been a more or less conventional pattern.

[140]

New York Silver

The lid of a well-known tankard by Peter Van Dyck, in the Garvan collection, is unique in combining with such engraved motives as foliate scrolls, flower-sprays, and a cherub head, a central embossed rosette and an outer border of gadrooning.

The early New York silversmith realized the decorative possibilities of coins and medals, as suggested by German and Scandinavian plate so ornamented. Occasionally medals but more frequently coins were inserted in the lids of the tankards. The Boelens, Schaats, Bogardus, Kierstede, Roosevelt, Hamersly, and others used them in this fashion, or sometimes as an ornament for the end of the tankard handle. The coins seem usually to have been such as might have been current in the colonies at the time and were chosen chiefly for their decorative qualities. They include English, Spanish, German, Austrian, and French money. The medals are even more interesting. A large medal by Sebastian Dadler, struck in 1634 to commemorate the death of Gustavus Augustus of Sweden (1594–1632), decorates the lid of a tankard made by Abraham Pontram and bequeathed by Jeremiah Owen in 1756 to the First Presbyterian Church of New York, to which it still belongs. A tankard by Bartholomew Schaats in the collection of Dr. Thomas H. Foulds bears in its lid a grave-medal inscribed, in Dutch: "To the memory of Samuel Hermans whom Our Lord has called, the fifth of September, 1688."

Most interesting and appropriate is the medal inserted in the lid of a tankard by Adrian Bancker, a medal struck in Holland in 1629, which commemorates and depicts the capture of the Spanish silver-

[141]

fleet by the Dutch in the preceding year. The treasure
thus taken was valued at 11,500,000 florins ($4,600,
000). One side of the medal bears a Latin inscription
relating that on September 8, 1628, the West India
Company, under the auspices of the United Provinces
of Holland and under the command of Peter Heyn,
captured near Matanzas, a bay of the Island of Cuba,
the royal silver-fleet of the Kingdom of Spain. A border inscription, also in Latin, pertinently quotes Jeremiah 51:33 and 48: "The daughter of Babylon is as a
threshing-floor . . . she shall be threshed by the spoilers
from the north at the time of her harvest." The en-
gagement of the two fleets is depicted on this face of
the medal, while on the opposite side is a map of the
western hemisphere, accompanied by another verse
from Jeremiah. It was the Spanish who first brought
to Europe vast quantities of silver, which they had
looted from Brazil and Mexico. They had also attempted to conquer the Netherlands and had subjected
them to the utmost cruelty. Consequently the highest
joy was experienced in Holland when Spain's pride
was thus humbled and her treasure taken by the
doughty Dutch admiral at Matanzas. Small wonder
that they quoted Scripture and likened Spain to the
daughter of Babylon and themselves to the spoilers
from the north. The bullion itself must have been a
godsend to the Dutch, so long besieged and ravaged
by Spanish armies. The medal suggests the romantic
story of silver plate of the period. Much silver was
captured by the Spanish in South America and taken
to Europe, where it was made into either plate or
bullion. Later some found its way to America, and was

eventually made into plate by the Colonial silver-smiths. This particular medal may have been an heir-loom in the family of the customer who ordered Bancker to fashion the tankard.

The hands that lifted these heavy tankards may sometimes have been unsteady, and to give them a firmer grip the handles were often furnished with a plain tapering strip known as a rat-tail. At other times this was developed (as in Plate XXIV) into what is rather inappropriately termed a beaded rat-tail. But the New York silversmith loved ornament, and saw in the handle an opportunity to expend some of his energy by designing such elaborate fashions as those shown in the sketch, taken from a tankard made by the silversmith P. V. B. and now owned by Mr. Gar-van. It employs such favorite motives as the cherub head, pendant fruit and flower sprays, etc. (Figure 13). A simpler mode of handle-ornament was the lion rampant, a device much favored by Cornelius Kier-stede, and found also in the work of Jacobus Van der Spiegel and Koenraet Ten Eyck.

The end of the handle in New England tankards is often decorated with cast cherub or other heads and this type of ornament also occurs quite frequently in New York. The New York silversmiths naturally em-ployed the cherub head and wings, as it was a favorite with them generally, and they used at times a man's head with a wig (Figure 11).

Peculiar to their work, apparently, is the elaborate design illustrated in the sketch, which combines a woman's face, clasped hands, caryatid figures, and other elements too intricate to distinguish. No European original is thus far known and it seems reasonable to suppose, considering how able these Colonial silversmiths were, that the design originated with them, although its elements were drawn from Continental

FIGURE 10

FIGURE 11

FIGURE 12　　FIGURE 13　　FIGURE 14

Characteristic Decorative Details on New York Tankards

sources. Perhaps only one silversmith in New York possessed the mold, but in any event tankards bearing the marks of Peter Van Dyck, Henricus Boelen, Benjamin Wynkoop, Everardus Bogardus, and the unknown P. V. B., show this handle-ornament, (Figure 10).

PLATE XXII   *See page 131*

DUTCH OR FLEMISH BEAKER, ABOUT 1700

New York Silver

The applied borders of foliation occasionally used in Holland, as illustrated by the beaker shown in Plate XXII, found their widest development in New York tankards. Four of the five early tankards illustrated in Plates XXIV and LIV have these charming cut-out borders around their bases. This is higher than the real average, but nevertheless indicates that they were very common. Figure 15 shows four such border patterns, taken from tankards by Van der Spiegel, P. V. B., Kierstede, and Henricus Boelen, and suggest characteristic variations. Kierstede generally chose this form of border (Number 3) for his tankards, nor has it thus far been found in the work of any other silversmith. How far a given design was limited to the work of one man, however, has not yet been determined but it would make an interesting subject for special study.

The broad expanse of the tankard drum offered the ambitious silversmith an opportunity to engrave a coat of arms with flowing mantling, as shown in the de Peyster arms on the Van der Spiegel tankard in Plate LIV. The styles followed by the New York silversmiths and engravers are discussed elsewhere (see pages 263–67 and figures 20–21).

In the tankard at the extreme right of Plate XXIV are set forth various later features representative of New York styles of about the middle or third quarter of the eighteenth century. This particular piece (Garvan collection) is stamped with the initials H & M, and is presumably the work of Hays and Myers. The later period is indicated by the more tapering lines of the drum or body, by the double-scroll handle with its scrolled termination, by the scroll thumb-piece, and by the applied drop on the handle just below the hinge. In all these features it differs from the early examples just described and has borrowed directly from contem-

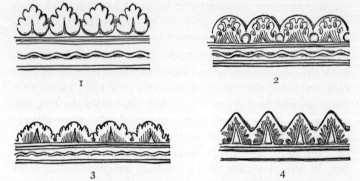

FIGURE 15. Characteristic Borders on New York Tankards
1. Jacobus Van der Spiegel, 2. P. V. B., 3. Cornelius Kierstede,
4. Henricus Boelen

porary English usage. Its New York origin still shows in its flat lid, in the engraved cipher on its lid, and in its generous proportions.

About the same period as that of the Hays and Myers tankard or a trifle later, there also appeared occasionally in New York a tankard with bulbous body. Judge A. T. Clearwater owns a tankard of this style made by Jacob Gerittse Lansing of Albany. The style enjoyed a great vogue in England and in Philadelphia in the second half of the eighteenth century. With these later styles, the corkscrew thumb-piece rarely occurs, its place being taken either by the scrolled form seen in the Hays and Myers piece and in Figure 12 taken from a tankard by Nicholas Roosevelt, or by the open-loop thumb-piece shown in Figure 14, both of which are inspired by English styles.

The earliest New York mugs, which are practically small tankards without lids, are straight-sided and tapering, and usually are girdled by bands of molding, sometimes with spiral wire and foliate borders. Straightforward, vigorous, and appealing, they win our interest more than do the more sophisticated bulbous mugs that were so generally made throughout the eighteenth century. Koenraet Ten Eyck (Plate L) and Simeon Soumaine (Plate XXV), among others, developed the early straight-sided mug. The Soumaine mug illustrated (Plate XXV) has the applied base border of foliation and a cipher enclosed within a medallion flanked by feathery sprays. This bit of engraving is characteristically New York, but in this case the engraver has been cramped for space and has not accommodated his design to it as well as he usually did. A mug by Jacob Ten Eyck, now the property of the Metropolitan Museum, has almost straight sides curving inward slightly at the base, and marks a transitional stage between the straight mug and the bulbous style much used in the eighteenth century.

Porringers must have been considered indispensable in all eighteenth-century Colonial households. While some were probably made in New England in the seventeenth century, presumably the New York examples date chiefly from the eighteenth, and may have been made in response to a demand on the part of incoming English settlers. The exact derivation of the

American porringer is still a matter for argument and is more fully discussed on page 330. The Dutch had somewhat shallow wide bowls with two pierced handles, which they used for broth-bowls. Fairly close to this form is the rare two-handled covered porringer in the Clearwater collection, possibly by Joseph Newkirke of New York, who is recorded as working in 1716 (Plate XXV; height with cover, 5″; length with handles, 11¼″). Among porringers with a single handle, New York offers one of the most attractive styles of handle-piercing, as represented in the work of Peter Van Dyck, Bartholomew Schaats (Plate XXV), and the unknown maker P. V. B. Another style which seems to have been more or less peculiar to New York is represented by the Figure 32. The great majority of New York porringers, however, follow the familiar Colonial style with so-called keyhole piercing (see Figure 30).

An early type of salt is illustrated in Plate LX, made by Jacob Ten Eyck and now the property of H. F. du Pont. The style, with its gadrooned borders, in European plate is late seventeenth century, but this piece dates from the early eighteenth. A similar salt by Ten Eyck belongs to Mrs. William Bayard Van Rensselaer. Examples are quite rare. The same fashion in New England has already been discussed (page 40); a salt by John Coney, belonging to the Museum of Fine Arts in Boston, is a delightful illustration of the type. A slightly later style, belonging to the first quarter of the eighteenth century, is represented by a pair of trencher-salts (Plate LX) made by the New York silversmith who stamped his work B L R, presumed to be Bartholomew Le Roux, who died in 1713. These are beautifully engraved with the de Peyster arms and belong to Frederic Ashton de Peyster, a descendant of the original owner.

Casters also find a place in early New York silver. Francis P. Garvan owns a large and handsome example, which is probably the work of Bartholomew Le Roux. It is circular in form and has a saber fastening for its lid. The latter is charmingly pierced with circular and heart-shaped openings and has an embossed whorl of leaves surrounding its elaborately molded finial.

The earliest New York tea-pots may not be remarkable for grace of line or for sophistication, but as steps in a fascinating story they have a strong appeal. One of the rarest, most interesting, and earliest in style is the spherical tea-pot by Jacob Boelen, in the collection of Pierre Jay and long in his family (Plate XXVI). Its shape must have come, more or less directly, from Chinese porcelain tea-pots. The molded base is comparable to the feet of certain Dutch beakers. In the straight spout no attempt has been made to beautify what was evidently considered a purely practical concern. A simple insetting cover is most commonly associated with rather early pieces; the Boelen tea-pot has such a cover, elaborated by a border of gadrooning and punched work. Though there is nothing dainty or self-conscious about this little tea-pot, it must have suited its use admirably, and appeals by its naïve directness. The coat of arms (Philipse) with scrolled mantling and cornucopias with which it is embellished shows, however, a trained hand and facility in the delicate art of engraving. Here, then, the silversmith divorced himself from practical matters and yielded to the purely decorative.

Probably the next stage in the evolution of the tea-pot in New York silver is represented by such a tea-pot as that by Peter Van Dyck (1684–1750), also in Mr. Jay's collection, or that owned by the New York Historical Society. Whether the latter is Colonial or European in origin has not been fully determined, but probably it is the former. Its shape apparently finds no exact counterpart in Dutch silver but does correspond fairly closely to other New York pieces. The coat of arms engraved upon it also follows New York fashions. It bears the maker's mark of a demi-horse or demi-unicorn without initials, which, if the piece proves to be American, is thus far the only instance of this sort of mark known.

Developing out of this simple and not too shapely form arose the pear-shaped style, which became the most popular in New York in the second quarter of the eighteenth century. Tea-pots like this were made by Charles Le Roux (Plate XXVII A, height 8″; Garvan collection), by John Le Roux, Peter Van Dyck, Simeon Soumaine, Jacob Ten Eyck, Adrian Bancker, John Brevoort, Nicholas Roosevelt, and Thauvet Besley.

Another development of the pear shape appears in the kettle owned by Miss Anne S. Van Cortlandt (Plate XXVII B). This most interesting and rare piece was made by Cornelius Kierstede of New York, later of New Haven. It is probably the only example of a New York kettle known; even in Europe silver

kettles are only occasionally found. Apart from this
distinction, this kettle merits study from the point
of view of its ornament. Kierstede had a distinctive
style, crude perhaps and more ambitious than his skill
sometimes justified, but nevertheless displaying a force-
ful and eager personality. The unusual style of acanthus foliation upon the spout is very similar to that
on a Kierstede snuffer-stand that was rather recently
presented to the Metropolitan Museum by Mrs. William A. Moore (née Clarkson). Both the Van Cort-
landts and the Clarksons are old New York families,
so that the authenticity of these two pieces is unques-
tionable. A bowl by Kierstede, embossed in the same
crude and conscious style, has already been described
on page 137.

Later New York tea-pots follow the same styles as
those seen in New England and Philadelphia, but often
continue to have a substantial quality and certain decorative features that are reminiscent of New York silver
of the earlier periods. A particularly swagger example
of one of these later tea-pots is that by John
Moulinar (Plate XLIII), with its strongly modeled
outline of inverted-pear type and with its well-con-
ceived and executed flat-chased decoration. Formerly
one of the outstanding pieces in Mr. Halsey's collection, it has subsequently passed into that of Mr. Garvan.

Presumably the earliest type of covered sugar-bowl
was the simple bowl with saucer-shaped cover of which
that by Simeon Soumaine (Plate LVIII A; Garvan collection) is a charming example. By way of embellishment it bears an engraved cipher on bowl and cover, as

simple as the plainness of the piece demands. The illustration (Plate LVII B) by Adrian Bancker proves that early New York creamers followed the general Colonial styles. This three-legged creamer is most amusing, standing on its sturdy little legs like an assertive puppy.

Another robust piece of mid-eighteenth-century New York silver appears in Plate LX D, a toddy-warmer made by Thomas Hamersly and mounted with a coin of William III of England in its bowl (Garvan collection). The use of the coin for decoration, the stout molding around the bowl, and the general heaviness of this little piece would make one guess its origin, even without the mark of its maker.

John Heath of New York fashioned the charming bowl (Plate XLVIII) that is engraved with the Van Cortlandt arms and belongs to Miss Anne S. Van Cortlandt. In form it is rather similar to bowls by well-known Boston craftsmen, such as William Homes and Paul Revere, in comparison with which it holds its own admirably. This bowl may well date from the middle or third quarter of the eighteenth century.

Of approximately the same period is the pierced dish-ring (Plate LIX) that bears the mark of Myer Myers of New York (became a freeman in 1746). This is probably the only known instance of a dish-ring made in Colonial America. It belongs to Mr. and Mrs. Roger F. Hooper.

The objects most commonly met with in New York silver prior to the Revolution, and especially those met with prior to 1750, have now been described—beakers and alms-basins in the churches; beakers, various types of two-handled bowls and cups, tankards, mugs, por-

PLATE XXIII   *See page 134*

TYPICAL NEW YORK BEAKER MADE BY JACOB BOELEN

ringers, casters, tea-pots, cream-jugs, and sugar-bowls for domestic use. The early silversmith often had occasion to produce other things, such as spoons, boxes large and small, seals for towns and churches—as one of the old advertisements writes it, "sundry other Things, too tedious to enumerate." Those made in New York bear the same general stamp of simplicity and sturdiness.

A rattle mounted with coral and hung with bells, made by Richard Van Dyck (Plate **XXVI**; collection of Judge A. T. Clearwater), suggests that these men sometimes worked for diminutive customers. The rattle is not unlike the gold one made in Holland that belonged to Johannes de Peyster and which the sober little boy in his stiff white dress held in his hand when his portrait was painted. Both portrait and rattle are now lent to the Metropolitan Museum by the de Peyster family. Another piece designed for a child is the silver-gilt spoon hung with bells, made by Jacobus Van der Spiegel probably somewhere near the year 1700 (Plate **XXVI**). The spoon comes from the Van Cortlandt family and still belongs to one of its members, Miss Anne S. Van Cortlandt. These pieces designed for children make one wonder whether the early New York silversmiths of Dutch ancestry may not also have made toys in silver, miniature beakers and tankards, or furniture and other things such as the grown-ups were using at the time. It seems highly probable, as such miniature objects were the delight of children in Holland. Their fragile nature and tiny size would make them things to be found to-day only in some old account-book, diary, or will.

[153]

Early American Silver

The desire to make his tankards or tea-pots, cups or bowls, in forms that would be eminently practical, imposed great restraint upon the early New York silversmith. Assuredly his fancy did not run riot either in the outline of any one piece or in the variety of styles he conceived. He allowed his imagination freer play in the matter of decoration, but had too keen a sense of the proper sphere of ornament, too much self-control and good judgment, ever to let the ornament become more prominent than the piece itself. Because Dutch silver is relatively rare in America and the literature on the subject is meager, it is difficult to speak with assurance, but presumably the early New York silversmith in his ornamentation followed rather definite conventions dictated by his fashion-arbiters in Holland and in the neighboring countries of Germany and Scandinavia.

The methods of enrichment were several—chiefly repoussé work, engraving, flat-chasing, and the application of cast ornaments. The silversmiths of Holland are famous for their repoussé decoration. They loved a profusion of natural forms, especially fruit and flowers, suggesting fertility and vitality—as though a horn of plenty had showered its wealth over the shoulders of the silversmith to rest upon his handiwork. It was such repoussé decoration that inspired the production of the English plate of the period of Charles II, especially caudle-cups, already discussed (page 30). Sometimes in Dutch silver the representation was naturalistic, sometimes it was formalized. In either case,

[154]

the ornamentation was opulent and boldly executed.

The reflection of this Dutch repoussé ornamentation appears most noticeably in New York silver in the two-handled bowls (Plate **XXI**) already described. Here the treatment is usually formal, representing flower-motives set in panels. Much of the lighter detail is undoubtedly rendered by flat-chasing. Elsewhere we find a foliate rosette within a border of gadrooning, embossed upon the lid of a Peter Van Dyck tankard. But repoussé decoration, which can only be executed upon relatively thin silver, is more appropriate on ornamental plate than on useful pieces, which must withstand wear. Probably for this very practical reason it does not find as wide exploitation at the hands of the New York silversmith, whose chief trade was in useful wares.

Engraved work, on the other hand, could be executed on heavily wrought plate, and was not so readily defaced by rough usage, for which reasons it would have commended itself to the Boelens, Ten Eycks, Van Dycks, and their fellows. They must have been familiar with some of the work of the great Dutch, German, or French *ornamentistes* and have accepted the conventions there established. If one cannot find line-for-line originals for the engraved designs of the New York silversmith, certainly the themes that he employed again and again in his own combinations are to be found in Continental design. For the New York silversmith built up his patterns by taking first a cherub head and wings, then a foliate scroll or two, then a cornucopia, then a flower-spray, and then a bird. On his beakers he kept fairly close to Dutch models, actually copying them on occasion, possibly in compliance with a customer's order, but probably more often simply following the general formula of interlacing strapwork, foliate scrolls, and medallions with figures.

On two tankards by Wynkoop and on others by Van der Spiegel and P. V. B. occur what may also have been an accepted fashion (see Figure 9), a design made up of cherub heads, scrolls, and birds, with the space in the center reserved for a monogram or cipher. These ciphers, which interweave not only the necessary letters but the same reversed, were a style of monogram much favored in Europe. Numerous books of patterns were printed, so that the individual craftsman might receive help if his own inventiveness was inadequate. As mentioned elsewhere, the inventory of a Rhode Island silversmith, Nathaniel Helme, lists "1 Book Cyphers." It is highly probable that such books circulated among the early New York silversmiths, for ciphers occur frequently on their handiwork. These monograms are cleverly devised and make graceful bits of ornament, as well as serving the practical purpose of indicating ownership.

Quite the most interesting and elaborate engraving done on early New York silver was the coat of arms, with its mantling of flowing scrolls, its cornucopias of fruit, and pendent flowers. Such arms are indeed handsome achievements, and greatly enrich and relieve the plainness of the tea-pot or tankard on which they occur. However, as the engraving of coats of arms is discussed in a separate chapter, little need be said here except to note that in early New York silver there seem to have been two principal styles, which are illustrated by Figures 20 and 21. Whether such engraving was done by the silversmith who wrought the individual piece, or whether it was later added by a man who was simply engraver or "chacer," is still a moot question. It seems reasonable to suppose that in the earliest Colonial silver, such work was done by the silversmith or by one of his more proficient fellow-craftsmen in the neighborhood. The silversmiths of the late seventeenth and the early eighteenth century throughout the colonies were particularly skilled and vigorous craftsmen. Later on, in the middle and second half of the eighteenth century, there occur many advertisements of men who engage to do engraving as a separate art, indicating that it had by that time become a specialty.

Because they were more durable than decoration embossed out of thin silver, cast ornaments must have appealed to the practical-minded smith of New York. He used them to reinforce the grip on his tankard handles, to ornament the end of the handle, to form the thumb-piece. On the more elaborate of his bowls he used finely modeled handles in caryatid form, as in the Wynkoop bowl (Plate XXI A). These, too, were quite conventional; they are strikingly like handles on New England caudle-cups, and go back to common ancestors in European plate. The New York silversmith also had plenty of precedent in German and Scandinavian plate for the use of medals or coins, material that he probably found ready to hand and

[157]

which, as he realized, added decorative quality to his work.

The New York craftsman made sure that his silver would withstand wear by reinforcing it with stout moldings. Sometimes the molding is a simple half-round or torus, but often ornamental bands with stamped patterns are added, as in the bases of beakers, bowls, tea-pots. He also made uniquely extensive use of the applied band of foliation (Figure 15).

In the matter of its decoration, as in that of its shape, New York silver of the second half of the eighteenth century tends to conform to English fashions, though, as we have said before, it still often betrays its origin by having a more substantial appearance and sturdier build, or by retaining some distinctively New York feature.

II. THE MAKERS OF EARLY NEW YORK SILVER

Passing from the silver to those men who wrought it, we find that much information concerning them has been brought together by R. T. H. Halsey, much of it published as introduction to the Metropolitan Museum's catalogue of an "Exhibition of Silver Used in New York, New Jersey, and the South," 1911. Searching in the records of early New York is an entertaining pursuit if one has time and imagination, for the Dutch spelled phonetically and were accustomed, to the confusion of later research workers, to give a child a Christian name and, in place of a surname, the father's Christian name with some such suffix as "sen" or "zen". Thus Jan's son might be Hendrick Janssen and the latter's son in turn might be Dirck Hendricksen. This of course was merely following Continental example. French and English names seem to have afforded difficulties, which were solved by spelling the names phonetically, or by giving a Dutch equivalent.

Despite the difficulty of tracing their names, these early silversmiths figure frequently in the public records, and their achievements in the political and social affairs of their day fully merit study, though it does not seem expedient to repeat them in much detail here. An early reference to a worker in the precious metals in New York mentions the name of Jeuriaen Blanck, "goutsmidt," in 1643. He married Tryntie Claes and presumably had come to New Netherland about that time. Stokes[1] notes that the Mayor's Court appointed Blanck and Albert Bosch, a cutler, in 1672 to measure weights.

Much of the earliest New York silver bears the marks of Jacob, Hendrick, and Henricus Boelen. Boele Roelofszen or Boelen Roeloffs, as his name is variously written, apparently came from Holland to New Netherland about 1660 with his wife Bayken Arents. Among their children were Jacob (1654–1729) who in 1679 married Catharina Klock, and Hendrick (1661–1692) who in 1686 married Anneke Cours. Hendrick is recorded as a "smith." The youngest of the eight children born to Jacob and Catharina Boelen was Henricus (1697–1755) who in 1718 married Jannetje Waldron and who had a son Jacob (1733–?).

[1] I. N. P. Stokes, "Iconography of Manhattan Island, 1498–1909," 1915–28. 6 vols.

Jacob Boelen (1654–1729) had a sister Aefje who married Dirck Ten Eyck, father of the silversmith Koenraet Ten Eyck (1678–1753).

Jacob Boelen (1654–1729) was an active and able silversmith. Mr. Halsey has already recorded many of the public offices which he held, such as assessor of the North Ward, 1685–1694; brantmaster, 1689; special assessor, 1693–94; alderman of the North Ward, 1695 and 1697. He was among those who petitioned to have the Bolting monopoly restored. In 1695 he and Cornelius Vanderburgh (Carol Van Brugh) were appointed as officers to regulate weights and measures used in the city, the old record describing them "as Persons of good Reputation and very fitt to be appointed by your Excellency for the keeping of the Standard of Silver & Gold weights and markeing all such as shall be used in this City & Province."[1] The first honorary gift of the freedom of New York was made in 1702 to "his Excellency Edward Viscount Cornbury Capt Gen^{el} And Governour in Chiefe of this Province &c." According to the records, the Common Council of New York, June 27, 1702[2] ordered a gold box made to contain this certificate and "Alderman Boelen is directed to make the said Box Convenient for the use." Other silversmiths, such as Charles Le Roux and Samuel Johnson, later made similar gold freedom boxes (Plate LXII).

The advertisement of silver stolen from Abraham Lefferts (quoted on page 228) includes a considerable amount made by Jacob Boelen and the quaint descrip-

[1] R. T. H. Halsey, "Early New York Silversmiths," 1911.
[2] I. N. P. Stokes, *loc. cit.*

PLATE XXIV

NEW YORK TANKARDS MADE BY VAN DER SPIEGEL, WYNKOOP, VAN DYCK, AND HAYS AND MYERS

tions succeed in presenting a vivid picture of its distinguishing features. Much plate made by both Jacob and Henricus Boelen is still in existence and includes many stout tankards, two-handled bowls of various sizes, beakers (Plate XXIII), a tea-pot (Plate XXVI), and a paten (Plate XXVIII).

Ahasuerus Hendricks, another early silversmith, swore allegiance to the King in 1675 and probably came to New Netherland already trained in his craft. He is chiefly known as maker of the silver beaker inscribed with the date 1678, a copy of a Dutch beaker of 1660, both belonging to the First Reformed Church of Albany.

Jacobus Van der Spiegel (working 1685–1705) was another puissant silversmith. He made capacious tankards, such as those shown in Plates XXIV A and LIV A. The second of these shows finely engraved arms, those of the de Peyster family. Van der Spiegel was also the maker of the child's spoon in Plate XXVI and of the baptismal basin (Plate XXVIII) which belongs to the South Reformed Church, New York. His brother Johannes was also a silversmith.

Another able silversmith was Carol Van Brugh, a grandson of Anneke Jans. In 1693 he fashioned the gold cup which was given to Governor Fletcher. With Jacob Boelen, as mentioned above, he was appointed surveyor of weights in New York. Two extremely interesting beakers by Van Brugh have already been described, one small, belonging to Francis P. Garvan, the other large and most unusual in the details of its decoration, the property of the Sanders family (see page 134).

Work by two early silversmiths of New York and Albany, Koenraet Ten Eyck (1678–1753) and his son Jacob, is illustrated in Plates L and LX. A splendid tankard by Koenraet Ten Eyck now belongs to H. F. du Pont.

Another important family of New York silversmiths were the Le Roux, of French Huguenot origin. The marriage record of Bartholomew Le Roux suggests that he reached America by way of England. In 1688, "Bartholomeus Le Roux, j.m. Van London, en Geertruyd Van Rollegom, j.d. Van N Yorck, beyde wonende alhier." Bartholomew was a doughty figure in New York and was one of those who urged that the city be guarded against a possible French and Papist attack. Considerable silver with the mark B LR (monogram) is now believed to be the work of Bartholomew Le Roux. Francis P. Garvan owns a cylindrical caster and also a handsome bowl, quite heavily wrought and decorated with flowers in compartments and with caryatid handles in a style similar to the Wynkoop bowl illustrated in Plate XXI B. The salt shown in Plate LX, one of a pair belonging to F. A. de Peyster, is also believed to be the work of Le Roux. He died in 1713.

His son Charles was a distinguished craftsman and for a long period served as official silversmith of New York. In this connection he had occasion to make many gold and silver boxes to contain the certificates of the granting of the freedom of the city to illustrious visitors or citizens. It is recorded that in 1732 he rendered the following bill to the Corporation of New York:

New York Silver

To 1 oz. 12 pwt. Gold to one **Box**	£10 :8 :0
To fashione and engraving the **Box**	4 :0 :0
	£14 :8 :0

and in 1733 he presented a bill for silver boxes:

To 3 oz. 13 pwt. of silver to two boxes	£1 :11 :11-1/2
To fashione of ye boxes	1 :10
To Engraving	1 : 4
To Guilding	2 :16
	£7 :1 :11-1/2 [1]

A tea-pot of characteristic New York shape made by Charles Le Roux is illustrated in Plate XXVII A. He also did much engraving, executing bills of credit for the province at various times between 1715 and 1737.

Probably the best known and the most proficient of the early New York silversmiths was Peter Van Dyck (1684–1750), who may have learned his trade from his father-in-law, Bartholomew Le Roux. Much silver by him is still extant, including tankards (Plate XXIV), tea-pots, porringers, spoons, a mustard-pot, bowls. His son Richard was also a silversmith and maker of the child's rattle shown in Plate XXVI. Peter Van Dyck willed to each of his daughters a piece of plate, as follows: "to my daughters Hannah and Cornelia each a silver mugg; to my daughter Lena my silver tea pot; to my daughter Sarah my smallest silver tankard; to my daughter Mary my largest silver tankard."

[1] "Valentine's Manual," 1844.

Early American Silver

Some excellent silver bears the mark of Bartholomew Schaats (1670–1758) including the porringer in Plate XXV, the charming tankard belonging to Mrs. Frederic Grosvenor Goodridge from which the arms shown in Figure 21 were drawn, and another tankard belonging to Dr. T. H. Foulds, which is distinguished by a grave medal set in its lid.

As yet unidentified, a silversmith whose initials were P.V.B. proved himself extremely able, as the tankard in Plate LIV B amply proves. Other New York silversmiths whose work was notable include Garrett Onclebagh, Benjamin Wynkoop, Simeon Soumaine, Cornelius Kierstede, Tobias Stoutenburgh, John Hastier, Nicholas Roosevelt, Christopher Robert, Thomas Hamersly, William Huertin, Adrian Bancker, who made extremely plain and solid silver, and John Moulinar. Myer Myers, a Jewish silversmith, was maker of the dish-ring shown in Plate LIX and also maker of plate for the Jewish Synagogue in Newport, Rhode Island. He was president of the New York Silversmiths' Society in 1776.

CHAPTER VI

SILVER OF PHILADELPHIA AND THE
DELAWARE VALLEY

WHEN the Quaker sect was first organized in England in 1652, its founder, George Fox, conceived the idea of establishing a colony in the New World, but the idea was not realized until fortuitous circumstances culminated in the royal grant to William Penn and the establishment of the Colony of Pennsylvania.

Penn's ancestors were landed gentry, probably of Welsh origin. From his father, who was an admiral in the British navy, the son inherited vigor, determination, and courage, but he coupled with them the peace-loving, liberal views of the Puritans and Quakers with whom he came in contact during his boyhood in Essex and his college days at Oxford. Traveling in Italy and France for two years after completing his studies at Oxford added greatly to his culture and to his knowledge of men and affairs. The range of his acquaintance included many of the greatest folk of his generation, both in England and on the Continent. Throughout his life Penn remained a surprising combination of courtier and Quaker, of man of the world and religious leader. Democratic, friendly, sagacious, he was able to keep the friendship of widely different, even antagonistic, groups, and to organize successfully a tremendous en-

[165]

terprise as no man of more limited sympathies and
contacts could have done.

When the Crown's debt to his family made possible the grant of the right to establish a colony in the
New World, Penn saw in the venture an opportunity
to release his fellow-Quakers from the danger of persecution to which they had been subjected and to develop a community in which there should be liberty
and toleration in all things. To this project he turned
his enthusiasm, energy, and sound judgment. Warmly
but without overstatement, he advertised the charms
and advantages of his new colony, the plenitude of
game and produce, the vesting in the people of the
legislative powers of government, and freedom for all,
regardless of nationality and religion.

His advertising campaign met with a gratifying response. It is estimated that 15,000 colonists came between 1681 and 1700. Of the early comers, the great
majority were English Quakers, people of culture and
moderate wealth, who came to America not in the hope
of personal aggrandizement, but because they sought
freedom from religious persecution. They brought
with them servants and plenty of household goods.
Though radical in their thinking, they were orderly
and law-abiding. Penn also showed his wisdom by
making a special plea for artisans and farmers: "In-
dustrious Husbandmen and Day Labourers, Laborious
Handicrafts, especially Carpenters, Masons, Smiths,
Weavers, Taylors, Tanners, Shoemakers, Shipwrights,
etc." Thus to natural thrift was added skilled industry,
and the success of Penn's colony was assured.

Gabriel Thomas, one of the earliest comers, apparently remained in the province for about fourteen years and then returned to England, where in 1698 he wrote "An Account of Pennsylvania and West New Jersey," which is one of the most illuminating documents of its kind, giving a vivid picture of the natural resources of the colony, its industries and trade. Philadelphia, he tells us, "contains above two thousand Houses, all Inhabited; and most of them Stately, and of Brick, generally three Stories high, after the Mode in London, and as many several Families in each. There are very many Lanes and Alleys." It is amusing to find this characteristic of the present city appearing at such an early date. So, too, Philadelphia's reputation for good living is foreshadowed in Thomas's comments on the abundance of game, fish, and fowl, which he concludes with the remark: "Excellent Food, most delicious, far exceeding that in Europe, in the Opinion of most that are Nice and Curious People."

Thomas attributes the rapid growth of the colony to "their great and extended Traffique and Commerce both by Sea and Land . . . They have constantly good price for their Corn, by reason of the great and quick vent into Barbadoes and other Islands; through which means Silver is become more plentiful than here in England, considering the number of People, and that causes a quick Trade for both Corn and Cattle. . . . A brother of mine sold within the compass of one Week, about One Hundred and Twenty fat Beasts, most of them good handsom large Oxen." Thomas also discusses local industries, estimates the wages paid a great variety of tradesmen, including carpenters, both house and ship; bricklayers and brick-makers; masons;

weavers; potters; butchers; brewers; pewterers, etc. "And for Silver-Smiths, they have between Half a Crown and Three Shillings an Ounce for working their Silver, and for Gold equivalent." There is, he says, no need for lawyers and physicians, so law-abiding are the people, so salubrious the climate. Because land is cheap and living easy, servants are tempted to set up for themselves and consequently, if they stay in service, demand high wages.

His comments on West New Jersey are of much the same import. Salem, its oldest town, and Burlington, he describes as fine market towns with "many stately Brick-Houses . . . many fine wharves, and most sorts of Tradesmen." Presumably conditions in these towns were generally much like those in Philadelphia, to which they were adjacent.

The English Quakers not only constituted the bulk of the population but because they were people of moderate wealth, of more than average culture, and of political ability, they also formed the governing class. They lived chiefly in Philadelphia. For these various reasons, their group consciousness was intensified, and they gave a definite English cast to the whole colony. In addition to the Quakers there were English Royalists, who belonged to the Church of England. At first they were so much in the minority as to have hardly any influence politically, but in time they became increasingly numerous and exerted more and more control in public affairs. Until the middle of the eighteenth century the Quakers predominated, but owing to various circumstances, such as the Indian Wars, they lost some of their popularity and prestige, and

PLATE XXV   *See pages 147–48*

MUG BY SIMEON SOUMAINE, PORRINGERS BY SCHAATS
AND I. N. (POSSIBLY JOSEPH NEWKIRKE)

from 1750 to 1775 the two groups, Quaker and Royalist, were more or less equally matched. After the Revolution, the Quakers passed out of power as a group.

Outside of the immediate vicinity of Philadelphia the colonists comprised rather distinct groups of Germans, Scotch-Irish, Welsh, Swedes, and Dutch, who engaged in agriculture quite exclusively and who never became a defined or controlling element in the political or social life. They later became the pioneering element, who pushed the settlement of the colony farther westward.

Politically the province had, if not an entirely serene, at least a consistently progressive development. It was always under royal control and subject to the will of its royal governor and of the Proprietor. It never enjoyed the liberty that Massachusetts Bay had during the first fifty years of the latter's existence, yet on the other hand it never had occasion to fret over the loss of former privileges. Its Provincial Assembly continually had disputes with the governors and representatives of the Proprietors, but usually the Assembly was holding out for some legitimate privilege or right, and it steadfastly held its ground, each struggle ending in a further advance in freedom for popular government. Therefore when the other colonies—especially Massachusetts, which had been the butt of England's most coercive measures—were eager to declare war and fight for independence, Pennsylvania was much less aware of wrongs suffered or privileges curtailed, far less interested in taking a positive stand for independence, loth actually to enter into war.

Up to the time of the Revolution the one serious interruption to the province's peaceful life was the French and Indian Wars. Penn's treatment of the Indians was considered by his European contemporaries and is still regarded as a model of fairness and honorable dealing. His colonists for a long period supported the same general policy, and the Indians were consistently friendly, by virtue of which relationship trade and agriculture prospered. Later, however, the border settlers, especially the Germans and Scotch-Irish, tended to disregard Indian claims to the land that they themselves wished to occupy, and drove out the Indians in a manner that roused the resentment of the red men. There were, moreover, high-handed and manifestly tricky dealings, such as the Walking Purchase, which unfortunately was countenanced by the Proprietor, Thomas Penn. All this destroyed the Indians' confidence and they turned to the French, who were eagerly seeking their alliance. In consequence, during the period of the French and Indian Wars the border settlements of Pennsylvania, wholly unused to such hostility and completely unprepared, were subjected to the most terrible ravages by the Indians. Bouquet eventually defeated the Indians and saved the colony from further depredations.

The colony's commercial expansion went on favorably from its beginning, which Gabriel Thomas has described. Pennsylvania not only built her own ships but was able to build them for others. She had an extensive trade with the other colonies, with Newfoundland, the West Indies, Spain and the Madeiras, and Great Britain. Despite the active commerce with the

See pages 149, 153

CHILD'S RATTLE BY RICHARD VAN DYCK, TEA-POT BY JACOB BOELEN,
AND CHILD'S SPOON BY JACOBUS VAN DER SPIEGEL

PLATE XXVI

Philadelphia and Delaware Valley Silver

West Indies which, as Thomas said, must have brought
in much silver, there was a much greater importation
of goods from England, so that, in common with all
her colonial neighbors, Pennsylvania found her silver
flowing out and her local trade handicapped by the
lack of a medium for exchange. New England's frequent issues of paper money had been all too hap-
hazard and ill-advised, and the currency itself had
become the object of speculation if the issue was insuf-
ficient, or had suffered depreciation if the issue was
overlarge. Philadelphia was slow to settle the question
and only came to a decision after careful study and
deliberation. In consequence, she issued just enough
for her immediate necessity, and it reflects much credit
upon the intelligence and moderation of men like her
great Secretary, James Logan, that her currency proved
so stable. The first issue of paper money occurred in
1722 and thereafter there were numerous other issues.

By virtue of her peaceful and prosperous development, Philadelphia attracted to herself large numbers
of desirable colonists. In 1720 the population of Boston must have been about twice that of Philadelphia;
in 1730 it was two and one-half times as great. Sometime between 1750 and 1760, however, the southern
town outstripped the northern. From that time until
about 1825 Philadelphia was the largest city in the
colonies. Nor was she distinguished merely by her
size, for throughout the eighteenth century she attracted
the most illustrious folk in the colonies, statesmen,
scientists, artists, scholars. The foundations of her
greatness in these fields had been established almost
from the beginning of her history. William Penn him-

self had not only encouraged artisans and craftsmen to come to his colony but had also induced an English architect, James Portius, to come to Philadelphia to design and superintend the construction of his proprietary buildings. To Portius and his fellows the early city owed much of the beauty and charm of its architecture. When he died in 1736, Portius left his library of architectural works to the Carpenters' Company, a guild formed as early as 1724 and modeled upon the Worshipful Company of Carpenters of London.

The early Philadelphia houses, patterned so closely upon English buildings of the period, and animated by the hospitable spirit for which Philadelphia has always been famous, called for furnishings in the same taste and of the same distinction. The ability of Philadelphia cabinet-makers throughout the eighteenth century has long been acknowledged. Much of the most elaborately designed and most elegant chairs, highboys, tables, and mirrors made in the colonies came from the workshops of such men as James Gillingham, Jonathan Gostelowe, William Savery, Edward James, John Elliot, William Wayne, and Benjamin Randolph —all of Philadelphia. Stimulated by the example of the architect-builders and the cabinet-makers, and seeking the patronage of a prosperous mercantile clientèle, the city's silversmiths naturally produced notable work.

The silver plate owned in Philadelphia from the time of its founding through the eighteenth century, if it could be viewed as a whole, would probably fall rather definitely into two groups, one comprising Eng-

lish silver imported by "world's people" and the other
plate made by Philadelphia silversmiths for Quaker
patrons, which, as suited the taste of the latter, was
simple and unpretentious. The English plate was probably like the average English silver used in Great
Britain by families of wealth and taste; presumably
it did not include the most sumptuous styles, such as
would have been used in England only for court occasions. A great deal of this Philadelphia-owned English
plate is still in existence, still in the hands of descendants of the original owners.

Penn himself represented both court and Quaker
parties in his personality, in his activities, and also,
it is interesting to discover, in his choice of silver.
When he came to Pennsylvania he had sent out in 1701
a quantity of plate, presumably English, of which a
list has been preserved. It offers an indication of the
pieces used in a household such as Penn's. "Plait carried to Pennsilvania—1 large Tankard, 1 Plaited, 1
Porringer with ears and a Cover, 1 Caudle cup with 3
leggs & a porringor to cover it, 3 tumblers 1 larger
2 lessor, 1 taistor, 6 spoons, 2 forks, 1 paire of snuffers,
1 handle cup, 2 things for Cruit tops, 1 new cup with a
covver, 2 tankerds was changed for 3 new Chaffendishes, 1 large 2 lesser & things to them to burn Spirits
in, 1 large Snuffer pan with Candle stil in it. 1 large
Plait with the Springets Arms that Springet's Grandmother Pennington Gave him. 1 little Candle Stick
marked W ^{P} G, 1 little Strong water bottle marked
G M S, 1 Saveall marked G S, 1 Extinguisher, 1 little
Standish with a drawer, 1 small Runnell marked

[173]

W P, 5 sweet meat Spoons, 1 childs drinking cup, 6 spoons with a Cross on them yt are used in the kitching, 4 came from Walthamstow 2 with a Cross 2 w$^{thot.}$ 1 we had before unmarked, 1 marked E B, 12 in all. 6 Egg spoons 3 marked with ye childrens names 3 marked W ^{P} G, 1 gone to Pennsilvania, 2 Cruit tops 2 taistors." There is also a shorter list included in the "Catalogue of Goods Left at Pensbury the 3rd. of ye Tenth Month 1701."

But the great Proprietor and Governor was also a staunch Quaker, who in democratic fashion engaged the services of local silversmiths. Thus there are entries in his cash-book for paying "Johan Nys Goldsmith . . . £2-10-0" in 1700 and "ye Goldsmith . . . Cesar Ghiselin £1-14-0" in 1701, and in the same year he paid Francis Richardson "for a paire of shoe buckles for Letitia," his daughter. Penn thus supplies some of the earliest and most trustworthy records concerning the first Philadelphia silversmiths.

In 1698, Gabriel Thomas, in giving detailed information concerning the wages received by various craftsmen and artisans in the colony, notes, as we have said, that the silversmiths received "between Half a Crown and Three Shillings an Ounce for working their Silver, and for Gold equivalent." He would hardly have given such specific information had there not at that time been several silversmiths at work in the colony. The first name so far discovered is that of César Ghiselin, a Huguenot refugee who came from England to Philadelphia, where he plied his trade. The earliest specific record concerning him is that already noted, Penn's

PLATE XXVII

See pages 150, 326

TEA-POT BY CHARLES LE ROUX
KETTLE BY CORNELIUS KIERSTEDE

payment to him in 1701 of £1.14.0. Thomas Coates paid him £5 for work in 1711, which proves that he was still in Philadelphia at that time. He seems to have worked in Annapolis from 1715 to 1728 and he died in Philadelphia in 1733.[1] Of the four pieces of silver known to be his handiwork, two are illustrated in Plate XXIX, a plate (diameter 9¾″) and a beaker (height 4¾″). Both are inscribed: "The gift of Margaret Tresse Spinstor to Christ Church in Philadelphia." Both pieces are plain and simple but pleasing in line, and suggest English antecedents. The other two pieces by Ghiselin are spoons, one belonging to F. P. Garvan, the other in a Philadelphia collection.

Another eminently interesting, because elusive, personality is John de Nise or Johan Nys, as he is variously called. Part of his history is known, part is surmised. Presumably his antecedents were French Protestants who fled to Holland and later came to America, living at some time in New York. Following the casual and phonetic methods of recording names, the old New York records list de Nys, Nice, Nyssen, Neuss, Nuson, etc., so that to trace any individual in the family involves much searching. John de Nise in all probability worked in New York long enough to become thoroughly familiar with Dutch silversmithing there, for his tankards are strikingly like those by New York silversmiths —so like New York silver of the late seventeenth century and so unlike that of any other locality that de Nise's residence in New York seems to be a certainty. Perhaps he reached Philadelphia by way of New Jersey,

[1] Information kindly supplied by Dr. J. Hall Pleasants and H. E. Gillingham.

where some of his relatives settled permanently. In any event he was in Philadelphia at least as early as 1700 and thereafter must have been actively at work, for almost a dozen examples of his handiwork still remain. There are three porringers with geometrically pierced handles, a pair of sucket-forks (or mulberry-forks) with a spoon-bowl at one end and a two-tined fork at the other, which were made for Hugh and Martha (Hunloke) Huddy of Burlington, N. J.; a brazier; and four or five tankards. That de Nise was still in Philadelphia in 1715 is proved by the will of Arthur Holton, made April 30, 1715, in which the latter bequeaths to his daughter a house "Situate in ye ffront Street in Philadelphia . . . and now in the Tenure and occupation of John Nys, Silver Smith."

A third very early silversmith of Philadelphia was Philip Syng, Sr. (1676–1739). He was born in Ireland and practised his trade in Cork before he came to Philadelphia in 1714 with his wife Anne (Murdock) Syng and his three sons, Philip, Jr. (1703–1789), Daniel, and John. There is record of his shop near the Market Place in 1720; he was working in Philadelphia in 1723, but later moved to Annapolis, where he died.

Philip Syng, Sr., and his son Philip between them produced a great deal of silver. Many pieces are late in style and can with certainty be assigned to the son, but concerning others there is still reason for debate. Some, such as a trencher-salt belonging to the Pennsylvania Museum, bear the early form of mark, P S in a heart, and are probably the work of the father. English silversmiths in the early eighteenth century

See page 136

PLATE XXVIII

PATEN BY HENRICUS BOELEN
BAPTISMAL BASIN BY JACOBUS VAN DER SPIEGEL

usually employed marks consisting of their initials, often with a device, enclosed within a heart, shield, trefoil, or other irregular reserve. Only very rarely did they use the initials alone within a rectangle, a custom that became general at a later time. Philip Syng, Sr., therefore, probably used the P S in a heart; his son probably used the P S in a rectangle.

The tankard illustrated in Plate XXX is assigned to Philip Syng, Sr., partly because it bears this heart-shaped mark and partly because it is finely engraved with a coat of arms in Hogarthian style, corresponding to English engraving of the early eighteenth century. It is not probable that engraving of this early style would occur on plate fashioned in the time of Philip Syng, Jr. The tankard has the domed lid characteristic of Philadelphia; a beaded rat-tail on its double scroll handle; a mid-band; and almost straight sides, which curve inward at the base in a manner corresponding to early-eighteenth-century mugs.

Three pieces have generally been assigned to Philip Syng, Sr.: a flagon (Plate XXIX) and a baptismal basin presented by Colonel Robert Quary to Christ Church, Philadelphia, in 1712; and a paten given to Holy Trinity Church, Oxford, Pennsylvania. However, as these pieces bear a form of mark—P S in a rectangle—found on silver known to be the work of Philip Syng, Jr., it has been suggested by Dr. S. W. Woodhouse, Jr., that these pieces may have been fashioned years after the date at which the donation was made, the assumption in such case being that the original gift took the form of land or money that was not converted into plate until much later.

Philip Syng's three sons and two of his grandsons, both named Philip, became goldsmiths or silversmiths. His eldest son, generally known as Philip Syng, Jr. (1703–1789), became the greatest of his family, as we shall later see.

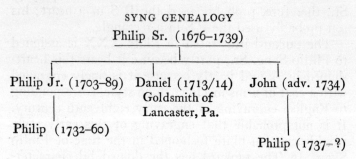

SYNG GENEALOGY

Philip Sr. (1676–1739)

Philip Jr. (1703–89)   Daniel (1713/14)   John (adv. 1734)

Philip (1732–60)   Goldsmith of Lancaster, Pa.

Philip (1737–?)

The fourth important Philadelphia silversmith working in the early eighteenth century was Francis Richardson (1681–1729), who, though born in New York, came to Philadelphia at the age of nine. By 1701 he was known as a goldsmith and was able to execute work satisfactorily for the Proprietor, for it was at the end of this year that Penn paid him for the "paire of shoe buckles for Letitia." Letitia's buckles are no longer to be found, but another pair made by Richardson were used by Elizabeth Paschall at her wedding in 1721. They were subsequently given by one of her descendants, Miss Lydia Morris, to the Pennsylvania Historical Society. Richardson also made the charming little patch-box, with its typical foliate border and floral rosette suggestive of a derivation from the Tudor rose of an earlier period. The box now belongs to the Pennsylvania Museum.

[178]

Philadelphia and Delaware Valley Silver

For some time it was assumed that Richardson did repair work only or made relatively small pieces of silver, because the latter were the only examples of his work that had been discovered. This theory seemed to gain support from his advertisement in the "Pennsylvania Gazette" for September 9-16, 1736, which read: "Very neat Clocks and Jacks made, sold, cleaned and mended reasonably by Francis Richardson, Goldsmith at the Corner of Letitia Court in Market Street." But more recently an excellently wrought tankard bearing his mark has appeared, proving that he attempted more ambitious work. The tankard (Plate XXX) is now lent by Isaac Starr, Jr., to the Pennsylvania Museum. The handle is inscribed "W M B," for William Branson. It is a stocky piece, broad, vigorous, and unsophisticated. It has straight sides girdled by a mid-band, a domed lid, and a beaded rat-tail ornament on the handle to reinforce the grip. It is stamped three times with the mark F R in a heart.

Richardson, like Philip Syng, became the head of a most illustrious family of silversmiths, the Richardsons and Syngs contributing a great quantity of splendid silver to Philadelphia homes throughout the eighteenth century.

GENEALOGY OF RICHARDSON SILVERSMITHS

Francis (1681–1729)

Joseph, Sr. (1711–1784)   John

Joseph, Jr. (1752–1831)   Nathaniel (1754–1827)

[179]

William Vilant's name would suggest that, like Ghiselin and de Nise, he too was of Huguenot extraction. Practically nothing is known of him except that in 1725 in the "American Weekly Mercury," as a "goldsmith of Philadelphia," he advertised that he wished to sell 250 acres of land in East Jersey. He was the maker of a number of tankards that, though they differ in size, have the same family likeness in general proportions and in details and show that he had a distinctive style. These tankards usually have a

FIGURE 16.
Tankard Handle
Ornament

rather slender, tapering body, a low domed lid, sometimes a beaded rat-tail ornament on the handle, and a shield-shaped cartouche enclosing a child's face as ornament for the end of the handle (see Figure 16).

One of these tankards by Vilant now belongs to the Pennsylvania Museum (Plate XXX). Several others belonged originally to Thomas and Beulah Coates, one of which is now in the hands of a descendant, while another is in the Clearwater collection. Still another was made for Isaac and Mary Norris and now belongs to Robert R. Logan.

A Vilant tankard in the collection of Lionel Crichton of London is of exceptional interest because it is decorated by a colonial engraver, Joseph Leddel, the younger, of New York.[1] In form, the tankard follows the regular Vilant formula in having a domed lid, scrolled thumb-piece, beaded rat-tail ornament on the

[1] E. Alfred Jones, "An Old American Silver Tankard," "Burlington Magazine," 1929, Vol. 54, p. 264.

handle, and a tip of the design shown in the sketch above (height, 6½"; weight, 28 oz. 16 pwt.). It is unique among American tankards, so far as known, because of the engraved panel around its body. The artist was Joseph Leddel, as is proved by an inscription on the base of the tankard:

L

I   M

Joseph Leddel

Sculp.

1750

This inscription also indicates that Leddel and his wife owned the tankard. As Mr. Crichton purchased the piece in England, it is quite possible that it was taken there during the American Revolution by some returning Royalist.

The engraved panel on the tankard has three scenes, illustrating subjects from Ovid, and their correspond-ing titles. Above each scene is engraved a portrait head. These, with the aid of an inscription on the base of the tankard, are readily identified as Philip, Earl of Chesterfield, Secretary of State; Simon Fraser, Lord Lovat, beheaded in 1747 after the second Scotch rebellion; and Philip, Lord Hardwicke, who as Lord High Steward presided at Lovat's trial. The full sig-nificance of the scenes and portraits is still to be interpreted.

There are relatively few examples that thus far have come to public notice to give us a fair concep-tion of the work of these earliest Philadelphia silver-smiths. As we now know it, their work appears to be simple, plain, not in the least sophisticated or pre-

[181]

tentious; it is sincere and vigorous, but still a bit tentative, and has not yet developed elegance or refinement
of line, qualities for which later Philadelphia work
was distinguished.

Though but few examples of early-eighteenth-century Philadelphia silver have thus far come to light,
it seems a fair presumption that in the course of time,
as more general interest in its early history develops,
a considerable number of other pieces will appear. Indeed, the exhibition held by the Colonial Dames in
that city in the spring of 1929 brought out an astonish-
ing array of most interesting pieces. These had been
in the hands of descendants of their original owners
and had never happened to come before the public
until the time of the exhibition. Even so, Boston knew
almost nothing about its early silver until the exhibitions of 1906 and 1911; since then great quantities
have been revealed. Perhaps it is true that relatively
little silver was made in Philadelphia in the first third
of the eighteenth century, but the indications would
point to a different conclusion.

The Quakers always chose plain and unostentatious
things but they also always chose the best of materials
and enjoyed in their quiet way most of the good things
of life. Sober in their dress, they sought other modes
of satisfying a normal desire for display. They certainly would have appreciated silver plate, and the
prosperity of their colony would have enabled them
to afford it. The indications seem to be that in the
early days of the colony there was even more silver,
comparatively, flowing into the colony from its West
Indian trade than flowed into New England from the

same commerce. Throughout the colonies there was experienced a need for silver currency for local use, which was met everywhere by the issue of paper currency. This need, however, was not insistent in Philadelphia until 1722, when the first paper money was made there. Although, owing to the wisdom of her public officials at that time, the currency remained remarkably stable, so that people could confidently invest their funds in this form and were not so tempted, as were their neighbors in Massachusetts, to convert them into plate, nevertheless despite this situation, it seems highly probable that with general prosperity and able craftsmen the colony must have indulged in a much greater quantity of native silverwork than we have thus far supposed. The writer's own theory is that the silver exists but public interest has not yet been sufficiently aroused to bring it to light in any adequate degree.

From the second quarter of the eighteenth century, the increasing size and prosperity of the colony brought to the fore splendid craftsmen of all sorts. The silversmiths who became prominent from about 1725 to about 1775 include the two greatest names, Joseph Richardson (1711–84) and Philip Syng, Jr. (1703–89), and also Elias Boudinot (1706–70), Peter David (advertised in 1739), William Ball (advertised 1759–82), John Leacock (advertised 1751), and Edmond Milne (advertised 1757–73).

Philip Syng, Jr., was prominent in the society of his day and was associated with many of the famous institutions of the early city. Thus he became a director of the Philadelphia Library Company, a member of

Franklin's Junto (forerunner of the American Philosophical Society), junior grand warden of the first
Masonic Lodge in America, trustee of the Public
Academy, which was later to become the University
of Pennsylvania, a charter member of the American
Philosophical Society, treasurer of the city, and provincial commissioner of appeals for the county.[1] He was
cultured, shrewd in business, and well-to-do, and, like
many other distinguished Philadelphians, had not only
his town house but also his country-seat.

His energy and marked ability placed him at the
head of his craft. He not only produced occasional
work of outstanding merit, but he also maintained an
extremely high level of performance throughout. His
most notable piece was the historic inkstand (Plate
XXXI; length, 10¼") made in 1752 for the Provincial Assembly of Pennsylvania at a cost of £25.16.0,
which was later used at the signing of the Declaration
of Independence and of the Constitution, and which
now fittingly has its place in Independence Hall. This
inkstand is interesting not only for its associations but
as an exquisite bit of handiwork. It follows European
styles that were current abroad at a slightly earlier
period. Other well-known pieces by Syng include a
charming brazier (Plate LX) belonging to the Pennsylvania Museum; a mug lent to this Museum by
Isaac Starr, Jr., which is skilfully engraved with the
arms of its original owner, Lynford Lardner; a splendid coffee-pot, belonging now to Edsel Ford; three-
legged creamers, salts, tankards, ladles, etc. Much of

[1] H. F. Jayne and S. W. Woodhouse, Jr., "Early Philadelphia
Silversmiths," in "Art in America," vol. 9, p. 258.

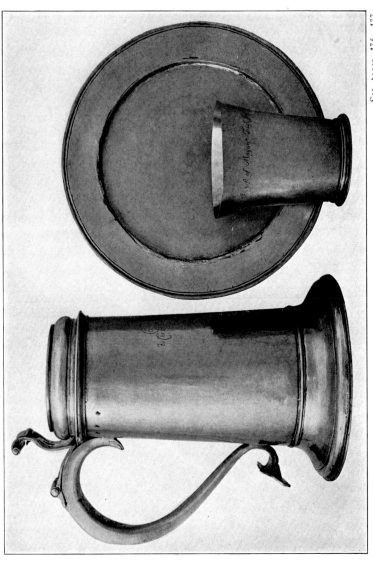

PLATE XXIX

See pages 175, 177

his work is very like English styles of the second and third quarters of the eighteenth century and though simple is excellently designed.

His son Philip, also trained as a silversmith, died at the age of twenty-seven. As he gave promise of being a proficient craftsman, well fitted to carry on the family tradition, his death must have been a sore grief to his father.

Joseph Richardson, Sr. (1711–84), son of Francis, fell heir to his father's business at his shop on Front Street below Walnut. He and Syng seem to have been on most friendly terms and to have interchanged business to some extent, as their account-books prove. Both men, being the leading silversmiths of their day, enjoyed the patronage of Philadelphia's first families, including the Logans, Willings, Hamiltons, Norrises, Coateses, and Powells. Richardson's work was extensive and many handsome pieces, too numerous to describe in detail, are still in existence.

The Pennsylvania Historical Society has three of Joseph Richardson's "day-books" covering the years 1733–40, and showing his accounts with numerous customers. The following is a characteristic form of entry:

1740   Anthony Morris is Dr.   oz.   dwt.
6 mo. 23d. to a 3 pint Tankard
                        wt.   37   12 to fashion £2-76-0
            to a pr of Pint Canns
                        wt.   23   3-18 to fashion 1-16-0
7 mo. 29 to 6 Poringers wt.   48   11 to fashion 3-12-0
                              109:   6:18
      to 1 oz 6 dwt 18 gr of Silver added to his Plate   12-0
                                                        £8-14-0

pr Contra   Cr.

   4 mo. 30   By 72 oz of Silver Recd.
   5 mo. 11   By <u>36</u> oz of Silver Recd.
               108
         By Cash Recd in full   £8-14-0

Richardson, a peace-loving but enterprising Quaker, was affiliated with numerous Quaker societies, such as the Friendly Society for Propagating Peace with the Indians by Pacific Measures. The organization of such societies reflects Pennsylvania's difficulties with the Indians along her western borders and her efforts to conciliate them and preserve their friendship. Richardson in 1757 struck silver medals for presentation to friendly Indians by this society, and for it he also made the gorget or neck-ornaments (Plate XXXII).

Syng and other Philadelphia silversmiths also executed commissions of a similar sort, as indicated by entries from the account-book of David Frank, an Indian trader (property of the Pennsylvania Historical Society):

  Mch 26–1761 To JOHN BAYLEY

                            oz. dwt. gr.
    9 doz. Silver heart brouches   ) wt. 5 18 6 @ 9/ £2-13-5
    3 do do stronger do   )
    Making the above 12 doz broaches @ 5/   <u>3. 0-0</u>
                                    £5-13-5

  1767 Dec. 28. To Philip Syng (Jr.)

                            oz. dwt. gr.
For 12 Moon and 12 half Moon Gorgets, wt. 42- 1- 12
                      @ 9/ pr. oz. £18-18-8
Fashion of 12 with Loops @ 12/ ea. do of 12 without
                       do @ 11/ea. <u>13-16-0</u>
                             £32-14-8

PLATE XXX   *See pages 177, 179, 180, 189*

PHILADELPHIA TANKARDS
MADE BY FRANCIS RICHARDSON, WILLIAM VILANT, PHILIP SYNG,
AND JOSEPH RICHARDSON

Philadelphia and Delaware Valley Silver

Edmond Milne was particularly busy with orders of this kind, making many silver ornaments intended to serve as propitiatory gifts to the Indians. Harrold E. Gillingham, in articles in the "Pennsylvania Magazine of History and Biography," has discussed the whole subject in detail and there quotes Milne's bill to George Croghan, property of the Pennsylvania Historical Society, which is interesting as showing the various types of objects offered. Croghan was at the time engaged as Indian trader and agent, and because of his recognition of the gravity of the situation was one of those who urged the building of a fort at the junction of the Alleghany and Monongahela rivers with the Ohio, as a protection against the French and Indians. In 1775 Croghan served as a captain under Braddock.

George Croughon Bought of Edmond Milne.

	£ Sᵈ
To 18 Doz of Broaches at 8/s pr Doz.	7-4
To 12 Doz of Ditto at 11S pr Doz.	6-4
To 8 Doz of Ditto at 11S pr Doz.	4-8
To 2 Doz of Crosses @ 12/	1-4
To 6 Arm Bands @ 20/	6-0
To 10 Rist Bands @ 8/	4-0
To two Gorgets @ 25/	2-10
	£31-10

Received Contents from
Geo. Croughan
        Edmond Milne. (Date about 1761)

Milne was among those who imported English plate but was also the maker of a considerable quantity of well-wrought silver. He is remembered as the maker of camp-cups which were used by General Washington during the Revolution.

His Excen^{cy}. Gen. Washington to Edm^d. Milne Dr.

1777
Augt. 20th
To makg. 12 Silvr. Camp Cups, wt. 11 oz. @ 14/ ea. £8-8-0
To the Whaist on   do   1.3
                              ————
                              oz. 12.3
Cr. By 16 Silvr. Dolls.   wt. 13.18
                              ————
           Remaining   1.15 @ 20/ p oz 1-15-0
                              ————
               Balance due   £6-13-0 [1]

Philadelphia silverwork made prior to the Revolution is, as a whole, based rather closely upon English styles, as one would anticipate from the fact that the leading class socially was of English descent and the additional fact that much English silver was continually imported directly into the town. That designed for Quaker patrons was usually quite simple and of a useful sort, such as tankards, braziers, porringers, tea-pots and bowls, salts, creamers, spoons. As these styles were less distinctive than those developed in Philadelphia after the Revolution, a relatively smaller number of the former are here illustrated. The tankards were much like their English contemporaries. Their lids were domed but practically never had finials, a feature that was widely used in New England. The earlier tankards had straight, tapering sides (Plate

[1] F. H. Bigelow, "Historic Silver of the Colonies and its Makers."

XXX) with or without a mid-band; later examples were often more or less bulbous, copying the English style of the second half of the eighteenth century. The Syng tankard (Plate **XXX**) shows a transitional stage, for its sides are almost straight but curve inward at the base. The bulbous style was made to some extent in New York but was more extensively used in Philadelphia than anywhere else in the colonies.

Relatively few tea-pots and coffee-pots of the period have thus far come to light. A straight-sided tapering coffee-pot made by Peter David and belonging to Mrs. John Cadwalader, and a pear-shaped coffee-pot made by Philip Syng, Jr., belonging to Edsel Ford, prove that both styles found favor.

The curves of the rococo period found expression in the three-legged salts, creamers, and sauce-boats made in the mid-eighteenth century. Usually such pieces were left undecorated. Once in a while a piece appears in which the silversmith apparently attempted elaboration of shape or ornament but had not had sufficient experience to accomplish it with distinction. The native silversmiths were most successful when they kept to the simple styles preferred by their Quaker patrons.

From about 1760 to 1795 Philadelphia was not only the largest but in many respects the greatest city in America. Here came Sons of Liberty from other colonies to confer as to the best means of coping with such harshly restrictive measures as the Navigation Acts. Here met the delegates who signed the Declaration of Independence and the Constitution. As the meeting-place of the Continental Congress the city

[189]

attracted great numbers of patriots; as the headquarters of Lord Howe during the Revolution, she was the scene of Tory festivities which culminated in that event of gaiety and splendor, the Mischianza. After the Revolution, she became, from 1790 to 1800, the nation's capital. Unfortunately, during this interval and especially in 1793 and in 1798, she was ravaged by epidemics of yellow fever, which depleted her population to a shocking degree and this, coupled with the removal of the capital to Washington, undermined her prestige.

In the halcyon days between the close of the French and Indian Wars and the end of the century, Philadelphia attracted the best and most active minds in the country, and her reputation for hospitality and social gaiety ever increased. In any considerable group of Philadelphia silver one finds numerous tankards and tea-services, symbolizing both the masculine and the feminine aspects of that expansive entertainment, which found its most brilliant expression in balls such as the Mischianza, and its quieter moments in teas and dinners in the homes of Philadelphians such as the Willings, the Binghams, and the Powells. The silversmiths themselves had abundant patronage and developed at this time their most distinctive styles. The leading craftsmen during this period were Joseph and Nathaniel Richardson, sons of Joseph Richardson, Sr.; Humphreys, Letellier, McMullin, Lownes, DuBois, Shields, Myers, Musgrave, Hall, John David, Haverstick, Wiltberger, Van Voorhis.

Joseph (1752–1831) and Nathaniel (1754–1827) were sons of Joseph Richardson, Sr. (1711–84).

See pages 184, 191

PLATE XXXI

INKSTAND BY PHILIP SYNG, JR.
TEA-POT BY JOSEPH AND NATHANIEL RICHARDSON

Philadelphia and Delaware Valley Silver

The younger Joseph worked for a time with his father, as a tankard bearing the distinctive marks of the two men proves. Like his father, Joseph, Jr., made a number of silver ornaments for gifts to the Indians. Plate **XXXII** illustrates one of these later Indian medals (weight 3 oz. 18 pwt.), which bears the figure of George Washington and the date 1793. It now belongs to the Pennsylvania Historical Society. The two sons, however, worked chiefly in partnership until about 1792, when Nathaniel left the silversmithing business and turned ironmonger. Some of their bills indicate that they were able to conduct their business even during the difficult days of the war. Their familiar I.NR stamp, with which they were wont to mark their silver, appears again and again on many splendid pieces. A charming tea-pot so marked is illustrated in Plate **XXXI** (height 5½"; property of Mrs. Adolpho Carlos Munoz). They also made the coffee-pot of inverted-pear shape shown in Plate **XXXIV** B (height, 12½"; property of Mr. and Mrs. Charles E. Ingersoll), which has the monogram of Jared and Elizabeth (Pettit) Ingersoll, married in 1781. Jared Ingersoll was one of the signers of the Constitution.

Because Philip Syng, Jr., maintained so high a standard of excellence, we turn with special interest to Richard Humphreys, to whom Syng left his business when he retired in 1772. According to the advertisement in the "Pennsylvania Packet" of August 24, 1772, Humphreys called his shop the Sign of the Coffee-Pot.

That he fully deserved Syng's confidence is proved

RICHARD HUMPHREYS,

GOLDSMITH,

HAVING taken the houſe in which PHILIP SYNG lately dwelt, hereby informs his friends and the public, that he now carries on the GOLDSMITH's Buſineſs in all its branches, at the aforeſaid place, a few doors below the Coffee Houſe, where he has for ſale, a NEAT and GENERAL ASSORTMENT of GOLD and SILVER WARE. Thoſe who will pleaſe to favour him with their cuſtom, may be aſſured of his utmoſt ability to give ſatisfaction, both in the quality and workmanſhip; ſuch favours will be gratefully acknowledged by their friend,

RICHARD HUMPHREYS.

THE ſubſcriber having lately removed into Upper Merion townſhip, hereby informs his friends and former cuſtomers, that they may be ſupplied as uſual, at his late dwelling, by the above-named RICHARD HUMPHREYS, whom he hereby recommends to them as a perſon qualified to ſerve them on the beſt terms, and whoſe fidelity in the above buſineſs will engage their future confidence and regard.

PHILIP SYNG.

by his later achievements. Particularly distinguished are a pair of sauce-boats with high scrolled handles, gadrooned edges, and finely engraved cartouche enclosing the monogram G E, which are now the property of Miss Hannah Fox. A mug and a bulbous tankard with the same monogram are also in Miss Fox's collection.

It is quite in the spirit of Philadelphia, the town so famous for its entertainment, that nowhere else in the colonies were made so many and such complete tea-services. A number were based on the inverted-

See *pages* 186, 191

GEORGE WASHINGTON
PRESIDENT 1795.

PLATE XXXII

GORGET AND PEACE MEDAL

Made for Presentation to Friendly Indians

Philadelphia and Delaware Valley Silver

pear shape that was also well represented in New England and New York. A tea-pot of this shape made by Joseph Richardson of Philadelphia now belongs to Mrs. A. Sidney Logan. Coffee-pots of this shape seem to have been even more numerous than the tea-pots of the same type, as the coffee-pots were also frequently combined, as we shall presently see, with straight-sided tea-pots. Of the coffee-pots of inverted-pear shape, a characteristic example is illustrated on Plate XXXIV, one made by Joseph and Nathaniel Richardson. Others by the same silversmiths are to be found in the Hare, Sinkler, Garvan, and Waln collections. The style was also developed by David Hall, John Letellier, and others.

With such coffee-pots there were frequently combined little straight-sided tea-pots, some of them oval in section, some circular. A splendid example of the oval tea-pot, decorated as they so frequently were with vertical flutes, appears on Plate XXXVII.

The most distinctive style of tea-pot in vogue after the Revolution in Philadelphia was that illustrated by the Letellier (Plate XXXIII) and Richardson (Plate XXXI) examples. The shape is reminiscent of the porcelain tea-pots made in China for the European and American market and taken out through the port of Canton. Many such services were brought from China by Philadelphia merchants and ship-owners. This particular kind of Chinese porcelain has unfortunately and quite erroneously become known as "Lowestoft" ware, sometimes as "Sino-Lowestoft," which is begging the question, and also as "European-market" porcelain. The little Chinese porcelain tea-pots are

[193]

characterized by a rather low, circular, straight-sided body with straight spout and usually an insetting cover. As developed in silver, the shape seems to have been practically confined to Philadelphia, where it enjoyed a great vogue. Many of these little tea-pots, made by Joseph and Nathaniel Richardson, Letellier, Humphreys, and others, were finished by a beading along the margin of the base and top; others had a pierced gallery around the top, and the Letellier set (Plate XXXIII), so far as is known, is unique in having this pierced gallery not only around the top but also around the base of the several pieces. The accompanying coffee-pot is of inverted-pear shape. This set formerly belonged to the North family of Charleston, South Carolina, and now belongs to Miss Mary Mills.

Toward the close of the Revolution, when it became fashionable to make the tea-service *en suite*, the use of urn shapes became established. Quantities of urn-shaped tea-services were made in Philadelphia, many of them of imposing proportions and elegant form, although they do not equal in charm some of their less pretentious and smaller forerunners. The tea-pot by John McMullin (Plate **XXXIV A**; height, 11 ⅜"), with its pierced gallery, so distinctive a feature of Philadelphia silverwork, is a fine example of the urn-shaped tea-pot, just as the set of tea-pot, sugar-urn, and creamer by Simmons and Alexander (Plate **XXXV**) shows how the urn forms were adapted throughout. Both groups are from the collection of Miss Ella Parsons.

Silversmiths of a given locality often develop a preference for some particular design or decorative detail. Thus on Philadelphia silver the pierced gallery outlining the tops of pieces (Plates **XXXIII** and **XXXIV**), the beading running down the spout of a pot (Plate **XXXIV**), and the ornamental framework for a monogram (see accompanying sketch and also Plate **XXXI**) have a most extensive use. The script

FIGURE 17. Philadelphia Bow-knot and Wheat-ear Design

monogram has above it a ribbon bow-knot and below it crossed wheat-ears.

Philadelphia silversmiths did not confine themselves to work in that metal. They often had occasion to write themselves goldsmiths, as their handiwork proves. There are still extant rings made by Philip Syng and Samuel Soumaine, clasps by Francis and Joseph Richardson, and other delightful bits of gold jewelry. That relatively few survive is not surprising; that much more was wrought is proved by the frequent inclusion of such items in contemporary advertisements.

Practically no attention has thus far been paid to the silver produced in communities adjacent to the important centers of its manufacture. In the course of time these small towns will receive their just due. From Gabriel Thomas's account of Philadelphia and West New Jersey, written in 1698, it would appear that while Philadelphia was developing much more extensively, the towns in New Jersey, especially Salem and Burlington, had many of the same advantages of climate, situation, and produce and that they were engaging in trade almost as actively, even though on a smaller scale than Philadelphia. There is reason, therefore, to suppose that local silversmiths may have enjoyed some patronage, though as the metropolis became more celebrated, its silversmiths gained greater prestige and wealthy folk of Burlington, for example, honored the latter rather than their local craftsmen. The case with Wilmington, Delaware, was doubtless much the same. The silversmiths in these smaller towns, however, enjoyed sufficient patronage to develop skill, as is proved by such a praiseworthy piece as the teapot with vertical flutings and bright-cut engraving, made by Thomas Byrnes, probably a Wilmington craftsman (Plate XXXVII). This particularly pleasing piece bears the monogram I M S and the date 1793, celebrating the marriage of Isaac and Margaret (Tatnall) Starr in Wilmington in that year. The teapot now belongs to their descendant, Dr. Isaac Starr, Jr. It is surmounted by a pineapple finial, reputed to symbolize hospitality.

The work of another Wilmington silversmith, Bancroft Woodcock, is represented in Plate LVIII B, a sugar bowl of inverted-pear form made about 1770 for James Smith, one of the signers of the Declaration of Independence.

[196]

CHAPTER VII

SILVER OF VIRGINIA AND MARYLAND

In Virginia and Maryland, the land was well suited for agriculture and peculiarly adapted to the cultivation of tobacco, which was raised in Virginia almost from the beginning of the settlement. The colonists realized that in exporting other produce they would be forced to compete with their Northern neighbors, but by devoting themselves to tobacco they could develop a monopoly and thereby secure high profits. In consequence, tobacco-cultivation became the all-important industry of these colonies. England dispatched large numbers of indented servants, who found labor in the tobacco-fields and in the course of five or six years generally became freemen and soon acquired small farms that they worked themselves. Many English yeomen also emigrated to this region. The natural increase in population over a period of years gave rise to a large class of independent small land-holders. Some men, who either possessed considerable wealth when they came from England or were equipped by superior intelligence or business acumen to become rich, gradually acquired large estates and began to buy slaves. This was the general state of Southern society throughout most of the seventeenth century.

As there was no limit to the land available, a man's wealth was determined not so much by the amount

[197]

of land he owned as by the labor he could employ in its cultivation. Toward the end of the seventeenth century the planters, realizing that slave-labor was cheap and admirably suited for use in the tobacco-fields, began to purchase negroes in large numbers. Those planters who had sufficient means to buy slaves rapidly acquired more wealth, while the small farmer who was too poor to buy labor and forced to cultivate his land himself, became still poorer and was often obliged to emigrate to other places where he would not have to meet the impoverishing competition of slave-labor. It was in the course of the eighteenth century that this situation became so intensified that Southern society became composed chiefly of a class of rich planters with extensive property holdings and troops of slaves, and a class of very poor small farmers.

The Southern planter sent his tobacco-crop to England; with the credit thus acquired he purchased English manufactured goods, and so had little or no occasion to develop local industries other than the most essential. Royal governors, visitors to these colonies, and other contemporary writers have commented on the reluctance with which these Southern colonists engaged in any manufacturing enterprise. The only industries recorded in the period about 1700 are cloth-making, tanning leather, and making shoes.[1] A great increase in the market for their tobacco at this period enabled the colonists to buy English goods even more extensively. Tobacco was a variable crop; the conditions of its market often changed suddenly and unex-

[1] M. S. Morriss, "Colonial Trade of Virginia and Maryland," "Johns Hopkins University Studies."

pectedly, and its price fluctuated accordingly. The planter endeavored to estimate what his crop would bring when sold in England and then, in order to expedite their delivery, ordered his London agent to ship him English goods to that amount. In many cases the crop failed to bring this return, and so it happened that sometimes for generations families were heavily in debt to their London agents. The general results of this system were to stimulate the importation of English goods and to intensify the sense of the colonies' close relationship to the mother-country. Ninety-five per cent of the population, it is estimated, were English. The sense of kinship was also heightened by the fact that the Anglican Church was the established church of Virginia.

Governor Yeardley of Virgina, who died in 1627, in his will left to his wife Temperance his plate, linen, and all housekeeping stuff. But the possession of plate was not confined to royal governors. As their wealth increased, the planters strove to live in more luxurious surroundings, to entertain on a more lavish scale, and to furnish their homes with such handsome appointments as silver plate. William Fitzhugh, one of the richest and most cultured of Virginia planters in the late seventeenth century, who frequently ordered plate from his London agent, expressed his point of view thus: "[It] gives myself the present use and credit, is a sure friend at a dead lift without much loss or is a portion for a child after my decease." Such well-to-do planters, who shipped their tobacco directly from their own wharves to London, naturally bought London plate, and would doubtless have scorned Colonial

Early American Silver

silver as too crude and provincial for their scale of living, even if local craftsmen had been active in their communities.

As his will proves, Fitzhugh acquired in the course of his life a very considerable quantity of plate. To his wife he left "one silver bason, three silver plates, one of the lesser silver candlesticks, half the silver spoons in the house, the second best silver tankard, a silver porringer, a large silver ladle, the great silver tumbler," and he desires that she should leave this silver to his youngest son John. In addition, his bequests include "2 silver dishes, six silver plates, one large silver salver Jappon, one small silver bread plate, one heavier, one larger silver salt, one silver porringer of the largest sort, a pair of large silver candlesticks, with snuffers, snuff dish and extinguisher, the great silver tankard and a set of silver casters. . . . 2 silver dishes, a small silver bread plate, one silver trencher salt, one silver porringer of the largest sort, and a silver candlestick with snuffers and stand . . . one silver dish, 3 silver plates, a silver porringer, a silver salt, and a silver candlestick . . . one silver dish, 3 silver plates, one silver porringer (if one is left), a silver salt, a silver candlestick, and the smallest silver candlestick . . . one silver bason, 3 silver plates, a silver salt, a small silver tumbler and six silver spoons . . . 2 large silver dishes." [1]

The Anglican churches in the South, like others of their denomination elsewhere in the colonies, frequently received gifts of sacramental plate from the English

[1] Will of William Fitzhugh, "Virginia Magazine of History and Biography," Vol. II, p. 276.

PLATE XXXIII

See pages 193–194

TEA SET BY JOHN LETELLIER

sovereigns. In other instances, these churches accepted
gifts of English silver from devout worshipers. Rarely
if ever, until the second half of the eighteenth century,
were they the recipients of silver of Colonial make,
and the earliest pieces they received appear to have
been the work of Philadelphia or Northern craftsmen.

Most of our conclusions about Southern silver are
still largely a matter of conjecture. It is well to remember that forty years ago many New Englanders possessed of ancestral plate assumed that of course it was
of English production. Similarly, in the absence of
definite means of identification, it has been supposed
that little if any silver was made in the South until
the late eighteenth century. The discovery in early
records of the names of men listed as silversmiths is
gradually modifying this point of view. E. Alfred
Jones [1] comments on the reference to "one Thomas
Howard, of Jamestown, whose name is recorded in
the register of the Virginia Company in 1620. That
he was a practical worker in the precious metals is
doubtful. He was probably like the silversmiths of
1608, mentioned by the redoubtable Captain John
Smith as employed for the purpose of finding gold in
Virginia, or a mere member of the Goldsmiths' Company of London, like Sir Hugh Middleton, Sir Robert
Vyner and other so-called goldsmiths in the seventeenth century." It is highly probable that men trained
as silversmiths in London emigrated occasionally to
the Southern colonies as they did to New York and
New England, but it also seems probable that they
found scant encouragement to pursue their craft in

[1] "Old Silver of Europe and America."

either Virginia or Maryland in the seventeenth and the early eighteenth century. The wealthy who could afford silver were buying it in London in exchange for their tobacco. The whole attitude of the colonists was opposed to engaging in any trades or industries unless compelled to do so by necessity. There were few towns and no definite trading-class. With the eighteenth century the division between the large landowner and the poor farmer became pronounced. The intermediate group, people of moderate means who would naturally patronize local craftsmen, was largely lacking. May we not conclude, then, that up to about 1725, let us say, such silversmiths as appear in the records of Virginia and Maryland had been trained abroad and found little opportunity to pursue their craft in the colonies, and that rarely if ever did conditions tempt a boy born in these colonies to undertake an apprenticeship in this craft?

Later on, however, with the rise of various industries, of towns, of a mercantile class, with the increasing intercourse with colonial neighbors, especially Philadelphia, there developed in the South a market for Colonial silver. That made in Philadelphia was first introduced, and then in the course of time a group of silversmiths resident in Virginia and Maryland and especially in Baltimore arose to supply local demand. In the years in which the Congress met in Philadelphia, many Southern members came to that city and returned home with plate wrought by its best silversmiths. This must have constituted a strong brief in favor of Colonial plate.

The recent publication by the Walpole Society of

See pages 191, 194

PLATE XXXIV

TEA-POT BY JOHN McMULLIN

COFFEE-POT BY JOSEPH AND NATHANIEL RICHARDSON

CHAPTER VIII

SILVER OF CHARLESTON, SOUTH CAROLINA

THE very active seaport, Charleston, is not to be
grouped with the tobacco-plantations of Virginia and
Maryland. The outstanding commercial town south
of New York, she developed more similarities to
Northern trading-ports than she did with other towns
in her own region. James Truslow Adams, in "Provincial Society," points out that while North Carolina
traded extensively with Boston, South Carolina and
especially Charleston traded chiefly with the West
Indies, the wine islands, and Europe. Plate was at
first imported from England and such, we may suppose, was that included in the property of a certain
resident of Edistoe,[1] situated fifty miles south of
Charleston, who in 1686 was robbed by "100 Spaniards
with negroes and Indians," who were able to land at
Edistoe and "carry away all his money and plate, and
13 slaves, to the value of £1500. sterling," a very
considerable sum at the time. Most impressive in comparison with other Colonial inventories of property is
that of Joseph Morton of South Carolina, who at his
death in 1723 had furniture in the "best chamber"
valued at £195, in the dining room at £126, in the
parlor at £135, and silver plate to the value of £600.[2]

[1] "Narratives of Early Carolina," 1911, p. 205.
[2] J. T. Adams, "Provincial Society," p. 71.

[205]

One source of Charleston's accumulating wealth is suggested by Governor Bellomont of New York, in one of his detailed letters to the Lords of Trade in London, in which he remarks that the master of a vessel from South Carolina says there is much disorder in money value in Carolina, "that the Dog Dollars, Rix Dollars, and the Seville, pillar and Mexican pieces of Eight have a currency there, but are not at a fix'd standard in value." [1] Unquestionably much of Charleston's trade was with Spain and the West Indies, by reason of which she had current a large amount of Spanish coin. Henry C. Kirk has advanced the theory that as the old Spanish and Mexican coins were less carefully refined than were the English, they contained appreciable amounts of tellurium, sulphur, and selenium, which rendered the metal hard and brittle. The presence of these impurities in the metal with which the Southern silversmiths worked was a constant source of difficulty. No amount of annealing could soften silver in which these impurities existed and it had a distressing way of cracking in the process of raising. Mr. Kirk contends that this difficulty, as its cause was not understood by the early silversmiths, accounts to a very considerable degree for the slow development of silversmithing in the more southern colonies. The more northern colonies, according to Mr. Kirk, although they had in circulation a certain amount of Spanish money, had the advantage of being able to use a larger proportion of English coins and the more carefully refined metal lent itself readily to shaping into ambitious forms. It is interesting to note, in con-

[1] "New York Colonial Documents," Vol. 4, p. 669, June 1700.

See page 194

PLATE XXXV

See page 203

PLATE XXXVI

SUGAR URNS MADE BY BALTIMORE SILVERSMITHS

GEORGE AIKEN, LITTLETON HOLLAND, J. LYNCH, AND LOUIS BUICHLE

CHAPTER IX

EARLY AMERICAN SILVERSMITHS AND THEIR METHODS OF WORK

It is not fair to consider early American silver merely crude and rather uninteresting provincial work, nor, on the other hand, is it reasonable to regard it as unique and original. Obviously it did not spring full-born, as Minerva did from the head of Jove. It had its immediate origins in the silverwork of England and Holland, the countries from which the colonists came and to which for many years they paid willing allegiance. It was also to some extent influenced, indirectly, by other Continental silver design.

The earliest silver made in New York was wrought by craftsmen who had emigrated from Holland and is directly inspired by Dutch models. Admirable illustrations are afforded by the tall beaker engraved with strapwork and foliate scrolls, made by Jacob Boelen (Plate XXIII); by the baptismal basin made by Jacobus Van der Spiegel (Plate XXVIII); and by the bowl embossed with flowers in compartments, made by Benjamin Wynkoop (Plate XXI). New Netherland, however, had been taken over by the English in 1664, and from that time on English colonists and English styles came in in ever-increasing quantity, with the result that much New York silver is a composite. Some of the old Dutch shapes persisted; the silver retained its heavy, sturdy character, and it continued to be embellished with engraved, embossed, and cast ornaments of Dutch inspiration. At the same time, however, certain English shapes and decorative details were adopted. The early New York tankards offer a delightful illustration of the manner in which Dutch and English elements merged, producing one of the most interesting and distinctive of Colonial types. Their shape, we find, was inspired presumably by English tankards; yet they are peculiarly massive in their proportions, and are frequently enriched, in a generous and spontaneous fashion, with foliate borders, engraved and embossed cherubs' heads, foliate scrolls, pendent swags of fruit and flowers, etc., derived from Dutch ornament. The influence of Dutch silverwork continued to show in New York silver even as late as the third quarter of the eighteenth century, sometimes in the shapes employed, more often in its general proportions or in features of its decoration. Probably nowhere else in the American colonies was this influence directly exerted, although it did occasionally enter indirectly.

Outside of New York, the predominant element in all the colonies was English, and the silver produced was primarily based upon English design. The succession of styles has already been traced in the story of Massachusetts silverwork. However, English silver itself often borrowed from Continental plate, and in turn passed these Continental elements on to the American craftsman. Specific instances have already been given. Thus bands of granulation, which were much used in Germany and Scandinavia, were sometimes copied by London silversmiths, as in the standing cup made in 1639 illustrated in Plate I (left). This cup was brought to America, and probably among others served to introduce the fashion that Boston silversmiths followed to some extent, as demonstrated by the beaker with a similar band of granulation made by Hull and Sanderson (Plate II, left). The silversmiths of Norwich, because of the town's proximity to Holland and the resultant commercial intercourse, made numerous beakers decorated with foliate scrolls and strapwork much like the customary Dutch beaker. It was presumably these English interpretations, rather than actual Dutch examples, that inspired such Boston beakers with engraved strapwork as that made by Hull and Sanderson belonging to the First Church in Marblehead, or that made by John Hull belonging to the Newman Congregational Church in East Providence, Rhode Island. More general instances of the transference of Dutch styles to America through the medium of English plate are offered by embossed floral decoration, derived from seventeenth-century Dutch models, used extensively in English plate of the Restoration period, and appearing in Massachusetts silver in such pieces as the caudle-cup illustrated in Plate IV B. The New England silversmiths might be said to have used an English translation of the Dutch original.

In considering the influence of French plate upon English and Colonial silver, it is wiser to generalize than to attempt to particularize. Numbers of Huguenots sought refuge in the American colonies, especially in Rhode Island, New York, Pennsylvania, and the

South, and if one lists the prominent American silver-smiths, one is impressed by the frequent occurrence of such names as Bartholomew, John, and Charles Le Roux; César Ghiselin; John de Nise; Elias Boudinot; René Grignon; Timothy Bontecou; William Vilant; John Hastier; Apollos Rivoire, who anglicized his name to Paul Revere. These men all possessed high ideals of craftsmanship and must have made a real, if intangible, contribution to the quality of Colonial silver, but it is difficult to determine whether they introduced French styles into the colonies. They seem rather to have devoted their skill to fashioning things in the styles current in the localities in which they settled.

French influence, however, was definitely if indirectly exerted upon American silver through the medium of English plate. England, which has always been much affected by French fashions, was deeply indebted to French designers during the seventeenth and eighteenth centuries. When Charles II returned to England from France in 1660, he brought with him a taste for lavish decoration in the French manner, and the acquaintance with French styles was steadily increased when, with the revocation of the Edict of Nantes in 1685, large numbers of Huguenots settled in England. French silversmiths were impelled to emigrate, not only because of religious persecution, but because of unemployment. The heavy taxation necessary to finance Louis XIV's wars and the building of his palace at Versailles had sunk France into such poverty that the silversmiths had practically no patronage. A royal order in 1687 called for the melting

Silversmiths and their Methods of Work

down of all silver plate in the kingdom and prohibited the further fashioning of it, so that the craftsmen were left no alternative but to leave France in search of employment.[1] These extremely able craftsmen, by their skill and high ideals, as well as by their fertility of invention, greatly enriched English art. Under Queen Anne, French influences were not so marked, the plate then made being severely plain. But from about 1725 to 1760 they were again in the ascendant, for the rococo styles that dominated England during that period had had their genesis and their most sensitive development in France. Though inspired by the French, the English were so different in temperament that their interpretation of French designs was distinctly individual. In general, the English adaptation lacked some of the delicacy, grace, and inventiveness of the original. It was more apt to be handsome than exquisite, was admirable rather than charming. The English, however, had a taste for elaborate plate and did not hesitate to follow the rococo style in its more extravagant phases, whereas the American colonists, as we shall presently see, had a marked preference for simple and practical things and so borrowed only the more restrained English adaptations of French design.

European styles entered the colonies through a variety of channels. Many a Colonial silversmith had been born abroad and served his apprenticeship to a London or a Haarlem master of the craft, so that he brought to the land of his adoption not simply his own skill and experience but also a knowledge of European design and the traditions of a long-established gild.

[1] W. W. Watts, "Old English Silver," 1924.

[213]

The coming of silversmiths thus trained was not confined to any one period or locality. Mention has already been made of John Mansfield, who came from London to Boston in 1634, and of Robert Sanderson, who had practised his craft in London before he came to New England in 1638. George Ridout's mark was registered in the London Goldsmiths' Hall in 1743. Shortly thereafter he came to New York, where he made an alms-basin that was presented in 1747 to Trinity Church by Robert Elliston. Daniel Christian Fueter's mark was also recorded in London in 1753, and in 1754, "lately arrived from London," he advertised in the "New York Gazette" that he "makes all sorts of Gold and Silverwork, after the newest and neatest Fashion." In the late eighteenth century Ewan, another London silversmith, traveling by way of the West Indies, eventually reached Charleston, South Carolina, where he became established in his trade. These instances, taken at random, suggest the steady and potent infiltration of European craftsmanship. Such incoming silversmiths not only directly reflected European and especially English styles in their own work but also passed on this knowledge to those men who served as their apprentices.

The acquaintance with European styles was also spread by a continuous importation of actual pieces of European plate. Some of these were brought in by colonists as part of their household goods, but many others were imported by dealers. Against the latter, Daniel Henchman, a native of Boston, complained bitterly when he advertised in 1773 that "he flatters himself that he shall have the Preference by those who

Silversmiths and their Methods of Work

are Judges of Work, to those Strangers among us who import and sell English Plate, to the great Hurt and Prejudice of the Townsmen who have been bred in the Business." Nevertheless, this competition must have proved highly stimulating to the local craftsmen, who would respond to changes in European fashion, turning to the imported silver as an index of current trends.

Just as Colonial builders and cabinet-makers turned for inspiration to imported books of architectural and furniture designs, such as, for example, the Batty-Langley series, the books by Ware and Abraham Swan, or the drawings in Chippendale's "Gentleman's and Cabinet-maker's Director," so the silversmiths may have had recourse to similar pattern-books planned for their trade. Much has been written from time to time about the printed books of ornament that the invention of engraving made possible. In Europe, from about the fifteenth century on, many craftsmen possessed of a special gift for design engraved and published books of their own designs, which were widely disseminated among less imaginative and resourceful craftsmen. Notable instances are the books issued by the Hopfer family, goldsmiths of Augsburg; Matthias Zundt; Virgil Solis; Peter Flötner; and Paul Flindt. In most cases, the designs in these pattern-books were not intended to be closely copied, but were suggestive and could be adapted by the practical craftsman to the work he had in hand.

Probably engraved designs of this sort occasionally found their way into the hands of the American silversmith, especially as a number of the early silversmiths were also engravers and would have instinctively bethought themselves of such aids. It seems highly probable, for example, that the Dutch silversmiths working in New York, who used a good deal of engraved ornament on their silver and observed rather definite conventions, turned to some such source of inspiration. The spontaneity that characterized their work, however, proves that they were themselves artists and not mere copyists.

In this connection it is interesting to come upon the item "1 Book Cyphers" in the inventory of the tools and other stock belonging to Nathaniel Helme, a Rhode Island silversmith, an inventory taken in 1789. The cipher or "reversed monogram" was composed of a series of letters and the same reversed and was a favorite decorative feature in European art of the seventeenth and eighteenth centuries. A French designer, Vérien, issued a book of ciphers in the late seventeenth century which doubtless served as a model for many issued subsequently. Jeremiah Marlow published in London in 1683 "A Book of Cyphers or Letters Reverst, Being a Work very pleasant & usefull as well for Gentlemen as all sorts of Artificers Engravers Painters Carvers Chacers Embroiderers etc." Copies of such books sometimes show that individual ciphers have been cut out, and doubtless they were stuck up on the work-bench as patterns for the craftsman. [1] The silversmiths in the colonies, and especially those in early New York, used these decorative monograms. Plate LVIII A, a sugar-bowl by Simeon Soumaine of New York, shows one quite clearly.

[1] Much of this information was kindly supplied by Dr. S. W. Woodhouse, Jr.

PLATE XXXVII

TEA-POT BY THOMAS BYRNES

See page 196

Silversmiths and their Methods of Work

Although the American silversmiths drew repeatedly upon European and especially English design for inspiration, they worked with discrimination, adapting the designs to the taste and character of their patrons, and created something fresh and distinctive. The qualities that thus distinguish early American silver were the direct result of the character and temper of the people for whom it was made and of the conditions then existent in the colonies. The early settlers were enterprising and hardy pioneers; naturally their silver was straightforward and vigorous in design. The rigors of living made utility a prime requisite; the early silver was, therefore, chiefly of a utilitarian sort and not intended purely for display.

Moreover, the development of native craftsmanship was fostered particularly in those communities which were most independent in spirit, such as New England, where the colonists had left England primarily because they were opposed to conditions there, especially as represented by the court, the nobility, and the Anglican Church. Because of these antipathies and because of their absorbing concern in the preparation for another life, the New Englanders tended to decry everything that savored of luxury and extravagance, and hence elaborate and purely ornamental silver was extremely distasteful to them.

The Southern colonies, on the other hand, were not so opposed to worldly things and had a taste for more luxurious appointments, but here local craftsmanship was discouraged by the economic situation. The concentration upon tobacco-culture and the consequent development of plantations at the expense of town life was at the opposite pole from conditions in New England. Instead of developing local craftsmanship like the North, the South kept in close touch with England, and wealthy colonists who could afford to own plate imported it from that country.

In New York and Pennsylvania, colonies that occupied a middle position between these two extremes, not only geographically but also from the point of view of the present discussion, there was likewise a distinct preference for plain and substantial silver. In New York, as Chapter V has stressed, the silversmiths of Dutch descent had an almost childlike love of engraved, embossed, and applied ornament, but even in their exuberance they never allowed it to interfere with the primary object, the usefulness of their silver. In other words, almost every piece they made was intended to serve a practical purpose; its ornamentation was incidental. In Pennsylvania, the dominant Quaker element, though often well-to-do, naturally preferred the simple and unostentatious types of silverwork, and the wealthy "world's people," who had a predilection for more showy styles, were sufficiently like their fellow-Royalists in Maryland and Virginia to give their patronage to London silversmiths in preference to what they were pleased to consider crude and provincial workmen.

Thus the taste of their patrons limited the scope of the early American silversmiths. What skill they might have developed in designing elaborate and fanciful pieces, had their customers so ordered, cannot be guessed; it can only be asserted that within their range they did highly creditable work. One is apt to

[218]

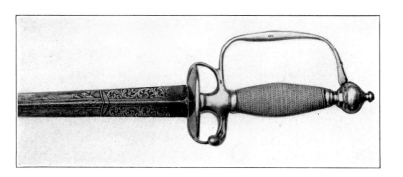

PLATE XXXVIII   *See page 64*

RAPIER AND TWO-HANDLED CUP BY EDWARD WINSLOW

think of English or Continental plate in terms of the more elaborate examples; presumably a relatively larger amount of this type has been preserved because its workmanship added materially to its value, while plain silver, once out of fashion, was worth little more than its value as bullion. In the seventeenth and eighteenth centuries, however, there must have been wrought quantities of plain, utilitarian plate. With such European plate the early American silver may fairly be compared, and in such a comparison the latter holds its own admirably.

Though the early American silversmith turned to foreign models for inspiration, only very rarely did he attempt to make a copy of another piece. One might mention the Haarlem beaker made in 1660, which was later presented to the First Reformed Church of Albany, New York, and the copy of it made in 1678 by Ahasuerus Hendricks. But the instances to which one can point to-day are so very infrequent that one can with assurance assert that the procedure was exceptional. The Colonial silversmiths, however, adapted the foreign models to which they had access, usually simplifying them more or less. But they could not have done even this successfully had they not themselves possessed sensitiveness and skill.

As a matter of fact, the character of their patrons set a wholesome restraint and at the same time served as a stimulus to these early silversmiths. The demand for simplicity kept them from slipping over to the bizarre and the ornate, yet the requirement that a piece be substantial and serviceable prompted the smith to make it vigorous and effective. He gave special thought to matters of proportion and balance, and in so doing succeeded in producing a result that is æsthetically satisfying. A tankard when full was heavy to lift; its handle must be stout enough to support the weight. Owing to this consideration, the handles appear well proportioned in relation to the tankards to which they are fitted. A caudle-cup, when full of wine, was raised and tilted by its two handles. There was reason, then, for the silversmith to strive to get a nice adjustment of weight. Only a sensitive and capable craftsman can accomplish these results; that the early American silversmiths did it repeatedly is proof of their skill and adds greatly to the merit of their handiwork.

A fine feeling for line, as well as the sense of balance, is exhibited in this early silverwork. Most of it was relatively plain and had to rely for its appeal upon its beauty of line and proportion. If the shape was weak and faulty, it was obviously so; it could not be concealed beneath a mass of decoration. On the other hand, while in general little decoration was employed, that which was used served primarily to emphasize grace or strength of line, as the case might be. Some of the earliest standing cups, such as those by Hull and Sanderson (Plates II and LI), are undecorated; they are beautifully proportioned and delightful to see. Others, like those by Dummer (Frontispiece and Plate VI) are enriched by a border of gadrooning that serves to emphasize the full curve of the cup and also affords a charming contrast of plain and fluted surface, with resultant play of light. The beaded rat-tail applied down a tankard handle served the practical purpose of strengthening the grip and the æsthetic ends of emphasizing the strength of the handle and of relieving a plain surface by a pleasant bit of contrast.

It is probable that these early silversmiths did not keep much stock on hand and that they considered each new piece of work a fresh adventure. Entries in the account-book of Joseph Richardson of Philadelphia (now the property of the Pennsylvania Historical Society) suggest the general procedure. On one side of the book Richardson enters the amount of silver coin brought to him by a customer; on the opposite page he enters his charge for the actual making of the piece ordered.

1745

| 7 mo. 16th | Rec'd of Sarah Robeson 39 oz. 6 dwt. of Silver and 7/6 Starling in English Silver to be made into 3 Poringers a Weighter & a pr of Salts. Markt S R. |

1745

9 mo. 29	Sarah Robeson is Dr to 3 Poringers & a weighter weighing 32 oz. 1 dwt.
	to making the above £2-9-0
11 mo. 14	Sarah Robeson is Dr to a pr of Salts wt. 5 oz. 13 to fashion £1-10-0

If a customer brought a little more or a little less coin, the piece finally delivered to him may have varied accordingly. The silversmith probably cut his garment to fit his cloth. There was not the modern demand for quantity production and uniformity. In the church in Farmington, Connecticut, for example, there are four caudle-cups made by Jeremiah Dummer of Boston and each varies more or less from its fellow, although alike in general design. It is these little variations which give the early silver much of its charm.

Moreover, while the silversmith strove for fine line and proportion and balance, he was not meticulous about mechanical precision. The side of a beaker, for example, will often be slightly irregular, yet it is just this deviation from absolute regularity that gives the silver personality. Allied to this is the quality of the surface. Looked at closely, it will reveal tiny hammer-marks, not glaring and pretentious as are those on some modern hand-hammered silver, but the sincere and knowing touch of the artist-craftsman. These tiny facets reflect the light at different angles and give to the old silver its mellow quality, as contrasted with the hard, brilliant, highly reflective surface of modern buffed silver. Too often old pieces are sent to ignorant or indifferent people to be polished and are subjected to buffing, a process that actually cuts away, by the use of rouge and emery, the old surface with all its delightful richness and play of light.

What gave the old silver its greatest distinction was the personality of the silversmith who wrought it. The work of some of the more prominent Colonial craftsmen has been discussed and illustrated in the preceding pages. No one will deny the skill of such men as Hull and Sanderson, Dummer, Coney, Winslow, Hurd, and Revere of Boston; of the Boelens, Van der Spiegel, Van Dyck, the Ten Eycks, Schaats, and Wynkoop of New York; of Vernon and Casey in Rhode Island; and of the Syngs and Richardsons of

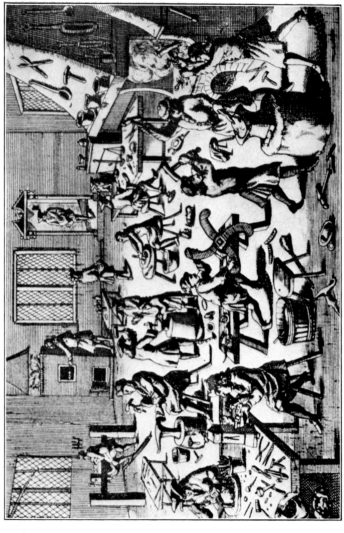

PLATE XXXIX   VIEW OF A LONDON SILVERSMITH'S SHOP, 1707

Philadelphia. But were these men exceptional? What of the rank and file? Were they merely regarded as tradesmen or were they respected in their communities and known for other merits than their abilities as craftsmen?

The skill of the Colonial silversmiths was based, first of all, upon a careful trade-training. In England from the late thirteenth and the early fourteenth century, a well-regulated system of apprenticeship had become established, which was enforced by gild and municipal authorities. By the Statute of Artificers, passed in 1562, the system was made uniform and national. The American colonists brought over with them the essential characteristics of this system, adopting what seemed expedient.[1] Fundamentally it involved the making of a contract between master and apprentice, which was publicly recorded and generally supervised by the colony or town authorities. The usual term of apprenticeship was seven years and this was not to be completed until the applicant had reached the age of twenty-one. This period ensured the development of skilled craftsmen. The indenture, in the obligations it imposed upon master and apprentice and also in its quaint phrasing, closely followed the English practice. The master was required to give his apprentice bed, board, and clothing, in addition to trade-training, and was also responsible for the latter's moral welfare. On his part, the apprentice promised to live with his master during the term of his apprenticeship,

[1] See Robert F. Seybolt, "Apprenticeship and Apprentice Education in Colonial New England and New York," Teachers College, Columbia, "Contributions to Education."

to obey his commands, keep his secrets, protect his interests, and abstain from evil behavior. Upon the satisfactory completion of his training, the youth became a freeman of the town and was permitted to practise his trade. A hint of the cordial relations frequently existing between master and apprentice is given by a letter written by the Philadelphia silversmith Joseph Richardson to his brother Nathaniel. The master was required to provide the boy, upon completion of the latter's training, with a suit of clothing. Accordingly Richardson writes: "Our Kelly's Indentures expired this day and he left us Since dinner full trim in his freedom suit, and if he is not a foot higher in reality I dare say he is in his own imagination." [1]

Massachusetts Bay had early passed definitive legislation governing apprenticeship and Connecticut closely followed her example. The customs in Rhode Island, New York, and Pennsylvania were generally similar. In the Boston town meeting of 1660: "It is therefore ordered that no person shall henceforth open a shop in this Town, nor occupy any place of manufacture or science, till hee hath compleated 21 years of age, nor except hee hath served seven yeares Apprenticeship, by testimony under the hands of sufficient witnesses." This system, following English precedent, endeavored to provide training and employment for children of poor or dependent parents, thus serving as a means of poor relief. In the colonies, it was often carried still further than the English system and used as a means of compelling elementary education by re-

[1] Mary T. Seaman, "Thomas Richardson . . . and His Descendants in America," 1929.

See pages 236-237

PLATE XL

METHOD OF RAISING A COFFEE-POT

quiring masters to teach ("or cause to be taught" in case they themselves were illiterate) their apprentices to read, write, and cipher. Thus it came about that the early silversmiths had received a substantial training before they were allowed to pursue their craft.

In addition to their craft knowledge, there is plenty of evidence to show that these early silversmiths often held enviable positions in the society of their day, that they played prominent parts in general civic affairs, that they were many-sided, that they were highly esteemed. Many of them belonged to distinguished families or won for themselves positions of honor. John Hull was an extremely wealthy merchant of Boston; Van der Spiegel was brother-in-law of Rip Van Dam, one of the most prominent men in early New York; Philip Syng, Jr., was connected with many of the most famous associations and institutions of early Philadelphia. The early silversmiths won their patrons not by systematic impersonal advertising, as is done to-day, but by direct acquaintance. Often silversmith and customer were members of the same church or of the same social group or met while serving together in public office. Such close association must have inspired the silversmith, for the sake of his own pride, to put forth his best efforts. One has but to read the biographical notes on the early silversmiths in such accounts as that given by Mr. Halsey in "Early New York Silversmiths" or in his introduction to the catalogue of the exhibition held in Boston in 1906, or to follow lines of research for oneself, to become impressed by the recurrence of these names in the annals of the day. In Boston, the names appear continually in the records of the Ancient and Honorable Artillery Company, the oldest militia in America. They also occur in other military annals, in lists of public officials, in positions of trust and importance in many fields.

Revere affords the best-known though by no means a unique example. As one of the Sons of Liberty in Boston, he was very active in the political affairs that immediately preceded the American Revolution. A fleet and trustworthy messenger and diplomat, he was frequently sent by the patriots at Boston with messages to their fellows in New York and Philadelphia. These public services must have taken a large part of his time and necessitated his being ever on call, yet he found opportunity to turn out a great deal of silver, to engrave biting political cartoons, to carve wood frames for some of Copley's portraits, to make cannon that were used during the Revolution, and to make bells in the same foundry when the declaration of peace made the former no longer necessary. Revere affords a picturesque instance, yet there were many others hardly less notable. Indeed, we must believe that many of these early silversmiths found time to ply their trade only in those intervals when public affairs or emergencies did not claim their entire attention. We must admire them for their public spirit, for their many-sided interests and activities, for their energy and enthusiasm, as well as for their skill as craftsmen.

People always have taken and doubtless always will take pride in the possession of handsome pieces of silver plate, but in early Colonial days there were special considerations that encouraged people to hoard their money in this form. If, for example, a wealthy Boston merchant acquired a comfortable surplus through his trade with the West Indies, he had no way of placing these funds in a bank, as there were then no banks in the colonies. New England paper currency fluctuated seriously in value, so that he might well deem it inadvisable to convert his funds into this medium. In the form of coin they could be readily stolen and if found again at all were not easily identified. But in the form of a silver tea-pot or tankard, stamped with the initials of a familiar silversmith and "cyphered" with the owner's initials or engraved with his coat of arms, his property could be advertised in the local newspapers as stolen goods and could be easily identified if discovered. Doubtless this gave the potential thief pause, lest he be apprehended with his loot with all the evidence marked against him. There are frequent advertisements in the newspapers of the Colonial period recording the disappearance of plate and describing its distinguishing features. In the "New York Gazette" for October 6, 1760, appears an advertisement of silver stolen from "Nicholas Burger's house in Queen St. in this city, one Silver Tea Pot, one Cream Pot, and six silver Tablespoons, a silver Sugar Tongs, and six Tea Spoons made by Mr. John Brevort, stampt with his Stamp thus I B V, in a circle, and marked on the bottom of the Tea Pot and Cream Pot thus N ^{B} I and on the handle of the Table Spoons, the same, and on the Tea-Spoons R ^{V} D" (probably Richard Van Dyck). The "Pennsylvania Gazette" for November 9, 1752, advertises: "Lost or stolen on the ninth or seventh of this instant Nov. a large silver spoon, marked I ^L M the Silversmiths stamp W. V. in two or three places. Whoever brings it to the New Printing Office will be rewarded and no questions asked." The "Boston Evening-Post" of April 18,1743, has this: "Lately lost or stollen, a Silver Spoon, mark'd T. F. the Maker's Name (if remembered right) W. Cowell. If it be offer'd to Sale, 'tis desired it may be stopped, and Notice given to the Printer."

Most interesting is the following advertisement, quaintly descriptive of early New York plate. "Stole from Flatbush on Long Island, One Silver Tankerd, a piece of Money in the Led of King Charles II, and the Led all ingraved, a Coat-of-Arms before (in it a Man on a Waggon with two horses) mark'd on the Handle L. P. A. One Silver Tankerd plain, with a piece of Money in the Led, mark'd on the handle A. P. or A. L. One Cup with twisted ears chas'd with Skutchens mark'd L. P. A. One tumbler Mark'd L. P. A. All the above was made by Mr. Jacob Boele, Stamp'd I. B. One large Cup with two cast Ears, with heads upon them, and a Coat of Arms Engrav'd thereon. One Cup with two Ears, a small Hole in the Bottom. . . . Whoever can inform Peter Lefferts of Flatbush on Long Island, or Abraham Lefferts in New York, so that it may be had again, shall have Fifteen Pounds Reward and no Questions asked." ("New York Gazette," October 8, 1723.)

If a wealthy merchant decided that the safest and most satisfactory method of investing his funds was in the form of wrought plate, his next move was to

Silversmiths and their Methods of Work

bethink himself of some silversmith of his acquaintance
with whose work and reputation for integrity he was
familiar. Going to the latter's shop, he would deposit
his bag of coins upon the work-bench and place an
order for the fashioning of a tea-pot or caudle-cup or
punch-bowl—whatever his desires might dictate or his
supply of silver make. The finished piece would then
cost him, as Joseph Richardson's account-book indicated, only the amount charged by the silversmith for
fashioning the piece and for adding suitable ornamentation.

Later in the Colonial period, when people desired
plate, they frequently depended upon the silversmith
to find his materials, in which event he added to his
bill the cost of so many ounces of silver. This is indicated by the two bills quoted below, both of which
were reproduced in the Boston Museum of Fine Arts
catalogue of 1911.

Mr. Norton Quincy to Danl Henchman Dr

To 1 Silver Tankard wt. 24-2-0 @ 52/ £62-13-6

To fashg Ditto   20- 0-0

To Engraving   1-16-0
                                                   ───────
                                    old tenor   £84- 9-6

Boston Septr. 4th 1768

Recd the Contents in full Danl Henchman

Moses Brown Esq.   Boston April 2 1789
         Bot of Paul Revere & son

	oz	
To Silv^r Tea-pot 16 @ 7		£5-12
Making & engrav^g oz		5-8
Silver stand for do 6		2-2
Making & Engrav^g		1-10
4 Silv Salt Spoons		18
		£15-10

	oz	
By Silver Salver 25 @ 7/		8-15
Rec^d pay in full		6-15

                     Paul Revere

A number of American silversmiths, especially in the second half of the eighteenth century, not only manufactured plate but also imported it from London. The advertisements of Edmond Milne of Philadelphia, in 1763–64, announce that "he has just imported in the last vessels from London, an elegant Assortment of Goldsmiths and Jewellry ware." This "large and neat assortment of the newest fashioned plate and jewellery" he proceeds to describe in great detail, affording an insight into the wide variety of articles fashionable at the time. But lest his imports seem his only trade, he adds: "He also makes up work bespoke in all its branches." Milne has already been mentioned in the chapter on Philadelphia silverwork as the maker of Indian silver ornaments and of the camp-cups used by General Washington.

Some of the earliest silversmiths' shops were crude and primitive affairs and were occasionally broken into. All readers of books on American silver are familiar with the oft-quoted entry in Samuel Sewall's diary for June 21, 1707, which reads: "Billy Cowell's shop is entered by the Chimney and a considerable quantity of Plate stolen." George Munson Curtis, in "Early Silver of Connecticut and Its Makers," writes that the shops of Joseph and Stephen Hopkins in Waterbury, Connecticut, were entered eight or ten times between 1765 and 1775.

So far no representation of the interior of a Colonial silversmith's shop has been discovered. Plate **XXXIX**, however, shows a London silversmith's shop of 1707. Though more extensive, better equipped, and carried on by more workmen than was the Colonial shop, this interior cannot but give us a better understanding of the tools and general equipment employed by the American craftsman.

Because he worked with simple tools and appliances, the achievements of the Colonial silversmith deserve special credit. The inventories are very enlightening. Mr. Halsey, in his introduction to the catalogue of the silver exhibition held at the Museum of Fine Arts in Boston in 1906, quotes the inventory of John Burt's tools, taken in Boston in 1745/6, and from this inventory deduces the methods employed by the Colonial workman at this period. Burt's business proved highly profitable, for he left a total estate of £6460.4.9, a large fortune for his time; tools, exclusive of the gold, silver, stones, and more or less completed work on hand, were valued at £238.7.6. As much of his handiwork remains and as the inventory of his tools is particularly detailed and complete, it is fairly easy

[231]

Early American Silver

to visualize the work that went forward in his shop. We cannot, therefore, do better than to quote this inventory again and base our discussion upon it, following Mr. Halsey's model.

INVENTORY OF JOHN BURT
Taken March 20, 1745/6

	£	s	d
316 oz 4 pwt of Silver @ 36/ p oz £569.3/ Gold 18 oz 11 pwt @ £27 p oz. £500.17/	1070		
Cash £100---33 oz of Correll @ 20/ pr oz. £33	133		
5 pair of stone earings & 3 sett of stone buttons £30 a parcell of old stones £7	37		
a parcell of Christalls for Buttons & Earings	32		
a parcell of old stone work	5		
2 Show Glasses. £5.0/ 53 pair of Chapes & tongs £10.2/	15	2	
11 Files, 33/ a pair of large and small bellows 40/	3	13	
a large Forgin Anvil 120 ld @ 2/ 6 p £15 ... 1 small do £9, ...	24		
9 raising Anvils 217 ld @ 3/6 p ld £37.19.6 2 planishing Teaster 39 ld @ 3/6 £6.16.6	44	16	
2 Spoon Teaster £26 . . . 2 planishing ditto 25/ 3 bench vises £12	39	5	
9 small vises 45/ 2 beak irons 20/ 40 hammers @ 8/ pr hammer 18.16.10............	22	1	
2 Melting Skillets £5. 37 bottom stakes & punches 155 @ 4/ £31..............	36		
a Drawing bench & tongs 40/ 11 Drawing Irons £11 10 pair of shears £6......	19		
2 brass Hollowin stamps £5. a pair of brass Salt punches 30/....................	6	10	

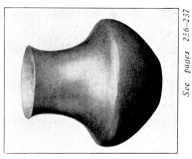

See pages 236–237

PLATE XLI

METHOD OF RAISING A COFFEE-POT

Silversmiths and their Methods of Work

1 Thimble stamp £4.10/ 6 pr. of flasks for casting £4.10/......................	9	
15 pair of tongs & plyers @ 5/ a pr. 75/ a pair of large scales and weights £8	11	15
4 pair of small scales & weights 40/ pewter and lead moulds 85 ld @ 1/6 £6.7.6	8 7	6
36 old files, 18/ 12 strainers 12/ 1 Oyl Stove 25, 3 small saws 25	4	
4 boreax boxes 5/ 3 burnishes 20/ 1 Triblet 10/ 2 boiling pans 60/...............	4	15
a parcell of punches £5, 1 Touch Stone 5/	5	5

John Burt (1691–1745) doubtless had his sons, Samuel (1724–54), William (1726–52), and Benjamin (1729–1805), as apprentices, and may have had other apprentices in his shop. Evidently he made jewelry, although none of it is known to the writer. He also made some flatware, chiefly spoons. The bulk of his work was simple, useful hollow-ware, in the production of which he was designer and craftsman. The processes he had occasion to employ included melting and refining bullion, hammering the metal into sheets, raising his shapes, annealing, embossing, casting, soldering, polishing, chasing, and engraving. The apprentice who set out to become proficient in such a variety of tasks possessed courage, initiative, and instinct for adventure. If he became, like Burt, master of his craft, he had developed facility in the execution of all of his many tasks and ingenuity in the solution of ever new and surprising problems. Let us consider what was involved in the making of an ordinary piece of hollow-ware.

[233]

Early American Silver

The silversmith's material generally came to him in the form of coins, presumably a mixture of those then current in the colonies—English, Dutch, Spanish, French, both true and counterfeit. These varied considerably in quality, according to the coinage standards of the several countries. The English standard for both coinage and wrought plate was known as "sterling" and was 925 parts fine, that is, in every 1000 parts there were 925 parts of pure or fine silver and 75 parts of alloy (or 11 oz. 2 dwt. pure silver in every 12 oz. or pound Troy). This regulation was consistently maintained in Great Britain except for a short interval from 1697 to 1720 when, for sufficient reasons, wrought plate was required to be of a finer quality, which because it was hall-marked with the figure of Britannia, was known as the "Britannia standard" (see page 58). Silver finer than sterling quality is too soft to be practicable for general use; indeed most of the Continental countries have not attempted to maintain as high a standard as the English and have contented themselves with the manufacture of plate and coinage of 800 or 900 parts fine silver.

The Colonial silversmith's first task, upon receiving a bag of coins from his customer, was to melt them down in a crucible and to refine the metal until he assured himself that it was of the requisite quality. This he often did by rubbing a bit of it upon the *Touch Stone* (mentioned in Burt's inventory) and testing the color of the mark or touch thus made with that left by a piece of silver of known quality. No one has yet determined what standard, if any, was adopted by the Colonial silversmiths. Those of English descent

See page 86

PLATE XLII

TEA SET BY PAUL REVERE

were naturally familiar with sterling and may well have made that their gage. They were, as a class, men of too great integrity and spirit to resort to inferior standards but as there were no laws or gild regulations in the colonies to control their work, it is possible that they did not keep to an arbitrary rule. They were continually forced to compete, however, especially in the eighteenth century, with men who imported and sold English plate. The latter established a criterion of quality and impelled the American craftsman to offer his customers some assurance that his silverware was of comparable merit. Sometimes, in advertising his work, he asserted that he "will warrant it to be true Sterling Standard." Until some one has opportunity to make careful tests of the quality of a sufficient number of pieces of Colonial silverwork, we shall not know just what the prevailing standard was.

Once assured that his molten silver was of the quality he desired, the silversmith poured it out into a *Skillet*, in which, as it cooled, it took the shape of a flat block of silver. This block the craftsman next hammered out on a *Forgin Anvil* and rolled out until it was as thin a sheet of metal as he required. But silver, under the repeated blows of a hammer, becomes more compact and brittle, and will crack unless it is reheated and made soft and malleable again. This process, known as annealing, was accomplished in John Burt's time by placing the silver in the heat of a charcoal fire that was fanned by *bellows*. Annealing has to be repeated again and again during the making of any piece of silver, to keep the metal in a workable condition.

[235]

Early American Silver

When the silversmith had beaten his silver into a sheet of the proper thickness, he was ready to begin "raising," the process by which a hollow object is brought up or raised, by the use of various hammers or anvils, from a flat sheet of silver. The Gorham Company has generously allowed us to reproduce a series of photographs (Plates XL, XLI) taken at their factory, which illustrate the process. With *saws* or *shears* (mentioned in Burt's inventory) the silversmith cut from his sheet of silver a circular piece slightly smaller in diameter than the combined base and side of the completed piece he had in mind. He probably began his work with a dapping hammer and a wood sinking-block furnished with shallow, saucer-shaped hollows, but as it progressed, he transferred it to a *raising anvil* and worked probably with a horn *hammer*. Leaving the central portion of this disc plain for the base of his piece, he struck blows in a series of ever-widening circles from the base toward the rim. Plate XL A shows the initial steps, Plate XL B the rough bowl-form soon attained. Unless properly controlled, silver may be stretched and strained unevenly. To ease it along, the silversmith sometimes beat in radial flutes (Plate XL C), and then, using a hammer with differently shaped head, he proceeded to smooth out these broad flutes and gain a more even surface (Plate XL D-E). If he had in mind a pot with bulbous sides, the silver must be brought inward again. Plate XL F shows how the preceding process was again resorted to, in order to contract the piece. These flutes were soon smoothed out (Plate XLI A-B) and the processes repeated (Plate XLI C-D) until a pot with

[236]

bulbous sides and contracted neck had been achieved. As long as the piece had the form of an open bowl, the silversmith could manipulate it upon a T-shaped anvil, but once he began to narrow the piece in toward the neck, he had to use anvils of various shapes, *beak-irons* and *stakes*, which would reach inside it. These tools were generally small and movable and were held in position for use by means of a *vise*. When a piece had thus been brought into shape, its roughly hammered surface was smoothed out by means of a *bottom stake* and *planishing Teaster*.

This series of Gorham photographs makes clear the principles involved in raising, and up to the time of the American Revolution, it was the process employed for the production of practically all hollow-ware. It seems a slow and laborious method, yet when it is carried through by a knowing and adept craftsman, who understands how to keep the metal of uniform thickness, or to reinforce it at the points most subject to wear or strain, and how to produce subtle and satis-fying curves, eminently desirable results can be ob-tained.

In addition to raising, there were a number of other processes to which the early silversmith had to resort. One of them was the making of silver wire and mold-ings. The wire that was used, for example, to form the handles on small things such as wine-tasters, was gen-erally made on a long, low *drawing-bench*, which was provided at one end with a winch, strap, and *draw-tongs* and at the other with cleats to hold in position a draw-plate or swage. This draw-plate was pierced with a series of holes of varying size and outline. The tapered end of a strip of silver was threaded through one of the larger holes and secured by the tongs. It could thus be drawn through the hole and then successively through holes of decreasing diameter until it was brought to wire of any desired gage and of circular, oval, or square section.

Moldings of more complicated outline were made by pulling a strip of silver through the opening between two dies set a given distance apart. By gradually reducing the size of the opening or altering its outline, moldings of various contours could be produced. These were useful in strengthening an object at its lip or base or wherever it might be subjected to special strain. The early American silversmiths designed their moldings with taste and restraint, generally depending upon classic styles for their inspiration.

Many accessory parts, such as handles, lids, etc., were hammered up by methods similar to raising. The hollow handles on tankards were made by soldering together two strips of silver, one flat, the other curved, and both hammered into an S-outline. When joined, these strips formed a handle that was flat on the outer side and comfortably curved to the hand on the inner surface. A hole was left at the lower end of the handle to serve as a vent for the escape of the confined air when the piece was heated for soldering. It was a practical and necessary feature and was not designed to serve as a whistle, as is often stated.

Soldering was in early Colonial days a more difficult process than it is now. *Boreax* was used to keep the surfaces clean and free of oxidization and to serve as a flux for the solder. Instead of having the con-

PLATE XLIII

TEA-POT BY JOHN MOULINAR OF NEW YORK

venience of the modern blow-pipe, which enables the workman to direct a hot flame upon his seam, the Colonial craftsman presumably had to depend upon a charcoal fire and so could not always apply the solder smoothly and thinly. Its lumpy appearance beneath the bases of the early tankards, mugs, and teapots bears evidence to the handicaps under which these silversmiths labored.

Polishing in early Colonial days was accomplished by rubbing the piece with pumice stone and then with a *burnisher*, which instead of actually cutting away any of the surface simply rubbed it smooth. For this reason old silver often retains the faint hammer-marks that show when it is held at the right angle and which lend it so much charm of surface.

Before describing the methods of decoration employed by the Colonial silversmiths, let us digress a moment to consider the processes employed at later periods for the production of hollow-ware. Under the influence of the classical revival in the last quarter of the eighteenth century, the effects sought in silver, as in the architecture and furniture of the same time, were lightness, slenderness, and elegance. Many of the shapes were quite directly based on classic forms, such as the urn-shaped sugar bowls, hot-water urns, columnar candlesticks, etc. Others bore no direct relationship to classic prototypes but nevertheless had a pseudo-classic quality. Thus the oval, straight-sided tea-pots, especially those of fluted sides, may have been derived from a section of a classic column (Plate XLII). While, like Hepplewhite and Sheraton furniture, they appear light and unsubstantial, their construction was

[239]

sound and based on expert craftsmanship. These straight-sided forms in silver were very simple to produce; they were made by cutting a section of sheet silver of the proper size, bending it around into circular or oval form, and soldering the seam. A circular or oval disc was added to serve as a base and another cut and shaped to serve as a top or lid. The spouts were similarly made of a section of sheet silver bent into the proper outline and seamed. Not designed to receive severe wear, they could be made of thin metal.

With the development of more complicated machinery in the nineteenth century, and the shifting of emphasis from quality to quantity production, radically different methods of producing hollow-ware came into general use. The old method of raising was all hand-work and each piece so made required just as much time as its predecessor. To-day, once the patterns are made innumerable pieces can be speedily turned out. The simpler forms are usually produced by forcing a piece of sheet silver into a die under the weight of a heavy drop-press. Others are fashioned by a process known as spinning, which serves admirably for shapes of more or less circular section. The pattern is first made of wood and fixed to a lathe. A sheet of silver is inserted in the lathe, centered with a pattern or "chuck," and then by the use of various tools is gradually forced to conform to the shape of a pattern as both revolve. Pieces so made sometimes show the fine concentric rings made by the spinning tool and the center point at which the silver was secured to the lathe, but these marks can be avoided. Presumably

PLATE XLIV   *See page 79*

KETTLE BY JACOB HURD WITH THE LOWELL ARMS

the early silversmiths sometimes employed a lathe as a means of truing up their shapes but not as a method of actually producing them.

The modern methods of producing silver under a drop-press or by spinning result in mechanical precision and perfect uniformity of shape and of surface. This effect is completed by the modern method of polishing—buffing—which, by the use of rouge and emery, actually cuts away the silver until every possible tool-mark is removed. By the old methods of raising and burnishing, the silver gained character and a subtle charm by virtue of the slight degree of variation in its form and surface. By contrast, modern silver is mechanically perfect, brilliantly polished, and has a hard impersonal appearance.

Returning to the old silversmith, whom we left at his work-bench making hollow-ware, let us see what he did by way of decorating his silver. While most of his work was relatively plain, he did employ some ornamentation, and the methods by which this was accomplished were various and interesting. One of the simplest means of securing a variety of surface with resultant play of light was fluting or gadrooning. This was generally accomplished by filling the piece with pitch, and with a blunt-edged tool beating in the lines between the flutes and then, after the pitch had been removed, by the use of such tools as *snarling-irons*, bossing out the flutes from the interior of the piece. A snarling-iron is a metal bar that is turned down at one end and secured by a vise, and turned upward at the other end and finished with a boss. When an object, because of its shape, cannot be hammered out from the inside by ordinary tools, a snarling-iron is inserted and blows struck on the iron near the vise will be carried along its length and serve to boss out the silver held against its other extremity.

Borders of fluting and gadrooning were a popular mode of decorating silver in England in the late seventeenth and the early eighteenth century and also enjoyed a very considerable vogue in Massachusetts, presumably at the end of the seventeenth and in the first quarter of the eighteenth century. In Massachusetts they were used principally as a means of emphasizing a broad curve and the flutes themselves were bold and round. At first they were usually vertical; later they were spirally whorled. They were used to form a surbase around the bowls of standing-cups, two-handled cups, beakers, etc. Dummer used them admirably (Frontispiece and Plate VI); so did Winslow in the chocolate-pot shown in Plate XIII and the two-handled cup in Plate XXXVIII. Coney, like Dummer, sometimes used them to emphasize the rise of a tankard lid. Of the spiral fluting, Cowell made particular use in two-handled cups such as that shown in Plate XI.

Flutings of a different sort appear in the later years of the eighteenth century as a simple but highly effective mode of enriching the straight-sided tea-pots made of sheet silver, and the urn-shaped sugar-bowls, creamers, and similar pieces (Plates XXXVI, XLII). Instead of emphasizing a curve, as did those used about 1700, these flutes were vertical and straight, and emphasized the upright lines of the piece. Instead of being full and round, like the earlier type, they were usually shallow and wide, producing a superficial and brilliant effect rather than a rich one like that of the earlier type.

In addition to such a simple and regular mode of embossing as fluting, there were more elaborate and freer types of embossing. Embossing or repoussé work consists of forcing out, by repeated blows upon the interior of an object, certain portions of its surface, which thus stand out in relief upon the exterior and form the desired pattern. It was a popular mode of decoration with the Dutch silversmiths of the seventeenth century, whose work found reflection in English silver of the Restoration period, in Massachusetts silver based on these English styles, and also in early New York silver that directly copies Dutch models. Its best expression in Massachusetts silver is in the freely rendered, naturalistic flower, foliage, and animal designs used in caudle-cups (Plates IV and LII) of the late seventeenth and the early eighteenth century. An interesting embossed design is the border of acanthus and palm leaves in the beaker shown in Plate L. Dummer, Coney, Winslow, and others made excellent use of this mode of decoration.

Embossing of this free order passed out of fashion with the plain styles inaugurated under Queen Anne, but returned again to favor in the rococo era. From about 1725 to 1775 in America considerable use was made of this sort of enrichment, the designs employed naturally following the current trend and including such typically rococo features as scrolls, foliation, flowers, masks, etc.

The effects obtained by embossing almost always

had to be sharpened by flat-chasing. As explained before, this latter mode of surface decoration was accomplished by working upon the outer surface of a piece with a blunt-edged tool that did not, as in engraving, cut away the silver but merely depressed it along the lines of the pattern. Not only was it used to supplement embossing, but it frequently served as the chief mode of decoration. Sometimes the lines of the pattern thus sunk were relatively deep and wide, as in the lines outlining the panels in some of the early New York bowls (Plate XXI). Flat-chasing proved a simple, popular type of decoration in English plate in the seventeenth century and finds its reflection in early Massachusetts silver, as demonstrated by the caudle-cup by Sanderson and Hull (Plate IV A). Finding little use in the time of Queen Anne, it too, like embossing, with which it was so generally combined, returned to favor in the rococo period. The teapot by Moulinar (Plate XLIII) is a distinguished instance of its use. Neither embossing nor flat-chasing found a place in the time of the classic revival. The former was too free and bold in effect to suit the formal classic styles of the time; the latter was not sufficiently brilliant.

A simple but telling mode of ornamentation that remained in vogue but a short time was cut-card work, chiefly used in the late seventeenth and the early eighteenth century in New England. As has been stated, these patterns were cut out of sheet metal by means of saws or shears and were soldered to the surface of the piece(Plate VII and XIII A). The earlier ornaments were generally left solid; later examples were frequently pierced, a progression that followed English precedent.

The process of casting was employed throughout the whole period of American silver-making. John Burt's *casting-flasks* suggest what was probably the most frequent and satisfactory method employed by the early silversmiths. A wooden model is made in two parts, each of which is embedded in sand in a casting-flask or box. The models are removed and the flasks clamped together, leaving a hollow impression of the whole model in the center. This hollow is then filled with molten metal poured through an inlet that has been provided. For more intricate designs the early silversmiths may well have used the *cire perdue* or lost-wax process. This consists of modeling in wax the object to be cast. The wax model is then embedded in clay or sand and baked. The wax melts and runs off through an outlet, and the cavity in the baked sand or clay is then filled up with molten metal. This method has the disadvantage of destroying the model, while in the preceding method the models can be used again and again.

Among the more elaborate of the early cast ornaments are the scroll handles with caryatid heads to serve as thumb-rests that are so frequently fitted to the embossed caudle-cups (Plate IV and LII) and bowls (Plate XXI) of the seventeenth and the early eighteenth century. Some of the more intricate and finely modeled designs are seen in the lion feet of the Coney inkstand (Plate L), in the eagle (Figure 4) and sun-and-dolphin (Figure 2) thumb-pieces on New England tankards, and in the masks used to decorate

[245]

the ends of tankard handles (Figures 1, 5, 16). These distinctive designs, some of them peculiar to American silver, some peculiar to that of a single locality, present one of the most interesting problems in American plate. So far as noted, no single design of which a number of instances have been found, is confined to the work of one silversmith. Thus the sun-and-dolphin thumb-piece occurs on tankards made by Winslow, Hurst, Millner, Vernon, and others. The grotesque mask that frequently appears as a handle ornament on tankards by Samuel Casey is strikingly like that on tankards by Homes, Minott, and Revere. The intricate design (Figure 10) used to ornament the ends of New York tankard handles is found on pieces bearing the marks of a silversmith whose initials are P. V. B., of Henricus Boelen, of Peter Van Dyck, and of Benjamin Wynkoop. The condition of the individual castings varies considerably, yet it would seem that, at least in many instances, they might have been taken from the same mold or model. On the other hand, the proportions and general outlines as well as freer types of decoration on these pieces vary considerably. The theory has been advanced by those familiar with the technical aspects of silversmithing that certain workmen, known as "raisers," concerned themselves primarily with the shaping of various pieces, while other silversmiths, in addition to such relatively simple work, made a specialty of executing cast ornaments, which they supplied, as it were, to the trade. In some cases, silversmiths may have borrowed the mold from its owner. If this theory is true, it affords a very early instance of specialization. It is even suggested that some of the molds were imported from abroad. This latter suggestion does not have so much support, however, as some of the designs seem to have been peculiar to American silver, and as a number of early silversmiths proved themselves so proficient in other tasks that they may well have accomplished this part of the work also.

In addition to these most interesting and elaborate cast ornaments, the Colonial craftsman used the casting-process frequently in the making of spouts, handles, finials. Sometimes the impression of the sand-grains will remain here and there and proclaim the method employed.

Engraving has always been one of the most important methods of ornamenting silver and finds its place in early American work. Its employment for the blazoning of coats of arms was so general and so significant that it has been made the subject of a special chapter (pages 261–72). Ornamental ciphers (monograms composed of a group of initials and the same reversed) were another common mode of indicating ownership, and have already received sufficient discussion (page 216). Much engraved work, however, is of a purely ornamental sort and follows the general style of the period in which it was produced. In this form it occurs frequently in the work of the early New York silversmiths (see pages 155–57). It was used to some extent also in the rococo period, especially as ornament around the lids of tea-pots (see detail from Casey tea-pot, Figure 6), and involves the masks, foliate scrolls, flower-festoons, and other devices favored by rococo designers. At the time of the classic

[247]

revival, when silver was made of thin metal and when brilliant and superficial effects were sought, engraving generally took the particular form known as bright-cutting, accomplished by a series of shallow gouges.

FIGURE 18.   Bright Cut Design

Simple border patterns, shields and oval medallions, flower-festoons, bow-knots, wheat-sheaves, and flower-baskets occur repeatedly (Figure 18).

Like casting, engraving seems to have become the special accomplishment of certain silversmiths. Gold-smithing and engraving have always been closely allied arts. It is not surprising to find, therefore, that a number of the most distinguished Colonial silversmiths also won fame for their engraving on metal. John Coney engraved the plates for the first paper money printed in the colonies, that issued by the Massachusetts General Court in 1690. Jeremiah Dummer printed and beyond a doubt also engraved the first paper money of Connecticut. According to the State records, in 1711–12 Governor Saltonstall laid before the Council Board "the account of Mr. Jeremiah Dummer of Boston, with this Colony, for the whole charge of printing 6550 sheets of bills of credit, to the value of ten thousand pounds." Charles Le Roux, official silversmith of the City of New York, engraved the plates for bills

James Knowles   To Joseph Richardson Dr.

1791

1st May To 6 Silver Table Spoons wt 11..19 — 2 dwt — £6.13.0

— To engraving Cyphers on ditto - - - - - .. 6

3/st — To a Silver Soup Ladle ..... 6 - - - .. 3.14.0

To engraving a Cypher on ditto - - - - .. 2 —

£10.15 —

By 5.11.10 of Silver a 10/6 . . . . . . 2.7.6   2 dwt gr

£ 8.7.6

Recw'd The above ballance in full

Joseph Richardson

PLATE XLV

of credit issued at various times between 1715 and
1737. John Waite of South Kingstown, Rhode Island,
executed the "new escutcheons and other such devices
as may be necessary for printing" the Rhode Island
bills of credit issued in 1776. Nathaniel Hurd, son of a
notable silversmith, Jacob Hurd, followed his father's
trade with success, as proved by the charming tea-pot
made by him (Plate XIV), but became far more re-
nowned for his engraving on copper. Many of the best-
known American book-plates are the work of his hand.
Others bear the name of Paul Revere, who was extremely able, both as silversmith and as engraver on
copper. The list of those who followed both pursuits
might be continued by the mention of numerous other
names.

There is every reason to suppose that such proficient engravers as Coney, Dummer, Hurd, and Revere proved themselves to be, engraved whatever ornament occurs on their silver. This is, in numerous instances, actually proved by bills rendered their customers. It is quite possible that their reputation for
such work was generally known and that they were
often commissioned to execute engraved ornament, including coats of arms, upon silver wrought by craftsmen who were not endowed with skill in this particular art. As the demand for silver plate increased in
the colonies, there presumably developed an increasing
amount of specialization, and hence it came about that
certain men advertised as engravers and doubtless often
worked in conjunction with practical silversmiths. In
1748 there occurs an interesting advertisement in the
"Pennsylvania Gazette": "Engraving on Gold, Silver,

[249]

or Pewter, done by Lawrence Herbert, from London, at Philip Syng's, Goldsmith, in Front-street." Peter Maverick, a well-known New York engraver, added the inscriptions and arms of the City of New York on numerous "freedom boxes" fashioned by Samuel Johnson. A gold box stamped by Johnson is thus engraved and signed by Maverick, as illustrated in Plate LXII. "Michael Cario, Goldsmith, From London, performs all sorts of Engraving Work either in Gold or Silver," according to his advertisement in 1736 in the "American Weekly Mercury" of Philadelphia. Five years later, in the "South Carolina Gazette," "Francis Garden, Engraver, from London," advertises that he "engraves in the best Manner, and after the newest fashion, in Gold, Silver, or any kind of Metal, Coats of Arms, etc." John Paul Grimke, a silversmith of Charleston, South Carolina, announces in 1760, "Having now a journeyman who is an extraordinary fine chaser, those who are inclined to have their old plate beautified, may have it chased in the newest taste at a small expence."[1] Such advertisements become increasingly numerous in the second half of the eighteenth century.

These later engravers continually stress their eagerness to provide their customers with "Coats of Arms, Cyphers, Crests, and all sorts of Devices, cut in the newest Style." The early colonists who had a right to bear arms had themselves come so recently from countries in which heraldry was a living thing that they were in no sort of doubt as to the blazoning of their

[1] Quoted from the Walpole Society, "The Arts and Crafts of Philadelphia, Maryland, and South Carolina, 1721–1785," 1930.

[250]

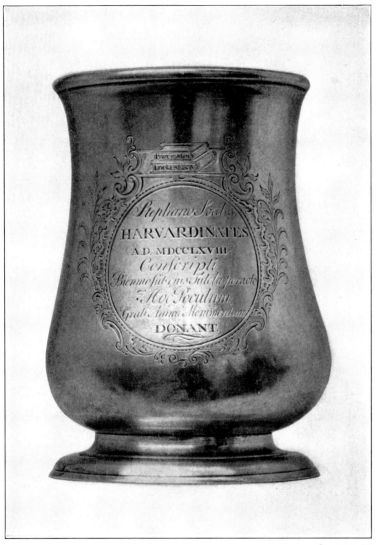

PLATE XLVI

See page 77

MUG BY PAUL REVERE

family coats. But later generations were sometimes ignorant of heraldic matters, and in some cases were anxious to display arms without understanding upon what terms they were granted. The engravers seem to have grasped this situation and striven to turn it to their own advantage. Thus Thomas Reynolds, a goldsmith and stone-cutter of London and Dublin, who had by 1785 established himself in Philadelphia, advertises[1] that, "realizing the difficulty to which gentlemen are liable here, in ascertaining and procuring the Armorial Bearings belonging to their families," he himself has obtained "a most extensive and curious collection of Coats of Arms, and Books of Heraldry; he therefore proposes to supply those who may apply to him from any part of the continent, with their Arms, truly and properly blazoned, at four dollars each. . . . Such arms as the subscriber cannot find in his collection, shall be sent for to Europe, as he has established large connections in the Heraldry line, in different parts." This system may account for difficulties sometimes encountered in identifying coats of arms.

While the engraver who added ornament to plate already fashioned seldom signed his work, the original silversmith practically always stamped his piece when he had completed it. In this, as in the styles he followed, he was keeping in mind European traditions and customs but modifying them according to his need and the conditions of Colonial life. During the Middle Ages the goldsmiths and silversmiths in Europe established powerful organizations or gilds. Reputable craftsmen for their own protection against unscrupu-

[1] See note on page 250.

lous workmen, purchasers who might be deceived by metal that was of inferior quality, and governments interested in the proper regulation of their national arts and industries, all gave their support to these craft gilds. In the course of time all the more important cities had their own gildhalls, to which all goldsmiths and silversmiths were required to bring their work so that it might be assayed and stamped with certain "hall-marks" guaranteeing its quality and lawful manufacture. In their simplest form, such hall-marks usually consisted of a town mark, which indicated that the metal was up to the standard required by the gild in that town, and a maker's mark. In cities such as London and Paris, where great quantities of plate were made, more careful supervision was necessary and more elaborate systems of hall-marking developed.

In numerous instances, as we have already said, silversmiths had practised their trade abroad, especially in London, before they emigrated to America. They were thus thoroughly familiar with the English requirements governing the making of plate and its marking. However, in early Colonial days communities were small and the few silversmiths at work were so well known to their patrons and fellow-townsmen that their personal reputations stood in lieu of gild guarantee. They therefore carried over from European custom only the maker's personal stamp on silver. Like contemporary English and Dutch marks, these Colonial maker's marks usually consisted of the silversmith's initials, enclosed within a circle, trefoil, heart, shield, or similar reserve, and frequently accompanied by a personal device. The latter was sometimes in punning allusion to the owner's name, doubtless borrowed from canting heraldry; thus John Coney used a coney in combination with his I C. Sometimes the device appears to have been arbitrarily chosen; Andrew Tyler used a cat with his initials. Silversmiths of Dutch descent working in New York rarely used any such device but sometimes conjoined their initials; Koenraet and Jacob Ten Eyck made a monogram of the T.E. Often, too, their Dutch names, like Peter Van Dyck, led them to use three initials instead of only two. New England silversmiths, copying English customs, sometimes enclosed their initials in a shield surmounted by a crown; in such case the crown had no real significance, although it may have been adopted to imply that the silversmith had been favored with royal custom. Coney's mark is an illustration.

Three characteristic New England marks of the early eighteenth century are represented in the illustration, Nos. 1–3 (John Coney, 1655–1722; Edward Winslow, 1669–1753; Samuel Vernon, 1683–1737), and a series of early New York marks in Nos. 4–7 (Jacob Boelen, about 1654–1729; Peter Van Dyck, 1684–1750; Koenraet Ten Eyck, 1678–1753; and Benjamin Wynkoop, freeman 1698). Following English precedent, the silversmith's initials came in time to be more generally enclosed in a simple rectangle, instead of in the more elaborate reserves of the early eighteenth century. Thus the work of Philip Syng, Jr. (1703–89), of Philadelphia, appears in a rectangle, accompanied by an impressed leaf (No. 8), and the mark of the brothers Joseph and Nathaniel Richardson, who worked in the second half of the eighteenth

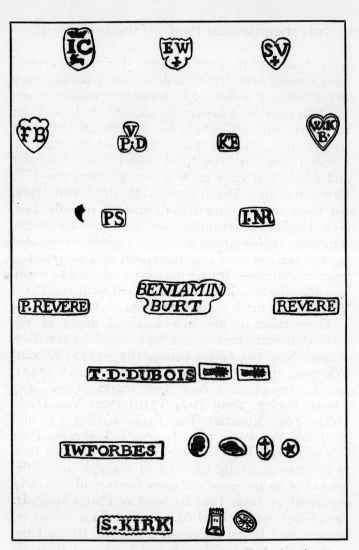

FIGURE 19. Characteristic Marks used by Early American
Silversmiths

See pages 67, 69, 267

PLATE XLVII

TAZZA BY ALLEN AND EDWARDS, STANDING-CUPS AND BEAKER BY JOHN EDWARDS,
CUP BY THOMAS EDWARDS

century in Philadelphia, also appears in a rectangle (No. 9).

In the course of time the centers of silver-making increased in size and a silversmith's initials ceased to be an immediate means of identification. Beyond a doubt, in early New York when stolen plate was advertised as marked with the initials I B, almost any person knew that it must be the work of Jacob Boelen. As communities grew in size and silversmiths increased in numbers, this would no longer be possible. In many cases two silversmiths might have the same initials and so to ensure identification of their work, they began to use either the surname, the surname and first initial, or the two names in full. Nos. 10–12 show how Paul Revere and Benjamin Burt marked their plate. Silversmiths who used this fuller form often found it too large a mark to apply to smaller pieces of work such as spoons, and for the latter they employed a small stamp consisting of their initials. Thus a large object, such as a tankard, will sometimes bear on the body the silversmith's name in full, but the cover, which was relatively small and fashioned separately, will bear the initials only.

Still later, as the situation became increasingly complicated, silversmiths sometimes further distinguished their work by adding the name of the place of manufacture. This seems to have been most frequently done in New York. Toward the end of the eighteenth and in the early nineteenth century, some silversmiths, especially those of New York (No. 14), added as marks on their handiwork other symbols suggestively like English hall-marks, quite possibly with the intention of making it appear to be English. In this they also had foreign precedent, for English silversmiths had frequent occasion to complain against the makers of Sheffield plate who imitated silver hall-marks in order that their work might be mistaken for the finer metal.

The first State law governing the hall-marking of American silver was that passed by Maryland in 1814, which required Baltimore silver to be 917 parts fine or 11 oz. fine silver in every pound Troy, and to be assayed by the assay officer and stamped by him as well as by the maker. For some years thereafter Baltimore silver usually bore the marks of the town (the arms of Baltimore), of the assayer, and of the maker, and a date-letter (No. 15). In 1830 the Maryland law was modified.

The identification of makers' marks on early American plate is not so simple as it may at first appear. The mere fact that the two initials in a given mark coincide with the initials of a known silversmith is in itself no guarantee that the mark is actually his. It may quite as well be that of some other silversmith with similar initials, working in some other place and at another period. One must secure definite proof. Finding a piece with both the mark that consists simply of the initials and a second mark consisting of the full name, establishes the identity of the maker. Bills that describe silver in detail, mentioning such things as "cyphers," coats of arms, or giving the weight of the plate, if they tally with actual pieces still in the possession of the family sometimes afford conclusive evidence of the identity of the maker. There are vari-

See page 152

PLATE XLVIII

BOWL BY JOHN HEATH OF NEW YORK

Engraved with the V a C oli h A

ous other means of securing proof, most of which involve considerable research and sound judgment. It is often extremely difficult to distinguish between the work of father and son where the two bore the same name, as in the case of the two Philip Syngs or the two Reveres. An added confusion arises in the nineteenth century, when, though the name may be given in full, there is the possibility that it represents not the name of the actual silversmith but that of a retailer. Gregg, Hayden & Co. of Charleston, South Carolina, offers an instance of such a distributing firm. For this practice there was English precedent.

A considerable amount of provincial English, of Irish, and of Scandinavian silver is marked only with the maker's stamp, and is sufficiently similar in design to American silver to give rise to confusion. Undoubtedly quite a bit of such foreign plate now masquerades quite innocently as Colonial silver. Unfortunately all such masquerading is not innocent. The high prices commanded by early American work have roused the cupidity of certain persons, who by cleverly removing the marks that would distinguish it as European, pass off on unwary and ill-advised collectors pieces of English or Continental plate that these unscrupulous dealers cheerfully affirm to be the work of some well-known Colonial silversmith. To risk the purchase of American silver, under the conditions of its present market, one should be very knowing and very cautious.

People are sometimes puzzled by the expression "coin silver." Most Colonial silver was presumably made out of coins, many of them Spanish dollars, which are so often mentioned in contemporary records.

For a very long period in Philadelphia quit-rents were payable in so many Spanish milled dollars, a fact that indicates the prevalence of this type of currency. But as already explained, the coinage standards of different European countries vary widely, so that "coin silver" is an expression that requires some definite interpretation. Some New York silversmiths of the late eighteenth and the early nineteenth century marked their work with the letters D or C, presumably for "Dollar" or "Coin." In the early nineteenth century the word "Coin" was sometimes stamped on plate. With the establishment of the United States Mint in 1792, the coinage standard had been fixed at .8924 fine, but in 1837 this was raised to 900 parts fine. As the word "Coin" as a mark on plate was open to some question, certain States passed laws requiring that plate so marked must be 900 parts fine. Similarly it was required that "Sterling" should indicate silver of 925 parts fine, the English standard. "Sterling" as a mark of quality appears on American plate from about 1865 on. The facts that such strict supervision was not necessary until a very recent date and that counterfeiting rather rarely appears as an offence among early American silversmiths bear eloquent testimony to the integrity and wisdom of these craftsmen.

In conclusion, it is not unprofitable to contrast the old and the modern system of work. The Colonial silversmith worked usually for his individual customer, and made each piece more or less unique, knowing that the demand of his purchaser was for quality and distinction, rather than for quantity. With the assistance of his apprentices, he did much of the work, from creating the design to raising, polishing, decorating, and stamping with his own mark the completed piece. He therefore became proficient in a wide variety of tasks, which exerted upon him a sort of interlocking control. He may have had his preferences, getting special joy in making fluted borders or adding engraving or free embossing. But these preferences rarely got out of hand. One aspect of the work acted as a curb upon another and the silversmith, seeking approbation for his completed pieces, made them all unite to secure that end. His methods seem laborious, yet they gave him an intimate knowledge and a command of his material that highly developed machinery rarely admits. Above all, his goal was quality, not quantity; distinction, not uniformity; excellence, not speed.

For more than a century, the metamorphosis of the artist-craftsman into artisan and factory-worker has been going forward. Where the Colonial merchant of 1690, let us say, had a few tankards and caudle-cups of silver that make us frankly envious, he sat down to a table where forks were rare, where the diners ate usually with knives and spoons, probably using pewter trenchers, and served themselves from a common dish in the center of the table. To-day we enjoy the convenience of individual knives, forks, and spoons of a wide variety of forms and even the poorer households can have plated silver. This convenience and accessibility we owe to large-scale factory production, and its advantages inevitably have their attendant disadvantages. The customer practically never deals directly with the producer. The cheapness of the individual pieces depends upon their being produced and sold in great quantity. This involves mechanical ingenuity that will make possible the rapid turn-out of great quantities of a model, and since it cannot be made the concern of a highly skilled and intelligent craftsman, it must have the merit of mechanical precision and uniformity. The more perfect the machine, the less is left to the human equation, the better satisfied we are. Now the artisan, in order to do his work with the utmost precision and despatch, is trained to do one small part of the total work of production, to do that one small task over and over again, monotonously but competently. Stop beside a workman in a factory. Show interest in his work. If he grows talkative, will he discuss the subtle relationship between the lines of the piece and the ornament upon it, or will he confine himself to discussing the merits of the engraved design he is cutting upon a dozen pieces, all alike, ranged in front of him? Even the designer, who more than any one else should be equipped to understand all the many aspects of the work and to correlate them into a cohesive whole, is often not trained as a practical craftsman before he begins to make designs for a material the possibilities, limitations, and subtle qualities of which he cannot comprehend. It is probably primarily in the designer that the weakness of our present system lies. If we ourselves had a truer appreciation of what constitutes excellence in silverwork, we would insist upon having the designers of our silver combine creative power with sound practical craft experience.

CHAPTER X

ENGRAVED COATS OF ARMS AS DECORATION ON SILVER

ONE of the less obtrusive but one of the most fascinating details of ornament on American silver is the engraved coat of arms. The fine lines of the engraving do not carry far and do not arrest the eye as do highly embossed patterns, but when a piece can be handled and examined carefully, the charm of this more minute work can be fully appreciated and its technical merits recognized. The embellishment of coats of arms varies in style much as do other engraved designs from period to period, and one might properly discuss the heraldic with other fashions of any given time. These heraldic decorations are, however, so much a group by themselves, are so elaborate in conception, and constitute such an important addition to the information to be gained from any piece, that they seem to deserve a chapter to themselves.

Arms were primarily planned to indicate ownership, and any one versed in heraldic matters can often learn the name of the family and sometimes even of the individual to whom the piece belonged. This search is not to be lightly entered upon, for heraldry is an intricate science, and the more one studies it, the more one treats it with respect and deference. The uninitiated

Early American Silver

may overlook a slight difference in the devices or in the tinctures and assign the arms to quite a wrong family. The identification of arms is complicated by the fact that the engravers themselves were sometimes ignorant of or careless about the finer points of heraldry, and while they drew the achievements gracefully, they did not always render them accurately. Our present concern is not, however, with the coat of arms considered from a heraldic point of view, but purely as decoration.

Though probably in the majority of instances the arms were engraved on a piece at the time it was produced, they were often, just as were initials and inscriptions, added at a later date, sometimes upon the occasion of the presentation of the piece, for example to a church. One cannot maintain that a given style ceased to be used at a specified date and that thereafter some other fashion obtained. Nevertheless, a sequence of styles in heraldic blazoning can be traced and some estimate made as to the general period at which any one style was dominant.

The arms engraved on English plate, which customarily bears a date-letter, or on English heraldic book-plates, many of which can be dated and concerning which there is a considerable literature, furnish an excellent starting-point for our study of the arms on American silver. John Buck, the pioneer writer on American silver, was sufficiently interested in the subject of heraldic decoration to devote a chapter to engraved arms in his book on "Old Plate." E. Alfred Jones has reproduced in line more than fifty of these heraldic achievements found on Colonial examples, de-

[262]

scribed in his volume on "Old Silver of American Churches."

Early New York, as pointed out in the preceding chapters, offers the one outstanding exception to the general rule that in the matters of form and decoration Colonial silver was inspired by contemporary English styles. So in the matter of heraldic ornament, early New York is again the one interesting exception. Since in designing coats of arms, New York engravers harked back to an older and more consistently maintained tradition than did those other Colonial engravers who drew their inspiration from English sources, it seems wise to discuss the New York types first. Before doing so, however, one should consider the Continental customs upon which the latter were based.

Artistic conventions in heraldry were developed with more precision and elaboration and were far more persistently followed in Germany, Friesland, and the Netherlands than they were in Great Britain. It would appear that the preëminent German designers and engravers, such as Dürer and Hans Sebald Beham, in the sixteenth century established certain arrangements of the shield, supporters, helm, crest, and mantling, which for centuries thereafter remained the recognized convention. Though this precedent was established, the individual engraver was so impressed with the decorative possibilities of these heraldic achievements that although he kept to the general scheme he worked with enthusiasm and ingenuity. His designs seem spontaneous and never pedantic.

Because these German and Dutch conventions were so definite, it is not surprising to find that the earliest

[263]

New York silversmiths and engravers, the majority of whom were of Dutch descent, kept rather consistently to the same rules. The most popular early New York style, as illustrated in the accompanying drawing,

FIGURE 20. Wendell Arms on Van Dyck Tankard

is a direct reflection of Continental types. Essentially it consists of a shield of this simple outline, surmounted by a helmet that rests upon its upper margin. The helmet in turn supports a torse and crest and from it depends a mantling of acanthus scrolls. Often swags of fruit, especially pomegranates, depend from the lower edge of the shield, as in this drawing. Occasionally instead of these swags there are cornucopias, as in the Philipse arms engraved upon the Boelen tea-pot shown in Plate XXVI.

The arms in the accompanying drawing are those of

See pages 81, 82, 272

PLATE XLIX

REVERE TRAY GIVEN TO LUCRETIA CHANDLER IN 1761

MINOTT ALMS BASIN WITH THE HANCOCK ARMS

Given by Thomas Hancock to the Brattle Street Church

the Wendell family, taken from a tankard made by
Peter Van Dyck (1684–1750) of New York. The
piece is in the collection of Francis P. Garvan. The
same style of engraved arms occurs in a Van der Spiegel
tankard (Plate LIV) and in a pair of salts probably
by Bartholomew Le Roux (Plate LX), which are de
Peyster family pieces and bear the family arms: azure
on a champagne, a tree between two sheep grazing ar-
gent. Handsomely engraved coats with similar acanthus-scroll mantling appear on silver made by Jacob
Boelen, Ten Eyck, Wynkoop, Onclebagh, P. V. B.,
and other prominent New York makers. These heraldic
achievements bear a strong family resemblance but
differ sufficiently in minor details and especially in the
technique of their execution to imply that they represent the work of several different hands.

In other instances there appears even more marked
variation in the manner in which the acanthus-scroll
mantling is rendered, as, for example, in the accompanying drawing, in which the scrolls, though retaining
the full swinging curves characteristic of New York
mantlings, differ from the preceding drawing in being
quite different in form and shaded by cross-hatching.
These arms, which occur on a charming tankard made
by Bartholomew Schaats (1670–1758), now in the
collection of Mrs. Frederic Grosvenor Goodridge, have
not thus far been identified (Figure 21).

Below the shield is drawn a cipher (monogram composed of a series of letters and the same reversed). The
charges, a harp resting on a champagne and a wyvern
or other fabulous beast are, like the ship in the Wendell arms drawn above, characterized by a spontaneity

[265]

and a pictorial quality that are much more akin to
German and Dutch heraldry than they are to the
English. A tankard by Wynkoop and a mug by Jacob
Ten Eyck, both belonging to the Metropolitan Mus-

FIGURE 21. Arms on Schaats Tankard

eum, are engraved with arms in which the charge is a
figure of Hope with anchor and dove, singularly like
the symbolic figures of Hope found on Dutch and New
York communion beakers. It is possible that these arms
belong to the Van der Hoop family.

As a group, these early New York heraldic achievements are very handsome. Though eventually supplanted by other styles, which were the result of increasing English influence in the colony, the early Continental conventions were sufficiently strong to continue well into the eighteenth century. Their acanthus
mantlings are rendered with great boldness and verve,

with a charming sense of proportion, and with great beauty of line and detail.

With the exception of these early New York coats, practically all the arms engraved on Colonial silver

FIGURE 22. Cotton Arms on Tazza Made by Allen and Edwards

directly follow English precedent. The earliest style thus to find reflection is that with a mantling of feathery plumes or scrolls, which occurs frequently on English plate of the second half of the seventeenth century. The probabilities are that this style was chiefly or only used in New England and that it passed out of fashion too early to be adopted elsewhere in the colonies. Examples are very rare. The accompanying Figure 22 represents the Cotton arms, which are engraved on the tazza made by Allen and Edwards of Boston, illustrated in the center of Plate XLVII. These

[267]

arms show the typical shield of simple outline flanked by feather-like plumes, but they lack a helmet to support the crest.

Another instance of the use of this style of feather mantling occurs on a baptismal basin made by John Coney (1655–1722) of Boston, which was bequeathed to the Old South Church by Mrs. Mary Saltonstall, widow of William Clarke, who died in 1710. The arms are those of the Clarke family. In this instance, the narrow border of the baptismal basin has necessitated the sidewise expansion of the shield and mantling and the separation from it of the crest. The latter is enclosed by similar feather scrolls and placed at the opposite side of the basin's border.

In England, as feather mantling was passing out of favor, there was introduced another style, that with acanthus scrolls, presumably derived from the same German or Dutch types from which the early New York coats were drawn. The New England silversmiths adopted this fashion, but their rendering is naturally, like that of the English, more restrained and less opulent than that characteristic of New York. Characteristic examples occur on silver made by John Coney, Jeremiah Dummer (see frontispiece), Edward Winslow, and numerous other Boston men.

This style of scrolled acanthus mantling evidently had a more considerable vogue in New England than it did in Great Britain and appears to have been in favor from the late seventeenth century through the first quarter of the eighteenth. Meantime, however, another style had come into use in England and had also been adopted in the colonies. The drawing of the

Livingston arms from the Coney punch-bowl (Plate XII), shows the decorative framework of heavy scrolls and foliation that surrounds the oval in which the arms are represented. During the first quarter of the eighteenth century many coats were enclosed in such

FIGURE 23.   Livingston Arms on Coney Punch-bowl

scrolled cartouches, which do not spring from heraldic usage at all but are inspired by contemporary ornament.   As in this instance, the helmet, wreath, crest, and mantling are often omitted. At this period the arrangement is always symmetrical.

More or less coincident with this type and akin to it are other heraldic decorations, of which the Quincy arms taken from a paten made by John Blowers (1710–48) of Boston, in the collection of F. P. Garvan, afford a typical example. The characteristic features of this type are a shield of scrolled, symmetrical outline set within but distinct from a heavy scrolled

[269]

and foliated framework. The intermediate space is generally relieved by imbrication or brickwork. The midpoint below the shield is sometimes decorated with a mask or shell, and the mid-point above either with a

FIGURE 24. Quincy Arms on Paten by Blowers

shell or with a helmet and the appropriate crest. Often such additional embellishment as the vase set at either side of the Quincy arms is incorporated in the ornamental framework. This style in book-plate engraving is generally termed "Jacobean." In American silver it enjoyed a wide vogue, especially from about 1730 to 1760, and was seldom seen to better advantage than on silver wrought by Jacob Hurd (1702–58). The kettle made by this silversmith and illustrated in Plate XLIV bears the Lowell arms enclosed in an ornamental framework of the type under discussion. Another instance appears in the arms on the tea-pot made by Samuel Casey of Rhode Island, shown in Plate XVIII.

[270]

Engraved Coats of Arms on Silver

In the course of time, with the full development of rococo fashions, the symmetrical arrangement gave way to one that was distinctly asymmetrical, a style that was especially favored in the third quarter of the

FIGURE 25. Provoost Arms on Fueter Tray

eighteenth century in America. The accompanying drawing of the Provoost arms on a tray by Daniel Christian Fueter of New York, the property of the Metropolitan Museum, well illustrates the style. The shield has a most irregular outline formed by scrolls and is surrounded by foliation, flower-sprays, shell-work and other typical rococo elements; the helmet and mantling are now exceptional. In book-plates this type of heraldic engraving is termed "Chippendale." In America it was extensively used in the book-plates designed by Paul Revere, Henry Dawkins, and Nathaniel Hurd, the son of the distinguished silversmith Jacob Hurd. Nathaniel was an engraver by profession but

[271]

also incidentally a silversmith, as several pieces bearing his mark attest. A tea-pot wrought by him, illustrated in Plate XIV A, shows the arms of the Gibbs family engraved in this style. The Revere tray shown in Plate XLIX bears the Chandler arms displayed on one of these scroll-shaped shields, with exuberant rococo enframement.

In marked contrast to the lack of symmetry and to the profusion of ornament and almost tumultuous fancy that these heraldic designs exhibit, are the delicacy, formality, and severe restraint characteristic of those which follow, under the classic influences of the late eighteenth century. The arrangement is balanced. The shield, which is usually spade-shaped, sometimes depends from a medallion and sometimes hangs poised in mid-air. The helmet is lacking, and the crest, when it occurs, is usually set upon the torse above and apart from the shield. Festoons of flowers or ribbons often hang above and at the sides of the shield. In many instances, instead of bearing a coat of arms, silver is engraved with a shield-shaped or oval reserve enclosing a script monogram, such as that illustrated by the drawing on page 248. The engraving at this period is almost invariably of the shallow, brilliant sort known as bright-cutting.

See pages 50, 281, 317, 314

PLATE L

INKSTAND BY CONEY, BEAKER BY S. D., SPOUT CUP BY JOHN EDWARDS,
AND MUG BY KOENRAET, TEN EYCK

CHAPTER XI

THE EVOLUTION OF THE PRINCIPAL FORMS IN EARLY AMERICAN SILVER

A PERSON interested in American silver may approach the subject from either of two points of view, each of which offers certain advantages. One method seeks to discover what shapes and modes of decoration prevailed at any given period, thereby stressing general style; this plan we have followed in detail in our study of Massachusetts silverwork. The other method traces the development of a particular object, such as the beaker, tankard, or tea-pot, from its earliest appearance in American silver through to the shapes in which it occurs at the end of the eighteenth century, the date we have chosen for the close of our study. While it involves some repetition of facts noted in the preceding chapters, it is well worth while to discuss American silver from this second point of view, in order to secure a more thorough knowledge of its characteristic forms and their interrelationships.

Practically all the objects that occur in American silver derive their form from European and especially from English prototypes. We must therefore briefly consider these foreign models in order to comprehend the genesis of American shapes. Many characteristic Colonial forms find illustration in the half-tone plates throughout this book, but as the latter are necessarily limited, all the types could not be so represented. For this reason, a series of outline drawings is appended to this chapter, designed to illustrate the principal forms that occur in American silver up to the beginning of the nineteenth century. An outline drawing is often more telling than a long paragraph of description and a group of such drawings makes vivid the progression and interrelation of many shapes. By the omission of detail, the outline drawing lays a sharper emphasis on form than does the photograph.

As American silver was not marked with a date-letter as was London silver, in many instances the only period that can be assigned to a given piece is the interval in which its maker was actively engaged in silversmithing. The more provincial a community, the longer a style may persist. For these reasons it is difficult to estimate when a given style came into use in the colonies and impossible to determine when it passed out of fashion. Some idea of the period in which it enjoyed its widest use may, however, be secured and this we have attempted to indicate in the accompanying chart. Even though at best it represents an approximation only, it may facilitate our study.

The objects, grouped according to type, such as the beaker, standing cup, etc., are described in the text and illustrated in the chart in the same order. This order is necessarily arbitrary. In general, drinking-vessels are placed first and those which came into use early are given precedence over those which were in vogue at a later date.

I. BEAKERS

Drinking-horns were much used in early times in

Europe and frequently received embellishment in the addition of metal tips and bands. Jackson, in his "History of English Plate," quotes from the will of Thomas, Earl of Ormond, dated 1515, "a lytle whyte HORN of ivory garnished at both thendes with gold." The greater convenience of a cup, made by cutting a section of horn and fitting the smaller end with a horn or metal disc to serve as base, gave rise to cups of this form, which in their turn yielded place to those of the same general shape made entirely of metal. Apparently an old German word, signifying such a wide-mouthed drinking-cup, passed over into English usage, where it became "beaker." In the Middle Ages, such vessels followed prevailing fashions in their general scheme of decoration and were frequently enriched with enamel or jewels. In the course of time, they became simpler and more purely utilitarian in character and certain national types tended to become established.

Domestic beakers in Holland and Germany were of varying size and were frequently ornamented with bands of granulation, with engraving or embossing. For the last method Germany seems to have shown some preference; Holland favored engraving. After the Reformation, the Dutch adopted the tall beakers as their chief type of communion cup and usually engraved them with interlacing bands of strapwork, with foliate scrolls, and often with symbolic figures of Faith, Hope, and Charity. Even though these designs were a convention, they did not become a mere formula, but were rendered with animation and spontaneity. The bases of such beakers were sometimes finished with

[275]

a heavy torus molding, sometimes they were flaring and convex and stamped with ovolo patterns.

A considerable number of Dutch traders and settlers established themselves in certain communities along the northeastern coast of Scotland and England, especially at Aberdeen and Norwich. They imported some of these typical Dutch beakers and also fashioned others, which, though they bore English hall-marks, were nevertheless distinctly in the Dutch style. The great majority of these Aberdeen and Norwich made beakers are tall, often six or seven inches in height, and have engraved strapwork and foliate scroll decoration and convex bases with stamped ovolo ornament. Most of those still in existence served as communion cups and date from the late sixteenth through the seventeenth century. Beakers of this Dutch style rarely bear British hall-marks other than those of Aberdeen, Norwich, and very occasionally London.

It seems safe to assume that beakers were a less popular type of cup in England than they were in Holland, even though we take into consideration the fact that in England they were more consistently used for domestic purposes and consequently a relatively larger number would in the course of time have disappeared. English beakers of the Charles II period were chiefly low and rather wide, with or without a molded foot. The majority were undecorated but some show the treatments popular at the time—engraving, embossing, and (later) bands of fluting. Eighteenth-century English beakers were usually plain with molded bases but are not common, as the beaker was outranked in popular favor by the more capacious tankard.

Evolution of Forms in American Silver

Beakers were attractive little cups and undoubtedly many of them came to America as simple but cherished personal possessions. Those which survived are chiefly those which chanced to be presented to Colonial churches. Among them, E. Alfred Jones found two of German origin, three of English, and seven of Dutch, the last named especially significant to us because of their evident influence upon Colonial silver. These imported Dutch beakers are listed on page 130, and discussed in connection with their relationship to early New York pieces. Of the seven, two belong to Boston churches, the other five to churches in or near New York. Plate XXII represents an unusually handsome example.

In discussing Colonial beakers, one must first of all distinguish between those made in New York after Dutch styles and those made elsewhere in the colonies, and especially in New England, almost invariably after English models. The early New York beakers form a definite group of which the distinguishing characteristics have already been described in detail (page 131). Usually they measure $6\frac{1}{2}''$ or $7\frac{1}{4}''$ in height, are engraved with strapwork, foliate scrolls, and sometimes also with symbolic figures in medallions, and have a stout torus molding at the base with a band of stamped ornament or an applied cut-out border of foliate pattern above (Plate XXIII). This style probably persisted from the second half of the seventeenth century (Chart: No. 13) through at least the first quarter of the eighteenth (Chart: No. 14). Later, New York beakers were often left undecorated (Chart:

No. 15) but they tended to keep their general height, even when made in more or less bell shape (Chart: No. 16).

Although two Boston churches were presented with typical Dutch beakers, this type does not seem to have directly influenced Boston silverwork. On the other hand, two beakers (Chart: No. 2), one made by John Hull (height 6⅜″) and presented to the Newman Congregational Church of East Providence, Rhode Island, and the other made by Hull and Sanderson (height 6″) and given to the First Congregational Church of Marblehead, Massachusetts, show Dutch influence, presumably derived not directly from Holland but by way of such English renderings as the Norwich beakers already described. The Hull and Sanderson cup has rather stiff foliate scrolls and strapwork and a convex base stamped with tongue or ovolo ornament. The Hull beaker is similar in the general character of its engraving but has a simply molded band at its base. The engraved scroll and strapwork designs on these two Boston beakers seem more stereotyped and less spontaneous than do similar designs on those made in New York.

Quite different are the characteristic Boston beakers, which follow more purely English styles. The earliest are relatively low and wide (averaging perhaps 3⅞″ in height and 3⅝″ in diameter at the lip) and have no reinforcement at the base. Some of the earlier examples are decorated with a band of granulation similar to that found on the English standing cup made in 1639 and later presented to the First Church, Boston (Plate I, left) and probably more remotely

ABOUT 1770-1810

ABOUT 1730-1775

ABOUT 1700-1735

ABOUT 1650-1710

BEAKERS
NEW ENGLAND

NEW YORK

derived from German and Scandinavian plate. Of these early Boston beakers decorated with granulated bands (Chart: No. 1), five examples remain: one by Hull belonging to the First Church, Boston; one by Hull and Sanderson belonging to the same church (Plate II); two others by the same silversmiths belonging to the First Church, Dorchester; and one by Dummer belonging to the First Congregational Society, Salem. Other beakers of the same general proportions are left undecorated; Hull and Sanderson, Coney, Winslow (Plate II, right), John Edwards, and Moody Russell made some of this plain sort.

Similar beakers equipped with a reinforcing molding at the base (Chart: No. 3) possibly represent a slightly later style, even though some actual examples of both types may have been made contemporaneously. These were usually plain, but an unusual example made by David Jesse (1670–1705), the property of the First Church of Dorchester, has an engraved border of strapwork, reminiscent of Dutch and Norwich-made beakers.

These typical seventeenth-century straight-sided beakers with a reinforcing base molding gradually developed into the typical eighteenth-century beakers, which are characterized by straight sides, usually flaring at the lip, and a molded base. In general proportions, they are more slender than were the earliest Boston beakers, but the eighteenth-century examples, among themselves, vary greatly in height. They are ordinarily plain, except for a line or two of inscription, which often chronicles their presentation to some church. This type of beaker was extensively used dur-

PLATE LI   *See page 284*

STANDING CUP BY HULL AND SANDERSON

ing the first half of the eighteenth century (Chart: No. 5).

A beaker of this general shape, which by virtue of its decoration is probably unique, now belongs to Judge A. T. Clearwater (Plate L). The ornamental band of erect acanthus leaves embossed around its base reflects a type of enrichment popular in English plate from about 1670 to about 1695. The only other known instance of its use in Colonial silver is on a tankard made by Timothy Dwight (1654–91), now belonging to the Shattuck family.

In the second half of the eighteenth century another type of straight-sided beaker appears in some numbers. It is made of rather thin silver and has no molding at the base, and compared with preceding styles appears lighter and usually more slender. Benjamin Burt (1729–1805), Zachariah Brigden (1734–87), and Paul Revere (1735–1818) made pieces of this sort (Chart: No. 6). The height averages perhaps 3¾".

In the late eighteenth and the early nineteenth century some low, wide, straight-sided beakers were wrought with stout moldings at base and lip. As a group, they completely lack distinction.

In addition to the straight-sided beakers there were made others of bell shape. The latter seem to have begun their popularity in New England in the early eighteenth century. At first they had almost straight sides with a slight incurve just above the base, and were generally set on a simple ring foot (Chart: No. 10). The general style finds illustration in the Madame Knight cup shown in Plate XI, which was made

[281]

by John Dixwell (1680–1725). While the majority were undecorated, a number were elaborated by a surbase of straight or spiral flutes and some also had a fillet of gadrooning below the lip (Chart: Nos. 8–9). While typically the beaker is a cup without handles, many Colonial examples, especially those devoted to use at communion, were either made with handles or had them subsequently applied. Bell-shaped beakers by Dixwell, Hanners, John Burt, John Glidden, and others were thus equipped (Chart: No. 7).

As the eighteenth century advanced, there was an increasing use of bulbous shapes, and this tendency is reflected in the bell-shaped beaker, which becomes more pronounced in outline, more sophisticated in appearance, and is set on a higher and more spreading base. Examples by Revere, Minott, Pierrepont, and Trott may be instanced (Chart: No. 11).

In the later eighteenth century, a small bell-shaped beaker with flat base and flaring lip, a style that had its origin in France, was current to some extent in the colonies (Chart: No. 12).

II. STANDING CUPS

For centuries, the Catholic Church has employed the chalice in the celebration of the Mass. The form of the chalice has, at any given period, been definitely prescribed. At the time of the Reformation, much of the old sacramental plate was destroyed. The general attitude is well expressed in the records of Wells Cathedral, which read: "The plate that beforetime was used to superstition shalbe defaced, and of the greatest

challaice shalbe made a fayer Communion Cuppe." [1]
The chalice, because used only by the priest, was relatively small. The communion cup was given to the
laity and was necessarily of larger size. Consequently,
in numerous instances two chalices were melted down
and the metal refashioned into one new and larger cup
for communion. But though it discarded the chalice
form, the Church of England adopted conventions of
its own governing the form of its communion vessels.
The Nonconformists looked with disfavor upon anything that savored too much of ritual and consequently
discarded the old sacramental forms and took over
for their own communion service many domestic objects, including various types of cups.

These several preferences were carried over to the
American colonies. In the Catholic churches the chalice
was used and was generally of imported silver. The
English sovereigns frequently expressed their approval
of parishes that followed the rites of the Church of
England by presenting them communion vessels of
London make. Trinity Church in New York, for
example, has communion flagons, cups, patens, alms-
basins, and baptismal bowls that were presented by
William and Mary, Queen Anne, and George III.
The Anglican churches generally had a relatively large
proportion of English plate, as compared with the
Colonial churches of other Protestant denominations.

In New York, aside from the Church of England
communion cups, there seems to have been displayed
little if any interest in standing cups. In the Dutch
Reformed Churches the preferred form of cup was the

[1] Quoted in W. W. Watts, "Old English Silver."

beaker. For domestic use, the Dutch colonists used tankards, beakers, wine-tumblers, and two-handled bowls.

The great majority of Colonial-made standing cups, both domestic and sacramental, come from New England. Here the English settlers brought with them domestic wine-cups, which in many instances they later presented to the Nonconformist churches in which they worshiped. Native craftsmen, quick to cater to the desires of their fellow-townsmen, made cups in the same style. Many of them may have been originally intended for domestic use but practically all that survive owe their existence to the fact that they were given to churches. As a domestic wine-cup, the standing cup did not persist to any extent in the eighteenth century, but for communion cups the shape has been retained.

In the preceding pages, a number of seventeenth-century English cups presented to New England churches (see Plate I) and the rather similar cups of Colonial make have been described and illustrated. The earliest standing cups of American production are the work of Boston silversmiths and are definitely related to contemporary English styles (Chart: No. 17). An excellent example is illustrated in Plate II, made by Hull and Sanderson and reminiscent of such English cups as that made in London in 1638 and later presented to the First Church of Boston, shown in Plate I, second from left. Plate LI shows another early cup by Hull and Sanderson. It is inscribed "B^{T}C" for The Boston Church, and "The Gift of a Freinde T.C.," and was presumably the gift of Thomas Clarke, a

ABOUT 1650-1710   ABOUT 1700-1735   ABOUT 1730-1775   ABOUT 1770-1810

STANDING-CUPS

17   18   19   20   21   22   23

CAUDLE-CUPS

24   25   26   27   28

TWO-HANDLED CUPS

29   30   31   32   33

wealthy Boston merchant who joined the First Church in 1647, became ruling elder in 1673, and whose will was proved in 1682-/3. Characteristic of cups of this period, it has a somewhat tapering bowl flaring at the lip, a stout baluster stem with a suggestion of foliation on the lower flange of its stem with a ring of beading just above, and a rather flat spreading foot. The bulb of the stem seems a trifle large; otherwise the cup is a delightful piece.

Standing cups of the late seventeenth and the early eighteenth century differ from this early type in having usually a slightly more straight-sided bowl and a higher foot. Frequently they are enriched with a type of ornamentation characteristic of this period, the border of straight or spiral fluting around the lower portion of the cup and at the rise of its base (Chart: No. 18). Handsome examples by Jeremiah Dummer (1645–1718) have already been described and illustrated (frontispiece and Plate VI).

Even if some of the eighteenth-century standing cups are not actually taller than the preceding styles, they have an air of greater slenderness (Chart: No. 19). This is probably due to the greater depth and smaller diameter of the bowl and to the fact that the whole piece is undecorated except perhaps for a lightly engraved inscription or a coat of arms. In the first half of the eighteenth century, the stems of these cups are generally slender with simple balusters and the bases are molded and stepped. Typical examples are illustrated in the cups made by John Edwards (1671–1746) of Boston, illustrated in Plate XLVII, and now the property of the Museum of Fine Arts.

Less effectual than these styles of the first half of the eighteenth century are such later types as that represented by No. 20 in the chart, which has a tall trumpet-shaped stem and foot. The extreme rococo styles of this period did not win favor in New England and so it is not surprising to see little if any reflection of them in the designs of standing cups of the third quarter of the eighteenth century.

Classic influences, however, did make a wide appeal, as is demonstrated by the standing cups made by Joseph Foster (1760–1839) illustrated in Plate XVI. The two shown are part of a group of six originally given to the Church in Brattle Street in Boston. The ovoid bowl, the reeding at its lip, and the general chaste severity are all characteristic of the period. These late-eighteenth-century cups (Chart: No. 21) may be more delicate than their predecessors but they are much less vigorous and convincing than are the finely modeled cups of an earlier day, such as those by Hull and Sanderson or Dummer.

Communion cups of Colonial make for use in the Anglican churches in the colonies are relatively rare. The shapes of several are suggested by the chart, Nos. 22–23.

III. CAUDLE AND OTHER TWO-HANDLED CUPS

In England, in the second half of the seventeenth century, there were made a variety of two-handled cups, which differed greatly in their shape and size, in the amount and character of their decoration, and in the uses for which they were intended. The large

Early American Silver

and elaborately decorated examples, which were usually accompanied by cover and stand of similar design, were for display or for occasional use in ceremonial drinking. These handsome cups were naturally tremendously esteemed in the Restoration period, with its taste for brilliant and sumptuous appointments. At the other extreme were the small two-handled cups of a size and shape suitable for porridge, which, according to Jackson, in his "History of English Plate," may properly be called "porringers." Between these extremes were cups intended to serve as domestic wine or beer cups, which varied in size and degree of enrichment with the taste and wealth of their owners. This constitutes by far the largest group, but because they were in constant use and were not especially valuable by virtue of their workmanship, countless examples must have perished. A considerable number used in the colleges of Oxford and Cambridge are still extant. Cups of this type were but rarely used for communion in the Church of England but were not uncommon in the Nonconformist churches of England. E. Alfred Jones finds that about fifty "important" examples thus preserved.

These domestic two-handled cups were not only used for wine and beer but also for such special beverages as caudle, "a warm drink made of wine or ale mixed with bread, sugar, and spices, and sometimes eggs," and posset, "curdled milk mixed with spiced wine or ale and very small pieces of bread or oaten cake." [1] The style to which the term "caudle-cup" is most generally applied is that with bulbous body and

[1] Jackson, "History of English Plate."

PLATE LII

See page 293

contracted neck, which had its greatest vogue from about 1655 to about 1675.

The making of cups of this sort in America was confined almost exclusively to New England. In New York the colonists either did not develop a taste for those beverages for which these gourd-shaped cups were peculiarly adapted or else they preferred to use as wine-cups the more open bowls with two handles of a shape similar to that in Plate XXI, which is of Dutch inspiration. In any event, no example of a New York-made caudle-cup is known to the writer. In a few instances, New York silversmiths moved to Connecticut and there made caudle-cups after the English pattern, as, for example, Kierstede and Quintard.

For different but equally potent reasons, caudle-cups were apparently not made in Philadelphia. In this case, the local silversmiths produced little, if any, silver before about 1700, when the style of the gourd-shaped cup had passed out of favor. In Virginia and Maryland imported English caudle-cups were undoubt-edly much used, but there were few if any local silver-smiths in these colonies at the period to imitate them.

In New England, on the other hand, where silver was made throughout the second half of the seven-teenth century in close imitation of current English styles, these two-handled cups enjoyed a wide popu-larity. The great majority came from the shops of Boston silversmiths, especially Hull and Sanderson, Dummer, Coney, Jesse, Savage, Pollard, Dixwell, and Winslow. A number were purchased by Rhode Island and Connecticut people. Evidently the gourd-shaped

[289]

cups, which passed out of fashion in England before
the close of the seventeenth century, became so established in New England that they there enjoyed a
longer vogue.

Though probably the majority were designed to
serve as domestic cups for wine or beer, like their
English prototypes, in the Nonconformist churches of
New England they proved quite acceptable and satisfactory as communion cups. Mr. Jones discovered
sixty-five examples of these two-handled cups among
the old Colonial churches. The earliest to which he
could assign a date was presented to the First Church
of Concord, Massachusetts, in 1676, the gift of Margaret Bridges. Its maker was John Coney, then but
twenty-one years of age. Unquestionably there were
many more such cups that began and ended their days
in domestic service. When they passed out of fashion,
or when their thin curved sides showed too much
evidence of wear, because they had only simple homely
associations and were not reverenced as were those
devoted to church use, they slipped quietly into the
melting-pot.

In these New England two-handled cups there appear not all the variations nor the same degree of
enrichment but the same general progression of styles
that characterized the English. The earliest style of
decoration (Chart: No. 24), which occurs in the work
of Hull and Sanderson and of Coney, consists of conventionalized flower (especially tulip) motives set
within panels around the sides of the bowl. It follows
English styles current about 1660. As cups of this sort
are quite rare, their variations become doubly inter-

esting and the individual pieces seem to be worthy of special description.

One of the earliest made is undoubtedly that by Hull and Sanderson, which is rather crude and tentative in form, decorated with six compartments, in each of which is a different flower, flat-chased against a mat ground. The two cast handles are scrolled and notched, are relatively small, and are set high on the sides. Pricked on the cup are the initials of Austin and Elizabeth Clement, by whom it was probably used as a domestic cup. At his death Austin Clement left his plate to his widow, who later, in 1678 gave this piece to the First Church in Dorchester, Massachusetts, which gave it to the Second Church a century later.

Another crude and early cup by the same silversmiths is decorated with four panels, each enclosing a tulip, and has very simple S-scroll handles. Engraved upon it are the Wentworth arms. Its height is two inches. Still another tiny cup by the same silversmiths has tulips in compartments; it is lent to the Museum of Fine Arts in Boston by Mrs. James Stuart Smith. .

The cup illustrated in Plate IV A is presumably slightly later in date than the preceding, since it shows more proficiency in handling. It has the typical decoration of formalized tulips in panels against a mat ground and handles in the shape of foliate scrolls.

Sanderson usually worked in partnership with Hull, but occasional pieces bearing only his mark appear. One such is the two-handled cup with six flowers in compartments and cast foliate scroll handles that bears the initials of John Foster (died 1681) and of his niece, Mrs. Silence (Baker) Eliot (1666–1744), by whom it was left to the Hollis Street Church, Boston. Mr. Bigelow queries whether this cup may not have been the work of Robert Sanderson, Jr. (1652–1714).

John Coney (1655–1722) was the maker of another of these early caudle-cups, which has simple punched designs in six square panels, formed by flat-chasing and punched dots and bordered at the top by a line of punched dots. The handles, rather more elaborate than those of the preceding pieces, are cast scrolls with female heads to serve as thumb-rests. This cup belongs to the Congregational Church of Stratford, Connecticut.

The two-handled cups thus far described are all decorated with conventionalized flower-forms in panels around the bowl. Evidence of a break with this style of decoration appears in another cup by Robert Sanderson, which has leaf-sprays rather freely drawn and slightly embossed against the mat ground. The usual row of punched dots serves to define the upper margin of the decorated band. Cast foliate scroll handles complete its ornament. The inscription: "Joanna Yorke/ 1685/ B.C." celebrates its donation as her bequest to the First Congregational Society (now Unitarian) of Quincy, Massachusetts. Previously, in 1660, she and her husband had removed to Stonington, Connecticut.

This freer style of decoration came into fashion slightly later than the compartment style, though doubtless both types were made for some years side by side in Boston workshops. As fully developed, the later type consisted of naturalistic designs of floral sprays or of bird or animal forms seen amidst foliage. It was directly modeled upon English cups with similar and often more elaborate decoration. Plate IV B shows a caudle-cup by Jeremiah Dummer (1645–1718) with freely rendered flower-sprays embossed about its bowl and with handles in the shape of dragons, one biting the tail of its fellow. In a cup by Sanderson, now in the collection of H. F. du Pont, the decoration consists of turkeys amid foliage, a Colonial variation of the English style that represents animals, especially the lion and the unicorn, coursing amid foliage.

An unusually large and imposing example (Plate LII) belongs to Edward Jackson Holmes and formerly belonged to Oliver Wendell Holmes. It has a wide embossed band around its bowl representing flower-sprays and the half-figure of a boy. The handles have caryatid figures to serve as thumb-rests. Such handles generally accompany these freely embossed cups. Another cup, very like this one, was given to Harvard College and bears the Cotton arms.

These early decorated cups have been described in some detail because they are rare and their variations are interesting. In point of numbers, they are completely outdone by the plain examples (Chart: No. 25). Mr. Jones, for example, found fifty-seven plain cups out of the total of sixty-five that he recorded as belonging to early American churches. It is obvious that the plain bowls of these cups would be easily dented and scratched, and when so battered, the whole piece would be of little value except as old

[293]

metal and so would shortly be converted into another and a newer shape. The cups that remain illustrate the skill of Coney, Dixwell, Jesse, Dummer, Noyes, Pollard, Winslow, Savage, and other Boston silversmiths.

A large and impressive cup with reel-shaped cover (Chart: No. 29) was made by John Coney and now belongs to Mrs. S. H. Bradlee. If one is interested in tracing forms back, not simply to their immediate antecedents but to their more remote origins, one should consider the similarity in outline between this Coney piece and certain Chinese bowls of the Ming period. The resemblance suggests that the European models which influenced Coney in their turn had been inspired by Oriental shapes.

A two-handled cup of unusual shape seems closely akin to certain early mugs. It has a definite, straight-sided neck and bulbous body and was made by Edward Winslow. It now belongs to the First Church of Milford, Connecticut (Chart: No. 26).

As in England about 1675, so in New England at a slightly later date, the form of the two-handled cup underwent a gradual transformation, changing from one with bulbous sides, contracted neck, and no distinct foot, to one with a cylindrical bowl rounding inward at the base and with a definite foot. About the period that this change was taking place, it became fashionable to employ a surbase of flutes by way of decoration. Consequently the new type of cup and the new style of decoration were often combined. In the earlier examples the flutes are generally vertical; a trifle later they became spirally arranged, and in com-

bination with them there was usually a fillet of gadrooning placed just below the lip of the cup. The two-
handled cup by Dummer shown in Plate VI (right)
is not of usual form; its shape is similar to the bowls
of contemporary standing cups, as demonstrated by the
standing cup placed next it in the illustration. It has,
however, the customary surbase of vertical flutes,
alternately concave and convex.

A particularly handsome two-handled cup, of proportions that suggest that it was intended for display
or for ceremonial rather than for everyday use, was
made by John Coney and belongs to Harvard University. It has finely cast caryatid handles and is engraved with the Stoughton arms. It was the gift of
Governor William Stoughton, who died in 1701
(Chart: No. 30).

Not unlike it in general character but a trifle later
in style is the great cup made by Edward Winslow
(1669–1753) and now in the collection of Mrs. Lois
B. Rantoul (Plate XXXVIII). In addition to the
fluted surbase, it has a fillet below the lip and gadrooning on base and cover (Chart: No. 31).

Smaller than these display pieces, and simpler in
detail, but of the same general form, are the drinking-cups such as that by William Cowell shown in
Plate XI. Cowell made a number of this sort, with
almost straight sides curving inward to a ribbed foot-
ring, with scrolled and notched handles and a fillet and
surbase of spiral fluting (Chart: No. 27). All of these
two-handled cups of moderate size proved so serviceable as communion cups that they were frequently presented to the churches.

[295]

The smaller two-handled cups seem to have passed out of favor as domestic drinking-cups in the course of the first third of the eighteenth century, but those of more impressive size, designed for ceremonial occasions or for display on the sideboard, continued to be in some demand. The English cups of the period of Queen Anne were very plain and generally had a deep ovoid body girdled by a molding and set upon a molded foot, two large scroll handles, and a domed cover. Although later, in response to rococo influences, the English two-handled cups became most elaborately decorated with embossed and chased scrolls, fruit, rockwork, and the whole gamut of rococo ornament, the Colonial examples seem to have clung to the plain style (Chart: No. 32). As they are one among the less appealing achievements of the American silversmiths, one does not regret that they are few. The late eighteenth century saw the production of some two-handled cups with ovoid bowls, high strap handles, and tall covers (Chart: No. 33) like that by Joseph Loring illustrated in Plate XVI.

IV. TANKARDS

In the northern beer-drinking countries of Scandinavia, Germany, and England, capacious covered drinking-cups known as tankards were extremely popular. In its most usual form the tankard consists of a large, cylindrical, somewhat tapering body; a hinged lid, with a thumb-piece to facilitate its raising; and a handle. Presumably this shape was evolved from early tankards fashioned out of a section of horn, fitted with

See pages 298, 303

PLATE LIII   EARLY NEW ENGLAND TANKARDS BY DUMMER AND DIXWELL

metal base, lid, handle, and reinforcing bands. In the course of time, the horn was discarded and the whole piece made of metal. There were also made at different periods occasional tankards with bulbous or pear-shaped bodies, doubtless suggested by similar forms in pottery and stoneware. The straight-sided tankards were, however, the more favored type, and were extensively made from the sixteenth through the eighteenth century. Their proportions, size, and ornamental details varied considerably from time to time and according to the decorative tendencies of the countries of their production. The majority of the English tankards, for example, were simple and plain, while those of Germany and the Scandinavian countries were usually considerably embellished with embossing or engraving, with inset coins or medallions, or with cast ornaments.

Strangely enough, apparently tankards were not made in Holland, though so generally made by her neighbors to the east and north. Excellent authorities on Dutch silver make this assertion. Had tankards been made in Holland, they would assuredly have been copied by the Dutch settlers of New York. As a matter of fact, the latter seem to have followed English models in developing the form of the New York tankards, so that in this colony, as in those originally settled by Englishmen, the shape of the tankard is derived from English types. However, though based upon the same models, Colonial tankards display many interesting and significant variations in form and decoration, which may most conveniently be discussed by considering them according to the locality of their production—Massachusetts, Rhode Island, New York, and Pennsylvania.

As Boston silversmiths were at work during the second half of the seventeenth century, the earliest Massachusetts tankards are modeled after the rather low, flat-topped English tankards of the period of Charles II. The body is usually broad, low, and plain; the lid is flat and in two stages; the handle is proportionately heavy and is frequently, especially in the earlier examples, attached to the body by a long spine-like projection by way of reinforcement. The great majority are relatively small, averaging perhaps 5½″ to 6¼″ in height (Chart: No. 34). An occasional early tankard, however, towers head and shoulders above its fellows, like the great tankard made by Robert Sanderson (1608–93) belonging to Mrs. Alexander F. Wadsworth, which is 7¼″ high and has an exceptionally broad and capacious body. Another, only a trifle smaller, was made by Jeremiah Dummer and now belongs to Mrs. Edward R. Warren. Both examples are of interest, not only for their size, but because the lid of each is engraved with a spiral whorl of four flowers, a primitive but pleasing bit of design. Several other great tankards bear the familiar mark of John Coney.

Admirable illustrations of this early style are two small tankards (height 5½″) made by Jeremiah Dummer (1645–1718) and now in the collection of H. F. du Pont. Though not identical, they are very similar. That shown (Plate LIII A) is inscribed "C C," and its mate is inscribed "R R to C C," commemorating its donation by Richard Russell to the Charlestown

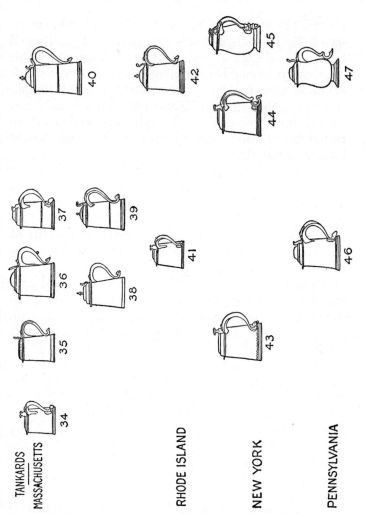

ABOUT 1650-1710   ABOUT 1700-1735   ABOUT 1730-1775   ABOUT 1770-1810

TANKARDS
MASSACHUSETTS

RHODE ISLAND

NEW YORK

PENNSYLVANIA

34 35 36 37 38 39 40

41 42

43 44 45

46 47

Church (First Parish Church, Charlestown, Massachusetts). By his will, dated 1674, proved 1676, Russell
left to this church a bequest of £100, with which this
plate was presumably purchased. The very low, flat lids
of these two tankards, their double-cupped thumb-
pieces, simple handle-tips, and narrow base moldings,
are all indicative of an early style. The tankard illustrated has the long spine reinforcing the junction of
body and handle.

Plate VII represents another tankard by Dummer
that, even if not necessarily made at a later date, is
a trifle later in style than the preceding, as indicated
by the more defined rise of the lid, the wider base
moldings, the shield-shaped ornament at the tip of
the handle, and the applied cut-card decoration at the
base.

Though the lid of the Massachusetts tankard generally remains flat, like its English antecedents, until
the time of Queen Anne, even in the late seventeenth
century there is a tendency to increase its height. As
a rule, these early tankards are undecorated except for
the ornamental thumb-pieces and handle-tips. In occasional instances, they received other enrichment, corresponding to contemporary English styles. For example, the cut-card ornament (Plate VII) or a surbase of acanthus leaves, which occurs in a tankard by
Timothy Dwight (1654–91) now belonging to the
Shattuck family. Fluting, which occasionally appears
around the lower part of the body of English tankards,
was apparently not so used in New England, but does
occur on the lids of some Boston tankards, where it
was employed to emphasize the rise (Chart: No. 35).

Evolution of Forms in American Silver

An early instance of a tankard with such a gadrooned band around its lid is one made by Jeremiah Dummer, probably about 1690, and presented to the South Parish, Portsmouth, New Hampshire. Three tankards made by John Coney (1655–1722) and a fourth made by John Burt (1691–1745) and given to the First Parish, Cambridge, Massachusetts, are decorated with bands of straight gadrooning around their lids. From the indications of the church records, two of these tankards by Coney seem to have been made about 1705.

In tankards, the thumb-piece, intended for the practical purpose of raising the lid, was always made a decorative feature. Often English models were copied in early Massachusetts examples. Simple and early styles are the double-cupped (Plate VII) and the split-scroll (Plate LIII). There also occur, possibly in the late seventeenth and certainly in the eighteenth century, more ambitious designs of a sculptural order, such as the cast lion, the eagle, and the sun and dolphin. The lion, finely modeled, occurs on a tankard made by Timothy Dwight (1654–91), the property of the Shattuck family, which is reminiscent of English and also, more remotely, of Scandinavian models. The eagle thumb-piece occurs on a tankard by John Coney (1655–1722), belonging to Mrs. W. Wanton Dunnell. The sun-and-dolphin thumb-piece (shown in Figure 2) was fairly common in New England, but was apparently not copied elsewhere, nor has any European prototype been discovered. It was used by John Dixwell, Edward Winslow, Henry Hurst, Benjamin Hiller, John Potwine, Thomas Millner, and

[301]

others. On tankards of the late seventeenth and the early eighteenth century, various forms of scrolled thumb-pieces were also extensively used.

A tankard when filled was a heavy thing to lift, and to give additional support to the hand some sort of grip was developed on the outer portion of the handle. In Plate LIII B is shown a vertical grooving of the handle that occurs fairly often in early New England tankards and which is generally terminated by a horizontal loop or tube of silver. Sometimes a long spine or rat-tail runs half-way down the handle to facilitate the grip. A tankard by Henry Hurst (1665–1717) in the Pickman collection has an elaborately embossed and applied handle decoration, so strikingly like the ornamentation found in New York silver that it suggests that Hurst may have seen and admired the work of some of his southern brethren. In many instances, however, the silversmith was content to add below the hinge of the cover and on the upper portion of the handle a simple bit of applied metal, by way of assuring the grip.

As might be expected, in the earliest examples, as in the tankard by Dummer (Plate VII), the end of the handle is finished in a rather summary manner. Sometimes it was given more definite shape and appears as a shield or an oval disc, while at other times, as with the thumb-piece, it received the most thoughtful attention of the sculptor-silversmith and was developed into a well-modeled cherub head. For this design, the silversmith had foreign precedent. A large number of New England silversmiths used the cherub head as a handle-ornament for their tankards, including Coney,

Hurst, Winslow, Burt, Hiller, Noyes, Potwine, and Millner.

Flat-topped tankards continued to be made in Massachusetts in the early eighteenth century, but changes soon developed, corresponding to those occurring in English tankards between about 1695 and 1710. There was a general tendency toward an effect of greater height and slenderness and more modeling. The changes that produced this effect were the doming of the lid, the increased tapering of the body, which continued through the third quarter of the century, the elaboration of the base moldings, and some reduction in the proportions of the handle. A mid-band, which became a common feature in eighteenth-century English tankards, was quite generally adopted in Massachusetts also. In English examples, the domed lid is most infrequently topped by a finial; in Massachusetts, after about 1725, this ornament became the general rule. There were various combinations of these features during the transitional period. Some tankards, like that by Dixwell (1680–1725) shown in Plate LIII, right, have a domed lid but neither finial nor mid-band (Chart: No. 36). Some have a domed lid and finial but no mid-band, as in examples by William Cowell, Josiah Austin, and by Allen and Edwards (Chart: No. 38). Others have a domed lid without a finial but have a mid-band, as in a tankard by Kneeland given to Harvard College in 1729 (Chart: No. 37). Still others have achieved the fully developed and customary eighteenth-century form of domed lid, finial, and mid-band (Chart: No. 39).

The earliest finials are rudimentary, so to speak,

[303]

merely a stumpy little excrescence, like those in several tankards by Coney. In the course of time, they assumed other simple but more shapely turned forms, corresponding quite closely to finials used on furniture of the same period. Still later, especially in the third quarter of the eighteenth century, they were elaborated into urn-and-flame, pineapple, and other designs. Meantime the grip on the handle was commonly made in the shape of an applied molded drop (see accompanying figure), a close counterpart of the applied drops on contemporary furniture. The handle end in eighteenth-

FIGURE 26. Molded Ornament on Tankard Handle

century tankards is generally of shield or oval outline or is cast in the form of cherub head or other masks (Figures 1, 3, and 5).

Many handsome examples of the typical mid-eighteenth-century tankard exist, the work of Hancock, Minott, Revere, Hurd, and Benjamin Burt. They are characterized by a tall tapering body with mid-band, high domed lid with urn-and-flame or other finial, erect scroll thumb-piece, molded drop on the handle, and somewhat convex base molding (Chart: No. 40).

See pages 139, 265

PLATE LIV   NEW YORK TANKARDS BY JACOBUS VAN DER SPIEGEL AND P. V. B.

Evolution of Forms in American Silver

At a still later date the increased height of the straight-sided tankard and of its high lid resulted in general proportions that are far from convincing. They seem to have passed their bloom and gone to seed. The bulbous tankard, which had its greatest vogue in England in the third quarter of the eighteenth century, seems to have won little favor in New England.

Rhode Island tankards, so far as known, all date from the eighteenth century and the majority date after the flat-topped style had passed out of fashion. The two outstanding Rhode Island silversmiths working prior to the Revolution provide us with numerous illustrations and upon these our deductions concerning Rhode Island styles are largely based. Early examples by Samuel Vernon (1683–1737) in the collections of Judge A. T. Clearwater and Mrs. Robert L. Montgomery show a stepped lid with a flat central section and no finial (Chart: No. 41). Others, presumably slightly later in date, show a rather similar lid with a simply turned finial. One belonging to the Worcester Art Museum is illustrated and another belongs to the Metropolitan Museum. The latter is notable for the well-modeled eagle thumb-piece (as shown in Figure 4). So far as noted, Vernon's tankards are all made without a mid-band and this seems to have been the general rule in Rhode Island tankards. Those made by Samuel Casey (about 1724–73+) represent a somewhat later style and have a full-domed lid and well-turned finial (Chart: No. 42). In a number of instances, Casey used a grotesque mask to ornament the end of this handle (as shown in Figure 5). That the design was not, however, peculiar to him is proved

[305]

by tankards with a similar ornament that bear the marks of Cary Dunn of New York, and of Jacob Hurd, William Homes, Paul Revere, Sr., and Samuel Minott of Boston.

Early New York tankards form a highly interesting and distinctive group, which has already received such full discussion and illustration (pages 138 ff.) that its characteristics need only be summarized here. There is no precedence for their shape in Dutch silver, but English styles of the Charles II period seem to have afforded the inspiration. Once established in New York, the form was consistently retained until the latter part of the eighteenth century. These tankards, like other early New York silverwork, are practically always heavily wrought, massive, and capacious. The essential parts are a flat lid in two stages; a large, slightly tapering body; and a proportionately heavy handle (Chart: No. 43). The decorative details, many of which appear to be of Continental, especially Dutch, inspiration, serve to distinguish the group from all other tankards. Almost invariably, at least until the second quarter of the eighteenth century, the thumb-piece is in the form of a cork-screw (as shown in Figure 8). The grip of the handle is sometimes reinforced by a plain or a beaded rat-tail, sometimes by an embossed and applied design of elaborate order. Jacob Boelen, Koenraet Ten Eyck, Jacobus Van der Spiegel, and Cornelius Kierstede sometimes used the figure of a lion applied to the handle of their tankards; this device was a special favorite with Kierstede. Wynkoop and Peter Van Dyck used a bunch of flowers by way of ornament. A number of silversmiths, including

Schaats, Wynkoop, Van Dyck, and Van der Spiegel, employed an elaborate combination of cherub head or woman's face, flower-festoons, and fruit-swags (as shown in Figure 13). Such a combination of masks and garlands is almost certainly derived from German and Dutch ornament.

The end of the handle in New York tankards is sometimes decorated, as in those of New England, with a cast cherub head and wings, with a shield or oval disc, and sometimes, following German and Scandinavian customs, with an applied coin. Coins and medals were also sometimes inserted in the lid. Peculiar to New York and presumably inspired by Continental design is the elaborate ornament for a handle-tip (as shown in Figure 10) that is found in the work of Peter Van Dyck, Benjamin Wynkoop, and numerous other prominent makers. Dutch and German influences also show in the embossed and engraved designs used on the lids and on the bodies of these New York tankards, particularly in the cherub heads, scrolls, birds, swags of fruit and flowers, and the mantling surrounding the coats of arms.

During the second quarter of the eighteenth century increasing evidence of English influence appears in New York silver and more similarities may be found between New England and New York pieces. Rarely if ever, however, does the domed lid and finial or the mid-band around the body appear. But scrolled and open-loop thumb-pieces and molded and applied drops on the handles do occur (Chart: No. 44). Bulbous tankards were made to some extent in New York in the second half of the eighteenth century (Chart: No. 45).

Early American Silver

Philadelphia tankards in general naturally show closer relationship to New England styles than to those of New York, for their inspiration was purely English. Curiously enough, however, several of the earliest Philadelphia-made tankards are as like New York types as two peas in a pod, because they were the work of a roving silversmith of Huguenot descent, John de Nise, who before he went to Philadelphia had in all probability worked in New York and had become so saturated with its styles that he took them to his new place of abode. But de Nise is an exceptional case. Philadelphia tankards as a class are closely modeled after contemporary English fashions (Chart: No. 46). Illustration of the work of four early Philadelphia makers is shown in Plate XXX. The example by Francis Richardson is very sturdy and has a low domed lid and stout mid-band round the body. That by Vilant is more slender and tapering and has no molding round the body. The tankard by Joseph Richardson is somewhat similar but has a lid. The fourth piece in the group is most interesting because it is an early example of a tankard with slightly bulbous sides. The tankard with definitely bulbous sides (Chart: No. 47) came into use later and apparently had a much greater vogue in Philadelphia than it had anywhere else in America. Elias Boudinot, Richard Humphreys, and Philip Syng, Jr., all employed this shape. Philadelphia tankards, almost without exception, lack finials.

V. FLAGONS

C. J. Jackson, in his "History of English Plate," traces the derivation of this term from the old French *flacon*, a pilgrim's bottle, and illustrates early flagons in which the bulbous body and contracted neck demonstrate their relationship to bottle prototypes. They differ from the pilgrim's bottle in having a hinged cover and a single handle. Toward the end of the sixteenth century in England another type of flagon came into favor, one with straight sides tapering toward the top. Other shapes, suggested doubtless by the forms of contemporary coffee-pots or mugs, were also employed at later periods, such as the urn-shaped flagons of the late eighteenth century.

Authorities differ more or less in their use of the terms "flagon" and "tankard." J. Starke Gardner, in "Old Silver-work," defines a flagon as an "elongated tankard of considerably greater capacity, handled and covered, and either with or without a lip or spout. Its introduction scarcely preceded that of the tankard, which its probable use was to refill." Jackson, on the other hand, while admitting that tall cylindrical tankards of the seventeenth century in domestic use were often referred to as flagons, in his book distinguishes between the two terms by employing "flagon" for "the vessel with a handle and cover for holding sacramental wine" and "tankard" for one "of similar form, but usually shorter, in secular use."

The distinction on the basis of use can hardly be sustained in Colonial silver, as so many cups designed for domestic use were subsequently employed as communion vessels. Gardner's definition fits the case more satisfactorily. As far as the writer knows, all existing Colonial flagons were designed for sacramental purposes; the tankards were in many instances designed

[309]

for domestic use, but as they could readily be adapted to the other, they were frequently pressed into service as communion cups, especially in New England.

The study of Colonial flagons is especially interesting, as it brings out in striking fashion certain of the differences between the Northern and the Southern colonies. The flagon was intimately associated with the rites of the Established Church in England. Most of the churches in Virginia and the Carolinas, and some in Maryland and Pennsylvania, were of this denomination, and so the flagon was an important part of their communion plate. However, the Southern colonists imported practically all of their early silver from England, as native craftsmanship had little opportunity to develop in these communities. In consequence, there is many a handsome English flagon to be found in the Southern churches. The earliest still extant was made in London in 1649–50 and given to the church in Yorktown, Virginia. An excellent record of these old communion flagons will be found in E. Alfred Jones's "Old Silver of American Churches."

In New England, on the other hand, where native silversmiths flourished from the early days, the flagon, because of its association with the Anglican Church, was not popular with the early Puritans. It was probably not until the early eighteenth century that this feeling of revulsion was wholly overcome. In the meantime at least one English flagon had been imported; in 1694–95 William and Mary had presented to King's Chapel (Anglican) in Boston a communion service made by Francis Garthorne of London, which included a flagon.

Evolution of Forms in American Silver

Apparently the first of the Colonial flagons were made in the early eighteenth century. One by John Noyes and another by Nathaniel Morse were presented in 1711 to the Brattle Street Church, Boston; one by Peter Oliver in the same year was given to the Second Church; in 1712 one by John Edwards and in 1713 one by Edward Winslow were given to the Brattle Street Church. Once the Bostonians became converted to the use of flagons, they seem to have accorded them whole-hearted support. All these just mentioned have the flat lid, double-cupped thumb-piece, and spreading convex base of English late-seventeenth-century models, with the addition of a finial that is quite characteristic of New England flagons and tankards but is an extremely rare feature on English ones (Chart: No. 48). Plate LV illustrates one of this series, that by John Noyes (1674–1749), which is inscribed within a lightly engraved foliate scroll border: "This belongs to the Church in Brattle street 1711." With other plate of the Brattle Street Church, this flagon has now become the property of the Museum of Fine Arts, Boston.

As in England, so in America, the flat-topped flagon soon gave place to one with domed lid, more tapering body, and widely splayed foot. The minor decorative features, such as finials, thumb-pieces, and handle-tips, correspond fairly closely to those on contemporary tankards. The chart (No. 49) indicates the general form, but gives no conception of the dignity and impressiveness of these eighteenth-century Colonial flagons. Among the handsome examples in this style may be mentioned those made by Samuel Burrill

[311]

(gift of Dorothy Frizell to the Second Church, Boston, in 1733); by John Potwine (gift of Mrs. Mary Lemon to the First Parish Church in Charlestown); by John Bridge (one the gift of Mary Hunnewell to King's Chapel in 1751, another the gift of the Reverend Mr. Welsteed to the Second Church in 1753); by William Cowell (gift of William Dummer to the Hollis Street Church in 1753); by Samuel Minott (gift of William Simpson to the Old South Church in 1764); by Paul Revere (gift of Zachariah Johonnot to the Hollis Street Church in 1773); and by Samuel Bartlett (gift of Thomas Waite to the First Church in 1775).

The flagons thus far discussed have all been the work of Massachusetts silversmiths. Several handsome flagons, closely patterned after English styles, were made by silversmiths of Newport, Rhode Island, including one by Benjamin Brenton given by Nathaniel Kay in 1733 to Trinity Church in Newport, and another by Brenton bequeathed by Kay in 1734 to St. Michael's Church in Bristol, two made by James Clarke, one of which was bequeathed by Kay in 1734 to St. Paul's Church in Wickford and the other of which was Kay's bequest to King's (later St. John's) Church in Providence.

Compared with the many flagons made in New England from 1711 up to the time of the American Revolution, those made in New York and Pennsylvania are surprisingly rare. An example of very tentative form, with low flat lid and body like an elongated tankard, was made by Simeon Soumaine of New York and later given to Immanuel Church in New Castle,

See page 311

PLATE LV

FLAGON BY JOHN NOYES

Delaware. One made by Philip Syng of Philadelphia is illustrated in Plate **XXIX**. It is a copy of an English flagon of 1708 given by Queen Anne to Christ Church in Philadelphia, to which the Syng flagon also belongs.

Occasional flagons were made of pear or bulbous shape (Chart: No. 50), corresponding to the bulbous tankard. One made by John Andrew was purchased in 1769 by the First Congregational Society in Salem, Massachusetts, and another was made by John David of Philadelphia and given by John Penn in 1773 to St. Peter's Church, Lewes, Delaware.

Later in the eighteenth century an innovation appears in the flagon with ovoid body, contracted neck, and high domed base, inspired by urn and vase shapes of the neo-classic period (Chart: No. 51). Judge Clearwater owns a flagon of this style, made by Rufus and Henry Farnam of Boston, which formerly belonged to the First Baptist Church of Salem, Massachusetts. Jesse Churchill of Boston also made flagons of this general style, which formerly belonged to the West Church in Boston.

VI. MUGS AND CUPS

Plain cups for everyday use were made in a wide variety of simple forms. The shapes in general follow the prevailing styles of their period.

Many mugs were like small tankards without covers. They were straight-sided and tapering and had reinforcing moldings at the base. Some of those of the late seventeenth and the early eighteenth century were girdled by moldings around the body and make delightfully straightforward and sturdy pieces. Two by New York silversmiths are illustrated; one by Simeon Soumaine in Plate XXV, one by Koenraet Ten Eyck (1678–1753) in Plate L. The latter belongs to the Metropolitan Museum in New York. Mugs of the same general shape continued to be made throughout the eighteenth century, many of them considerably larger and quite plain (Chart: Nos. 53–58).

Other cups, fairly common in the first half of the eighteenth century, were made with straight sides that tapered inward to the base. Dixwell made a number of this sort (Chart: No. 52).

A very common type in the eighteenth century was the bulbous mug, often described as a "can." The style began with almost straight sides curving inward slightly at the base, but with the progress of the century the shape became much more pronouncedly bulbous and the foot more defined (Chart: Nos. 59–62). The early handles were a simple scroll; later this developed into a double scroll, often ornamented with an acanthus scroll by way of thumb-rest. Some of the larger examples are girdled by a band of molding.

These were the more usual types found in the colonies. There were also numerous other styles that appear occasionally, such as the little cups by Coney, one of which is illustrated in Plate IX.

A special type of cup was the little wine-tumbler, a small bowl-shaped object with rounded base. Though made of thicker metal at its base, it must have been rather unstable when full of wine, tempting the drinker to dispose speedily of its contents. Most Colo-

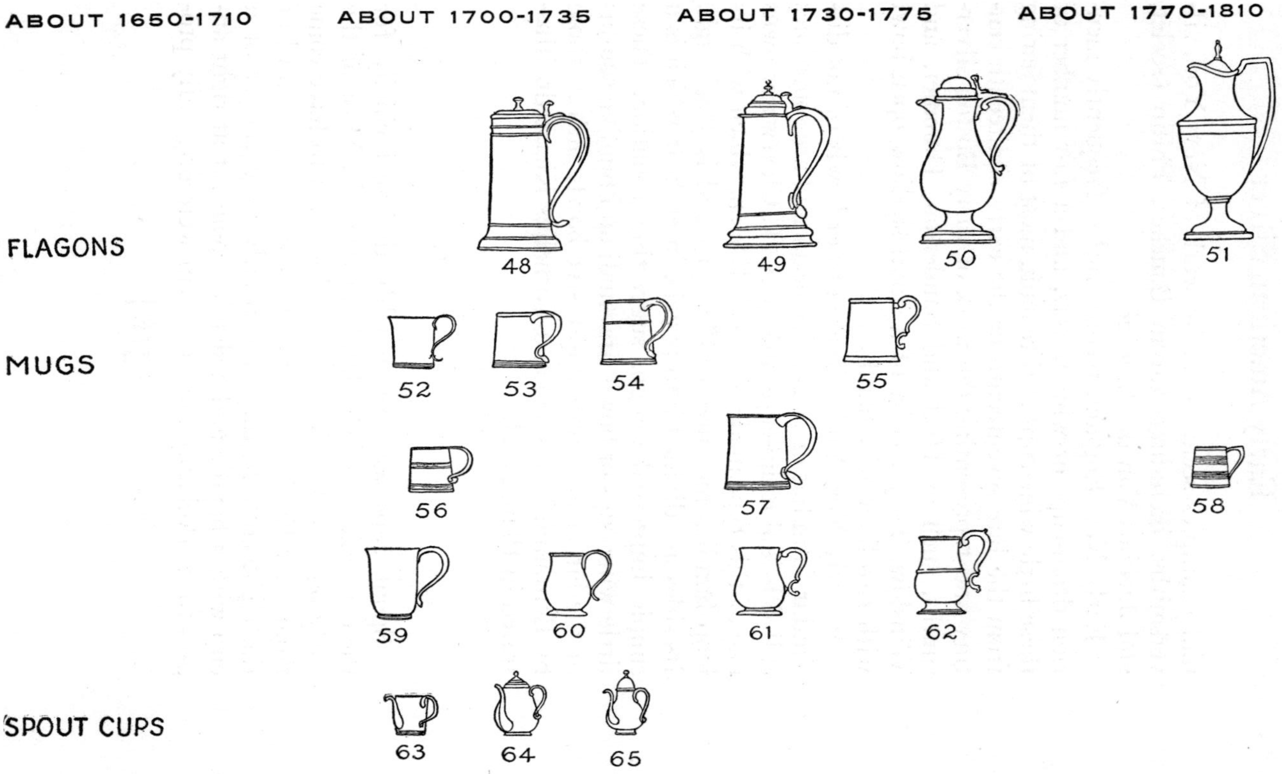

ABOUT 1650-1710   ABOUT 1700-1735   ABOUT 1730-1775   ABOUT 1770-1810

FLAGONS

48   49   50   51

MUGS

52   53   54   55

56   57   58

59   60   61   62

SPOUT CUPS

63   64   65

nial examples seem to be the work of New York silversmiths, including Adrian Bancker, Philip Goelet, and Jacobus Van der Spiegel.

Early New England records rather frequently mention dram-cups or wine-tasters, and a fair number of these little wine-cups still remain, most of them dating from the late seventeenth or the early eighteenth century and representing the work of early Boston silversmiths, such as Hull and Sanderson, Dummer, and Winslow. They consist of a small shallow open bowl with two little wire handles.

In early New York, silver cups or bowls of not dissimilar form but of larger size occur and are sometimes called bridal dram-cups. Judge A. T. Clearwater owns one of this type made by Jacob Boelen, which with its loop handles measures 6¼″ across and is 1⅝″ high. Its sides are divided into panels, in each of which is a simple impressed design, suggesting foliation. These little wine-cups or bowls are small and humble cousins of the larger and more impressive bowls such as those by Benjamin Wynkoop and Cornelius Kierstedt, illustrated in Plate XXI.

VII. SPOUT CUPS

Spout cups were presumably designed chiefly for the convenience of children and invalids. Most of the early ones of American production seem to have come from New England and to date from the first third of the eighteenth century. Essentially they consist of a cup with a handle and a slender spout set at right angles to it. Probably most of them were originally provided with covers, but in many instances the latter have been lost. Though spout cups are relatively uncommon pieces, they are interesting because they show a wide variety of form, corresponding to the cup and pot shapes most favored in the first third of the eighteenth century. An early type is illustrated in Plate L, a spout cup by John Edwards, now the property of the Metropolitan Museum, which has a full bulbous body and vertical ridged neck, closely corresponding to certain English and American mugs, which in turn had probably derived their form from stoneware jugs of German and Flemish make. Similar shapes also appear in English pottery.

Another spout cup by John Edwards (1671–1746), now the property of the Worcester Art Museum, is interesting not only because its cover is ornamented with cut-card work but also because the body is of the unusual high-shouldered gallipot form found also in the chocolate-pot by John Coney shown in Plate X. Dixwell made a number of straight-sided little cups that taper toward the base; the same shape was used by Moody Russell for a spout cup. Another of this shape, belonging to Philip L. Spalding, was made by Samuel Vernon (Chart: No. 63).

More common are the spout cups of pear shape, corresponding closely to the bulbous mugs and also more or less to the pear-shaped tea-pots of the first third of the eighteenth century. These sometimes have a domed lid and finial, quite like contemporary tankards or tea-pots. Occasionally the lid is hinged to the spout cup but more frequently it is separate and insetting (Chart: Nos. 64–65).

[317]

Early American Silver

A cup of hot tea or coffee was assuredly not numbered among the contributors to cheer and comfort among the earliest settlers in America, for until the middle of the seventeenth century these beverages were but little known even in western Europe. Tea was first drunk for medicinal purposes, but its wider possibilities were soon realized. For a time it was so expensive to import that during the Commonwealth its price ranged from £6 to £10 per pound. The price soon became lower, but the commodity itself was so much esteemed that the East India Company in 1664 deemed a gift of 2 pounds 2 ounces a suitable present for the king. The custom of coffee-drinking, meantime, was probably introduced from Abyssinia by way of Arabia and Turkey. For a while both beverages were looked upon with disfavor by some folk who, suspicious of new and strange pleasures, maintained that tea and coffee "are permitted by God's Providence for the lessening the number of mankind by shortening life, as a kind of silent plague." [1] Chocolate was made from cacao imported from the West Indies and was first used in England in the second quarter of the seventeenth century. The importation of all three beverages increased steadily during the rest of that century. Chocolate fell out of favor for a time in the second quarter of the eighteenth century, but the taste for the other two seems never to have shown any diminution.

When Europeans first adopted the Chinese custom

[1] Quoted by W. W. Watts, "Old English Silver."

of tea-drinking, they naturally followed Oriental precedent to a large extent, taking their tea clear and serving it in pots and cups of Chinese porcelain or pottery. While such imported wares were enormously esteemed, they were inevitably expensive to import, and the European potters and silversmiths at once strove to cater to the demand with wares of their own. In some cases they endeavored to imitate Oriental shapes and materials; in others, they selected the most promising of European forms and adapted them to the new requirements. As the use of tea, coffee, and chocolate developed during the same general period, the forms of the respective pots were closely related and hence it seems simplest to discuss them as a group. In fact, it is believed that the earliest pots were used interchangeably for tea and coffee and only later was the coffee-pot made taller and larger than that for tea. The early chocolate-pots were distinguished by having a hole in the lid with a removable stopper or finial, which was generally secured by a chain, the other end of which was fastened to the hinge of the lid. The purpose of the hole was to permit the insertion of a stick with which the thick chocolate could be stirred in the course of its preparation.

Undoubtedly the earliest tea-pots used in England were of Oriental porcelain or pottery; similar shapes were carried over into silver by the English silver-smiths. Of the chief early forms employed for tea, coffee, and chocolate pots, the globular, gallipot, and pear shapes were presumably of Oriental inspiration. The lantern-shaped pots, which have a tapering, straight-sided body and conical cover, were probably derived from European forms. These lantern-shaped pots, as it happens, provide us with the earliest examples still extant. There are, for instance, in the Victoria and Albert Museum to-day a silver tea-pot made in 1670 and presented to the East India Company by one of its members, Lord Berkeley, and a silver coffee-pot made in 1681, given to the Company by Richard Sterne. These are the earliest known examples of London-made tea and coffee pots. This style, with modifications that will be noted in their place, persisted for a long period, and coincidentally there developed other shapes, such as the globular, the gallipot, and the pear.

J. H. Buck quotes from old Boston records for 1670–71: "Mrs. Dorothy Jones is approved of to keepe a house of publique Entertainment for the Selling of Coffee and Chuchaletto." In 1690, "Benjamine Harris and Daniell Vernon are licensed to sell Coffee, Tee and Chucaletto." Even with evidence that these beverages were thus early known in the colonies, it is to be doubted whether any of the American tea, coffee, or chocolate pots of silver now extant date much before 1700. Unquestionably one of the earliest is the little globular tea-pot figured in Plate XXVI. This piece, made by Jacob Boelen (1654–1729) and now the property of Pierre Jay, is extremely simple and unsophisticated, has a full round body, a plain straight spout, a ring foot with stamped ornament, and an insetting cover. All of these features point to an early dating. Inspired by some similar pot in Dutch or English silver, its real ancestor must have been a Chinese piece (Chart: No. 66).

TEA-POT MADE BY JACOB HURD

PLATE LVI

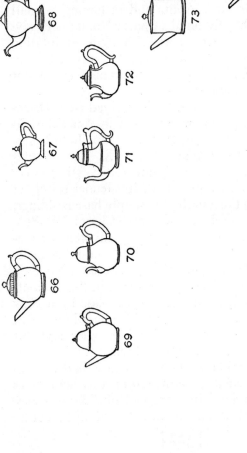

ABOUT 1650-1710   ABOUT 1700-1735   ABOUT 1735-1775   ABOUT 1775-1825

TEA POTS

66 67 68 69 70 71 72 73 74 75 76 79

KETTLES

77 78

Later developments of this globular shape occur in the second third of the eighteenth century in such tea-pots as those shown in Plates LVI, XIV, made by Jacob Hurd and by Nathaniel his son. These differ from the Boelen pot in being more compact and re-strained in form, in showing greater refinement of spout and handle attachments and in having a small hinged lid and shapely finial (Chart: No. 67). Evolv-ing from these came tea-pots with more undulating outline, such as those by Moulinar (Plate XLIII) or Casey (Plate XVIII), a style current from about 1765 to 1790 (Chart: No. 68).

The gallipot shape, presumably derived from Orien-tal vase forms, was not widely used in American sil-ver. A chocolate-pot of this form made by John Coney (1655–1722) is illustrated in Plate X. The features that mark this piece as early are its insetting cover with wide rim and simple finial, its slender spout set at right angles to the handle, the simple base moldings, and the general simplicity of form (Chart: No. 80).

As the globular shape was greatly favored for tea-pots, so the lantern shape with its later refinements provided a popular type of coffee-pot (Chart: No. 83). A fairly early example of its use occurs in the straight-sided tapering body of the coffee-pot made by a New York silversmith (Plate XX A). The handle is set at right angles to the spout, which is slender and but slightly elaborated. The cover, though hinged, evi-dences an early period by its high domed shape.

This straight-sided tapering form was sometimes developed in England in octagonal outline and may have received such treatment in America, although no example is known to the writer. With the mid-eighteenth century, the shape had become more refined, as illustrated by the Pygan Adams coffee-pot in Plate **XX B**. The spout and handle attachments are scrolled in the rococo manner. The lid has become a low and carefully modeled dome and has a rather high turned finial (Chart: No. 84).

Just as the straight-sided mugs probably gave rise to those with almost straight sides that curved in just above the base, so the straight-sided pots were altered in the same manner to produce a shape such as the Winslow chocolate-pot shown in Plate XIII A. This is an early piece, as demonstrated not only by its form but by the bands of straight fluting around its lid and base, by the high domed lid, by the early split-scroll thumb-piece, and by the slender simple spout with its cut-card ornament (Chart: No. 81).

As the curves of such a pot became more exaggerated it would take on a definite pear shape, as illustrated by the chocolate-pot by Coney in the same Plate **XIII B**. This has its handle set opposite its spout, a later fashion than the preceding example. Its lid is lower than that of the Winslow pot and altogether, whether or not actually made later, this Coney piece represents a later style than the Winslow (Chart: No. 82).

The shape was very serviceable for coffee-pots. Rococo influences later modified it to correspond to the tea-pots of inverted-pear form. Examples by Revere (Plate XV) and by Joseph and Nathaniel Richardson (Plate **XXXIV B**) are characteristic of these late developments (Chart: No. 86).

Pear-shaped tea-pots, comparable to the pear-shaped chocolate-pot illustrated (Plate XIII), appear in the early eighteenth century. One by John Coney, with high domed lid, ring foot, and duck-neck spout, belongs to Judge A. T. Clearwater (Chart: No. 70). A very early and unsophisticated example, presumably by a New York silversmith, belongs to the New York Historical Society (Chart: No. 69). This was succeeded by a tea-pot of more pronounced curves, such as that by Charles Le Roux of New York (Plate XXVII B) and others of slightly different outline that were made in New England (Chart: Nos. 71–72).

The foregoing were the chief types developed in American silver up to the time of the American Revolution. In general, the earliest features are a separate insetting cover, a straight spout often set at right angles to the handle, and a ring foot. Succeeding the straight spout came the duck or goose neck style, and following this came the spout with scrolled ornamentation in the manner of the rococo. The foot meantime had become higher and molded. The cover ceased to be insetting and was hinged and changed from one of high domed outline to one that was lower and more shapely.

The little straight-sided, circular pots of Chinese porcelain made for the European and American market, to which the name "Lowestoft" has been erroneously applied, set the fashion for pots of similar form in silver. The style seems to have been greatly favored in Philadelphia (Plates XXXI, XXXIII) but rarely appears elsewhere in America. Its popularity was most

ABOUT 1650-1710   ABOUT 1700-1735   ABOUT 1735-1755   ABOUT 1755-1775   ABOUT 1775-1810

CHOCOLATE POTS

80 81 82 83

COFFEE POTS

84 85 86 87

CREAMERS

88 89 90 91

SUGAR BOWLS

92 93 94 95

pronounced just before and just after the Revolution (Chart: No. 73).

During the last quarter of the eighteenth century, tea and coffee pots with their attendant pieces were made in new shapes to accord with other furnishings designed in the classic taste. Many of these new pieces were made of sheet silver, with flat base and vertical sides in either circular or oval outline (Plates XXXVII, XLII, and Chart: No. 75). About the end of the century, this style was succeeded by that with slightly curving sides and full curved spout (Chart: No. 76). All these tea-pots were generally supplied with trays to prevent their heat from marring the polished tea-table. At the same period many tea-pots and coffee-pots were wrought in urn or vase shape and are usually tall and impressive (Plates XXXIV, XXXV, and Chart: Nos. 74, 87).

IX. TEA-KETTLES AND URNS

Tea-kettles were relatively rare in England and consequently did not develop as wide variety of form as did the more popular tea-pots. Nevertheless, the same general styles were followed by both. In American silver kettles are far more rare than in English plate. Fortunately, we are able to illustrate the two more prominent types and one of the later tea-urns. The first of the group is the pear-shaped kettle made by Cornelius Kierstede (about 1675–1753) and now belonging to Miss Anne Van Cortlandt (Plate XXVII). Undoubtedly it once had a stand, now lost. Its form is most interesting and vigorous and implies an early period. So, too, do the shape and decoration of its spout. As this kettle belongs to an old New York family, it seems safe to assume that it was made before Kierstede removed from New York to New Haven, Connecticut, about 1722 (Chart: No. 77).

More sophistication and more feeling for outline is expressed in the bulbous kettle (Plate XLIV) by Jacob Hurd (1702–58), belonging to Mrs. Stanley Cunningham. This is representative of mid-eighteenth-century types (Chart: No. 78) and follows closely the form of tea-pots of the same general period.

During the last third of the eighteenth century tea-kettles were supplanted by the tall tea-urns (Chart: No. 79), which correspond in general outline and decorative detail to the urn-shaped coffee-pots and tea-pots. A characteristic example by Paul Revere (1735–1818), belonging to Mrs. Charles F. Russell, shows the slender elegance and brilliant decoration of the style (Plate XVI).

X. CREAMERS

As Europeans had no Oriental precedent for the use of cream in tea, when in the early eighteenth century they became thoroughly converted to its use they had to employ ingenuity in adapting some familiar European shape to serve as cream-jug. They were familiar with helmet-shaped ewers of French and Italian design, which, accompanied by basins, were passed around the table for hand-laving at banquets. Evidently this form commended itself, as some of the earliest creamers, though much smaller in size, were of this open, helmet shape. Other early English cream‑ers were made much like sauce-boats.

Of neither of these two styles has any American ex‑ample been found. The account-book of Joseph Rich‑ardson of Philadelphia mentions a "milk youre," which may have indicated a jug of ewer shape or may merely have been a current term for any early creamer.

Succeeding these early types in general favor there came the pear-shaped cream-jug, which was the com‑monest style through the second and third quarters of the eighteenth century. Early examples have a small pinched spout and ring foot (Chart: No. 88). Brown University owns one of this sort, made by the elder Revere. Plate LVII A shows one by Jacob Hurd, now belonging to Hollis French. Much more numerous are the slightly later creamers with scroll-cut lip and three scroll feet (Chart: No. 89). A plain creamer of this sort by John Waite is illustrated in Plate XIX. Less frequently these jugs are supported by a circular molded foot. A later example with more undulation of form and with embossed floral festoons (Plate LVII C) was made by Abraham DuBois of Philadel‑phia, presumably to match an English sugar-bowl with similar decoration (Chart: No. 90).

During the last quarter of the eighteenth century the helmet creamer enjoyed a great vogue. In some cases, the shape is broad and open, as in the Letellier creamer (Plate XXXIII), but more typically it is slen‑der and the feeling of height is intensified by a high scroll handle and often by vertical fluting on the body (Chart: No. 91). That by Revere belonging to Judge Clearwater (Plate XLII) is a characteristic example.

PLATE LVII

See pages 328, 151, 328, 348

CREAMERS BY JACOB HURD, ADRIAN BANCKER, ABRAHAM DuBOIS,
CASTER BY ISAAC HUTTON

Evolution of Forms in American Silver

Although long known in England, by the end of the seventeenth century sugar was still an expensive luxury, and no piece had been specifically adapted to hold it. Probably it was sometimes served in simple bowls. With the eighteenth century it became more readily procurable and sugar-bowls become more common as part of the tea-equipment.

An early Colonial style, corresponding to English fashions, is represented in Plate LVIII A, a simple bowl on a ring foot, provided with a saucer-shaped cover with a similar ring to serve as foot when the cover was inverted. This early sugar-bowl was made by Simeon Soumaine of New York and is now the property of Francis P. Garvan. Admirably suited to its simple outlines is the engraved cipher on bowl and cover, their sole decoration. Bowls of this form were made by several other Colonial silversmiths and correspond rather closely to what in England is sometimes called a college cup, which owed its origin quite obviously to Oriental porcelain shapes. In early examples, as in the Soumaine bowl, the foot is a ring (Chart: No. 92). Slightly later, this changed to a spreading base and the top of the cover was similarly altered. Two rather rare examples by John Coburn and Josiah Austin of Boston are set on three scroll feet. Occasionally, like other pieces made during the first half of the eighteenth century, sugar-bowls were wrought in octagonal form.

Shortly before the American Revolution there came into fashion the bowl of inverted-pear form, to ac-

Early American Silver

company tea-pots and coffee-pots of the same outline.
A sugar-bowl of this style (Plate LVIII B) was made
by Bancroft Woodcock of Wilmington, Delaware, and
is now the property of the Pennsylvania Museum.
Another is to be seen in Plate XXXIII, the work of
Letellier of Philadelphia. The fashion persisted for
a while after the close of the war (Chart: No. 93).
Before it had been discarded, those sugar-bowls inspired by the classic revival had been introduced.
These tall sugar-urns (Plates XXXVI, XLII) are
imposing, and were made *en suite* with other pieces in
the tea-service. Another type made at the same period,
but evidently less popular in America, is that of oval
basket shape with bail handle (Chart: Nos. 94, 95).

XII. PORRINGERS

Tyltyl in "The Betrothal" had the amusing experience of seeing all his ancestors ranged before him,
some vagabonds, some gentlemen in fine lace, some with
garments made of skins, some with clothes of embroidered satin. Could the silver porringers that graced
early Colonial tables have shared this experience and
summoned forth their remote ancestors, they might
have assembled as motley a crew. For in their distant
parentage must have been numbered medieval broth-
bowls of wood and pewter, more sumptuous dishes of
silver and gold, seventeenth and eighteenth century
French two-handled bowls with covers, which adopted
the family name of *écuelle*, and Scottish cousins which
were known as "quaighs" and also had two "ears."
The family in England seems to have become more

Evolution of Forms in American Silver

FIGURE 27

FIGURE 28

FIGURE 29

FIGURE 30

FIGURE 31

FIGURE 32

professional, and was commonly associated with the craft of the barber-surgeons and with the pleasant practice of cupping and bleeding. By the time they reached America, these bowls had become incurably

[331]

domestic, were known as porringers, and served the
household as a dish for porridge, bread and milk,
berries and cream, broth, and other semi-liquid comes-
tibles. Aware of their domestic associations, they were
frequently engraved with the initials of the husband
and wife to whom they may have been given as a wed-
ding-present. As the ancestors of the porringers for
generations had proved the convenience of a pierced
handle to keep the heat of the contents of the bowl
from being conducted to the hand, the Colonial bowls
uniformly continued this feature.

Porringers, like so many other things that derived
their form from English models, were first made in
New England. The early silversmiths were content to
pierce the handles in the simplest patterns, which
served the practical ends admirably and at the same
time were quite in harmony with the plainness of the
bowl itself. The latter was shallow, with a flat base
slightly domed in the center, and the single pierced
handle was set nearly flush with its rim. Three characteristic examples made by early Boston silversmiths,
John Dixwell, Jeremiah Dummer, and William Cowell, are illustrated in Plate X. That in the center is
probably the earliest in style and is of what is generally termed the geometric pattern. That at the right is
described as a crown cresting, which appears in the
work of John Edwards, Andrew Tyler, John Potwine,
and William Cowell. The porringer at the left has
what is called a "keyhole" handle and proved by far
the most popular eighteenth-century style. Various
other styles of piercing were used in New England
but cannot all be illustrated here.

Evolution of Forms in American Silver

As the Dutch were familiar with shallow two-handled bowls, usually somewhat greater in diameter than the average American porringer, but nevertheless quite similar in general form and purpose, this fact may account for the ready adoption of the style by New York silversmiths of Dutch descent. Two styles of piercing that were more or less peculiar to New York are represented by Figures 31 and 32.

The natural asceticism of the Puritans who settled New England was fortified by the character of the land to which they came. It yielded them food rather grudgingly. Many families contented themselves with a breakfast of bread and milk and this custom may account for the wide prevalence of porringers in New England households. The English folk who settled Pennsylvania chanced upon a country that offered an abundance of food of every description. These Quakers knew how to enjoy in moderation most of the good things of life and had no occasion to keep to so frugal a diet as did their northern neighbors. Perhaps this condition accounts for the scarcity of porringers in Pennsylvania.

XIII. BRAZIERS OR CHAFING-DISHES

In the list of plate which Penn "carried to Pennsilvania" there are included "3 new Chaffendishes, 1 large 2 lesser & things to them to burn Spirits in." These may well have been objects of the same general shape and use as the rather charming pieces of early Colonial silver that are now commonly called braziers. Relatively little seems to be written in books on Eng-

[333]

lish plate concerning these stands, which were evidently designed to keep hot such things as tea-pots, plates, etc. Objects of much the same type in Dutch silver are called *komfoor*.

Of such braziers or chafing-dishes, a fair number of American examples have survived. Two are here illustrated, an early one by John Coney of Boston (Plate IX) and another, probably of slightly later date, by Philip Syng of Philadelphia (Plate LX). The essential features are a shallow open bowl, and a pierced and removable bottom plate, beneath which is a shallow compartment with pierced sides. The bowl is supported by three feet, which terminate above the rim in three scrolled supports designed to hold whatever object is to be kept hot. Early examples, such as that by Coney, are often without a handle, but most of the later ones are provided with a straight wooden handle by which the brazier itself and the object resting upon it might be conveniently carried about. The Syng brazier is unusual in showing no piercings around the sides of the bowl; it displays a Quaker simplicity throughout.

The majority of the braziers in existence to-day bear the marks of Boston silversmiths and date from the first half of the eighteenth century. Among them are a number by Coney (1655–1722), John Burt (1691–1745), Thomas Edwards (1701–55), John Potwine (1698–1792), Nathaniel Morse (1685–1748), Joseph Kneeland (1698–1760), Jacob Hurd (1702–58), and Paul Revere, Sr. (1702–54).

In support of the contention that these braziers were used chiefly as stands for tea-pots or kettles, one may

ABOUT 1650-1710   ABOUT 1700-1735   ABOUT 1730-1775   ABOUT 1770-1810

BOWL

CADDY

PORRINGERS

PUNCH BOWLS

CHAFING-DISHES

SAUCE BOATS

96
97
98
99
100
101
102
103
104
105
106
107

refer to two paintings illustrating English tea-services of the period of about 1720 to 1730. One is Hogarth's "Walpole Family," the other Thomas Hudson's "Gay Family," both paintings now in the collection of Lionel Crichton and both reproduced in "Country Life" (Vol. 57, page 420) in an article by H. Avray Tipping.

XIV. DISH-RINGS

Pierced silver rings used to support various dishes were a fashion that was confined almost exclusively to Ireland. They were usually spool-shaped and circular, with a solid border above and below and a pierced section between, which was often also engraved or embossed. C. J. Jackson, in his "History of English Plate," states that "one was used all through dinner as a stand for the support in succession of the earthenware soup bowl, the wooden potato bowl, the glass fruit dish and the silver punch bowl." In addition to many handsome Irish dish-rings, occasional English examples occur; one American, the work of Myer Myers of New York (freeman, 1746), is also known.

This Myer Myers ring (Plate LIX) belonged, according to family tradition, to Sarah Saunderson Campbell, wife of Robert Campbell, about 1780, and descended through Robert Campbell's sisters or nieces to its present owners, Mr. and Mrs. Roger F. Hooper. It is engraved with the script monogram SSC, in the heart that forms the central motive of its pierced sides. Myers has stamped the piece twice with his mark. Because it is apparently a unique American dish-ring, this piece is of exceptional interest.

[336]

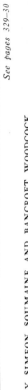

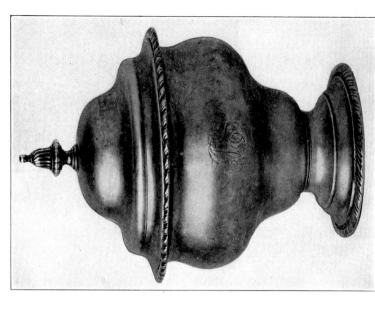

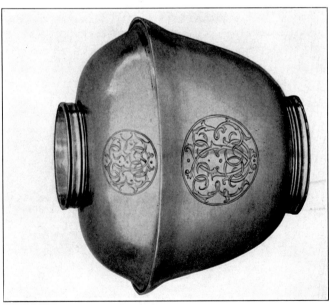

See pages 329–30

PLATE LVIII   SUGAR BOWLS BY SIMEON SOUMAINE AND BANCROFT WOODCOCK

Evolution of Forms in American Silver

Englishmen in the seventeenth century developed a taste for a number of new beverages, including tea, coffee, chocolate, and punch. The last, "a kind of Indian drink," was known as early as 1632, and from the many punch-bowls made in that and the succeeding century evidently became widely popular. The English silver bowls appeared in a variety of styles, with ornamentation corresponding to that of other plate of the same epoch. Relatively few American punch-bowls have yet come to public notice, but those which have are most interesting pieces.

English punch-bowls of the time of Charles II were made with or without handles and the rim, which was not detachable, was cut in a series of indentations corresponding to the vertical grooves that separated wide panels around the bowl. The rim thus had a somewhat crenelated appearance. Presumably the amenities of life in New England at this period were too limited to admit of such luxuries as punch-bowls, for no example of an American-made bowl of this style has been found.

Succeeding this style in England came the famous "Monteith," which implies a bowl with a notched and removable rim and which derived its name from this amusing legend: "This yeare (1683) in the summer time came up a vessel or bason notched at the brim to let drinking-glasses hang there by the foot, so that the body or drinking place might hang in the water to cool them. Such a bason was called a 'Monteigh' from a fantastical Scott called 'Monsieur Monteigh' who at that time, or a little before, wore the bottome of his cloake or coate so notched." [1] English Monteiths of the late seventeenth or the early eighteenth century were often decorated with vertical flutes or flat channeling; no American example of this style is known.

With the early-eighteenth-century preference for rather heavy, plain types, many English punch-bowls were made with practically no decoration except a stoutly molded rim, which was usually removable, a molded foot, and a little engraving on the bowl, perhaps a monogram or a coat of arms. One of the handsomest pieces of American silver illustrates this style (Chart: No. 101). It is the large punch-bowl by John Coney (1655–1722), which now belongs to Mrs. Henry Parish (Plate XII). Though the scalloped rim is now riveted to the bowl, it was originally removable, so that the piece may be properly called a Monteith. Beneath one of the scallops on the rim is a finely designed script cipher, and on the bowl is a beautifully engraved coat of arms, that of the Livingston family (as shown in Figure 23). Like contemporary English bowls, this example is without handles. A high molded base supports it and completes its good proportions. It belonged to the Alexander and Livingston families (height, 9″; diameter, 11⅝″).

A famous punch-bowl by an American silversmith was made by Daniel Henchman (1730–75). A removable rim, with elaborately scalloped edge formed by heavy scrolls, puts it into the class of Monteiths (Chart: No. 102). The bowl portion is plain except for an inscription signed with the initials of the en-

[1] Quoted by W. J. Cripps, "Old English Plate."

graver, Nathaniel Hurd, brother-in-law of Henchman. According to this inscription, "His Excellency John Wentworth Esqr. Governor of the Province of New Hampshire, And those Friends who accompanied him to Dartmouth College the first Commencement 1771. In Testimony of their Gratitude and good Wishes, Present this to the Revd Eleazer Wheelock, D.D. President And to his Successors in that Office." According to Francis Hill Bigelow, "Sir John Wentworth, created a baronet in 1795, gave its charter to Dartmouth College; and Rev. Eleazer Wheelock was its founder and first president." The bowl still belongs to Dartmouth College (diameter 10¾").

The elaborately rococo English bowls of the mid-eighteenth century were apparently not sufficiently popular in America to produce much if any imitation. But simpler bowls of this period do occur, and several historic examples may be mentioned (Chart: No. 103). One plain bowl without any decoration at its rim was made by William Homes (1717–83) and is engraved with the Dawes arms and the inscription: "The Gift of the Field Officers and Captains of the Regiment of the Town of Boston to Thomas Dawes, Esqr. for his past services as Adjutant to said Regiment Sept. 13, 1763." It was presented to the Museum of Fine Arts at Boston by Mrs. Ambrose Dawes.

Another large plain American punch-bowl is perhaps the most famous of all American silver pieces. It was made by Paul Revere (1735–1818) and bears inscriptions commemorating the spirited defence of constitutional government made in Parliament by John Wilkes and also the courage of the "glorious

Early American Silver

NINETY-TWO: Members of the Hon^bl House of Representatives of the Massachusetts-Bay, who, undaunted by the insolent Menaces of Villains in Power, from a strict Regard to Conscience, and the LIBERTIES of their Constituents, on the 30th of June 1768, voted NOT TO RESCIND." When the English Parliament, just prior to this time, had set new checks upon her American colonies, the Massachusetts House of Representatives had sent a letter of protest to the Ministry in London and a circular letter to the other colonies urging them to united opposition against such British policies. The Ministry became much incensed and ordered the Massachusetts House of Representatives to rescind the letter, but the latter, by a vote of ninety-two against seventeen, stoutly refused, thus making "the Illustrious Ninety-two" a symbol of American patriotism. This bowl by Revere was ordered by the fifteen Sons of Liberty whose names are inscribed upon it: "John Marston, Ichabod Jones, John Homer, Willm Bowes, Peter Boyer, Benj^a Cobb, Caleb Hopkins, Nathl Barber, John White, Willm Mackey, Danl Malcom, Benjn Goodwin, John Welsh, Fortescue Vernon, Danl Parker." It now belongs to Mrs. Marsden J. Perry.

The foregoing examples have all been the work of Boston silversmiths. A fine New York bowl (Plate XLVIII), made by John Heath, is in general style very much like those by Revere and Homes. It is plain except for the Van Cortlandt coat of arms engraved on its side. It belongs to Miss Anne S. Van Cortlandt, who is a descendant of the original owners.

[340]

Evolution of Forms in American Silver

XVI. STANDING SALTS

In medieval times the standing salt, frequently described as the great salt, occupied a position of chief importance on the banqueting-table and was placed near the host and his honored guests. Often the table was supplied with other salts of smaller size. In the course of time, the standing salt lost much of its prestige and eventually, at the close of the seventeenth century, passed out of use altogether. Its use was served thereafter by trencher-salts.

A standing salt in the form of a spool-shaped receptacle came into vogue in England in the second quarter of the seventeenth century. Some were circular in section, others had a square top and base, and others, later, had octagonal base and top. The flat top had a well to contain the salt, which when not in use was covered by a napkin supported by three or four scroll brackets attached to the top. Harvard University owns a spool or reel shaped salt made in England about 1629, which was brought to America by Elizabeth (Harris) Glover and bequeathed to Harvard College by her brother Richard Glover, one of its first tutors.

American standing salts are extremely rare, as the fashion passed out of favor at an early date, presumably before Pennsylvania or Southern silversmiths had occasion to produce them and before New York was sufficiently under English influence to adopt them. Of the examples known, all are the work of Boston silversmiths (Chart: No. 108). One illustrated in Plate V (height 5½″) was made by Edward Winslow and is now the property of Philip Leffingwell Spalding. Its base and top are of octagonal outline and are bordered by gadrooning in the fashion of the late seventeenth and the early eighteenth century. The middle section is circular and enriched by a gadrooned molding. It bears the initials I ^{C} M. Another standing salt, made by Jeremiah Dummer, belongs to Charles H. Tyler and is in general plan similar to the preceding. Still another was made by Allen and Edwards and belongs to Nathan Hayward. [1] Its height is 6″, its weight 13 oz. It is inscribed with the initials S ^{S} E for Solomon and Esther Stoddard. Solomon Stoddard was minister in the church of Northampton, Massachusetts, from 1672 to 1729. Probably all three salts were made in the late seventeenth or the early eighteenth century.

XVII. SALT-CELLARS

As table manners became more refined, communal dishes were reduced in number and individual dishes and utensils, such as knives and forks, ceased to be looked upon as a mark of extreme fastidiousness and gradually were accepted as essential table-appointments. Partly because of this desire for greater convenience and delicacy, and partly because salt itself was more readily obtainable, the standing salt, which previously had held such a place of honor, now drifted into the discard, and the individual salt-cellar, which took its place beside the trencher, was increasingly in

[1] "A Unique Early Colonial Salt," by S. W. Woodhouse, Jr., and Horace H. F. Jayne, in "Antiques," Vol. 2, p. 17; Pennsylvania Museum, "Catalogue of Exhibition of Silver held in 1921," No. 39.

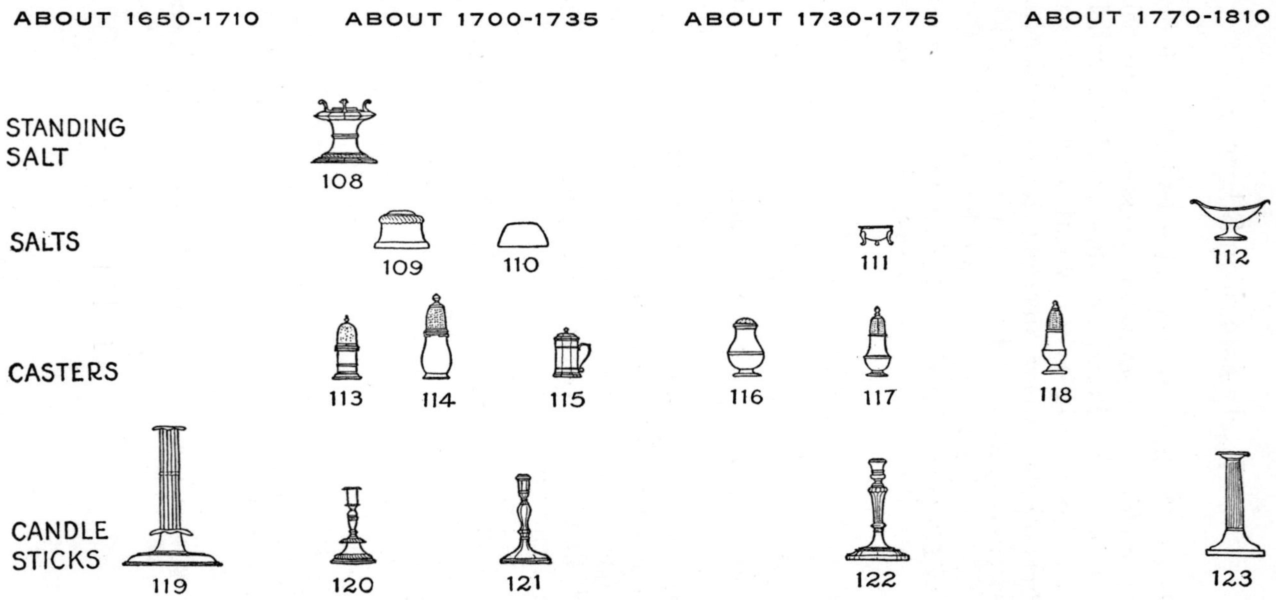

ABOUT 1650-1710 ABOUT 1700-1735 ABOUT 1730-1775 ABOUT 1770-1810

STANDING SALT

108

SALTS

109   110   111   112

CASTERS

113   114   115   116   117   118

CANDLE STICKS

119   120   121   122   123

evidence. The latter form was known in English plate by the middle of the seventeenth century and probably somewhat before. Because of their small size and liability to injury, relatively few early examples remain.

Probably the earliest American trencher-salts extant (Chart: No. 109) are of the form illustrated in Plate LX, a charming little piece made by Jacob Ten Eyck, son of Koenraet Ten Eyck of New York and Albany. Jacob is said to have begun in 1719 his apprenticeship to Charles Le Roux, a distinguished New York silversmith of Huguenot extraction. This salt was inscribed with the owners' initials H $\overline{T}$ M and has passed by inheritance to its present owner, H. F. du Pont. It is relatively high (2⅜″), is somewhat contracted at the waist, and is bordered at top and bottom with a series of lightly impressed lines suggesting gadrooning. Very similar to it is another salt by Ten Eyck that is a family piece belonging to Mrs. Bayard Van Rensselaer. Still another example of this early style, in the possession of a Philadelphia collector, appears to bear the mark of Jacobus Van der Spiegel of New York. These New York salts are in general style much like a trencher-salt with gadrooned border around its top that was made by John Coney of Boston and belonged to Sarah Middlecott, who married Louis Boucher in 1702.[1] All of these Colonial examples probably date from the first third of the eighteenth century and resemble English salts of the late seventeenth century.

[1] F. H. Bigelow, "Historic Silver of the Colonies and Its Makers," p. 255, illustrated.

See page 336

DISH-RING BY MYER MYERS OF NEW YORK

PLATE LIX

Evolution of Forms in American Silver

A style that is slightly later, although actual examples may have been made contemporaneously with the preceding type, is the salt-cellar of circular or octagonal outline, and sides that either are simply curved or follow the outline of a series of moldings (Chart: No. 110). Plate LX illustrates such a circular salt, one of a pair, probably made by Bartholomew Le Roux of New York, and now the property of Frederic Ashton de Peyster, to whom they have come by inheritance. They are plain except for the de Peyster arms engraved on the side. Charles H. Tyler of Boston owns a rare and interesting pair of octagonal trencher-salts.

Rococo influences developed another style of salt, that consisting of a shallow bowl with rounded base supported by three feet (Chart: No. 111). The fashion was much followed in the colonies in the middle and the third quarter of the eighteenth century. The general style is indicated by a salt (Plate LX) made by John David, who was working in Philadelphia in 1763. The edge of the bowl is gadrooned and it rests on scallop-shell feet with similar shell ornaments at the knees. The feet of other salts were in scroll, bird's claw, animal-hoof, or spade form, all good rococo features.

When classic styles supplanted those of the rococo period, these little three-legged salts were displaced in popular favor by those of an oval boat-shape on an oval base, a form not unlike that of the boat-shaped sugar-bowl (Chart: No. 112). These late-eighteenth-century salts sometimes have two strap handles high arched above the rim.

[345]

Early American Silver

Sets of three casters, a large one for salt or sugar and two small ones for Jamaica and Cayenne pepper, were made in England in the time of Charles II. In the early eighteenth century, the three silver casters were often accompanied by two glass bottles or cruets for oil and vinegar and were set in cruet-frames. In most instances, these early frames have been lost and the bottles broken, but a fair number of the silver casters survive.

So far as the writer knows, there is no early American cruet-frame in existence, though Colonial silversmiths unquestionably had the skill to execute them and may well have made them. A large number of separate casters and pepper-pots have come down to us but sets or even pairs of early date are extremely rare.

The seventeenth-century English casters are cylindrical, with pierced lid, generally secured to the body by what is known as a saber or bayonet fastening. A few American examples following this style are to be found (Chart: No. 113). One by John Coney (1655–1722) in the Spalding collection is figured in Plate XII. The body is circular and straight-sided, with spreading molded base. The pierced lid is topped by a simply turned finial and secured to the body by a bayonet fastening. Presumably this caster dates from the early eighteenth century. A particularly handsome and rare piece of this early style is a caster made by Garrett Onclebagh of New York (freeman 1698), formerly in the Palmer and Tiffany collections and

[346]

See pages 344, 345, 152, 334

PLATE LX

SALTS BY JACOB TEN EYCK, BARTHOLOMEW LE ROUX, AND JOHN DAVID
TODDY-WARMER BY THOMAS HAMERSLY, BRAZIER BY PHILIP SYNG

now in that of Edsel Ford. Not only is the top finely pierced but also the piece is the more interesting because it has a cut-out foliate border applied just above its molded base, illustrating this type of decoration on a New York piece other than a tankard or beaker. Like late-seventeenth and early-eighteenth century English pieces, it is decorated with borders of gadrooning. Though the Coney and Onclebagh casters follow late-seventeenth-century English styles, probably both were made in the early eighteenth century. Comparable to these casters in general form are the straight-sided cylindrical casters or pepper-shakers with a handle and low-domed pierced cover.

Baluster or pear shapes appear extensively in English silver of the early eighteenth century and find reflection in American work (Chart: No. 114). Illustrative of these new styles is an unusual pair of casters by John Coney (Plate XII), in the collection of P. L. Spalding, which have a slight incurve of the body just above the simple base. The lids are secured to the body by the early bayonet style of fastening. As pointed out above, a pair of casters of this early date is rare indeed.

Out of these two main types, the cylindrical straight-sided and the baluster, develop most of the numerous variations of the eighteenth-century American casters. In the first quarter of the century octagonal and hexagonal shapes were very popular in England and were used to some extent in America (Chart: No. 115). Judge Clearwater owns a pepper-caster of this sort made by Moody Russell, with low pierced lid and simple strap handle. Another, made by Andrew

Tyler, belongs to Hollis French. A third and later version of octagonal straight-sided caster, made by Jonathan Otis of Middletown, Connecticut, and Newport, Rhode Island, is in the Clearwater collection.

Fully developed baluster forms predominate in the eighteenth-century types of caster. Occasionally there appears an octagonal one, such as that by Arnold Collins, of Newport, Rhode Island, now in the Ford collection. This is a well-proportioned piece and beautifully executed. The majority of baluster casters, however, are circular in section (Chart: Nos. 116–117). Those of the mid-eighteenth century are generally slender and shapely (Plate XIX). From about 1765 to about 1790 many were made with the extra curve in the body corresponding to inverted-pear shapes in other objects, such as coffee-pots and creamers (Chart: No. 118). The vase-shaped caster of the late eighteenth century, a shape suggested by neo-classicism, is illustrated by an example by Isaac Hutton of New York, in the Clearwater collection (Plate LVII).

XIX. CANDLESTICKS

We who affect soft candlelight like to think of our ancestors as dining at trestle tables with candles for cheer. Undoubtedly they did so, using sticks of iron, brass, or pewter when they could not afford silver. George Francis Dow in his researches has discovered the invoice of some English goods shipped to New England about 1690, which in its quaint phrasing sheds much light upon the variety of equipment then in use. In "wrot Brass" there are listed "2 pr of 8

Evolution of Forms in American Silver

Square Monument Candlesticks, 4 square ditto, Round ditto." "6 hanging Candlesticks" are of "Tinnerie Ware" while certain "New-fashion'd Candlesticks" are of pewter. The list also includes "Brass Snuffers," "Snuffers Stands," and "Snuffers panns."[1] But candles, which in 1630 sold for 8 shillings a dozen, remained more or less a luxury during the seventeenth century and were not the ordinary mode of lighting, but were reserved for "occasions."

Early American candlesticks are now extremely rare, which seems the greater pity in that those which do exist are among the most sumptuous pieces of plate wrought by the Colonial craftsman. William A. Jeffries has inherited the magnificent candlestick shown in Plate LXI (Chart: No. 119), one of a pair made by Jeremiah Dummer (1645–1718) of Boston. In early records it might well have been described as a "4 Square Monument Candlestick." It closely resembles English columnar candlesticks of the Charles II period, which owed their form to a brief revival of interest in Gothic architecture. The shaft is formed by a group of engaged colonettes and is rectangular in section. It is topped by a wide nozzle and a corresponding flange below separates the square shaft from a short circular section, which in turn merges into the wide square base. This stick is of impressive size, measuring 10¾" in height. It belonged to David and Elizabeth (Usher) Jeffries, who were married in 1686 and whose initials are engraved on the base. In the four corners of the base are engraved the arms of Jeffries, Usher, Lidgett (Elizabeth's maternal grand-

[1] George Francis Dow, "Domestic Life in the Seventeenth Century."

father was Peter Lidgett), and Clarke. According to tradition, the Clarke arms were added in 1713, when David and Elizabeth Jeffries presented this candlestick to their son John upon his marriage to Anne Clarke. [1]

A most interesting candlestick of square columnar form, following styles of the William and Mary period, was made by Cornelius Kierstede of New York. It was exhibited at the loan exhibition at the Washington Centennial in New York in 1889 and is illustrated by J. H. Buck, in "Old Plate," page 122. At that time it belonged to T. S. Clarkson.

A candlestick (Plate IX, left and Chart: No. 120) made by John Coney (1655–1722) represents a step between this columnar type of candlestick and the fully developed baluster forms of the eighteenth century. The central portion of its shaft is a simple baluster, much like the stems of some seventeenth-century English standing cups. The circular base, flange, and nozzle are all bordered by gadrooning, following late-seventeenth-century English fashions. This Coney candlestick dates from the late seventeenth or the beginning of the eighteenth century. It has come by inheritance to its present owner, Dudley L. Pickman. Another rare candlestick by Coney, one of a pair also belonging to Mr. Pickman, is shown at the right of the same illustration. Though not necessarily made later than the preceding, it represents a slightly later style, for it is a fully developed baluster stick made up of numerous turned sections.

[1] "Heraldic Journal," Vol. 2, p. 166, and F. H. Bigelow, "Historic Silver of the American Colonies and Its Makers."

PLATE LXI   *See page 349*

CANDLESTICK BY JEREMIAH DUMMER

Evolution of Forms in American Silver

Both baluster and octagonal forms enjoyed wide popularity in the first quarter of the eighteenth century in England. A direct reflection of both styles is found in a pair of octagonal baluster candlesticks (Chart: No. 121) made by John Burt (1691–1745), which were given to Nicholas Sever, a Harvard tutor, by his students in 1724 and subsequently presented by one of his descendants to Harvard College. They are now shown at the Fogg Museum in Cambridge, together with other silver belonging to Harvard.

A later style of candlestick with molded baluster and square base with notched corners is represented by a pair made by George Ridout, a London silversmith who came to New York about 1745 and opened a shop "near the Ferry Stairs." The pair now belong to Francis P. Garvan.

Rococo influences in the mid-eighteenth century gave rise to a more elaborately molded candlestick with ribbed and fluted shaft and base of irregular curved outline (Chart: No. 122). A pair by Jacob Hurd belongs to Judge A. T. Clearwater. The full flower of the rococo, however, never found expression in Colonial silver.

Of the later eighteenth-century English styles of finely conceived Corinthian-column candlesticks, which began their vogue about 1765, no American example has thus far been discovered. Thomas Lynde (1748–1812) of Worcester, Massachusetts, made a pair, now belonging to the Worcester Art Museum, that have octagonal bases, finely fluted shafts, and festoons of drapery at the shoulder. Other late-eighteenth-century candlesticks are of simpler design (Chart: No. 123).

[351]

Early American Silver

If any one is disposed to think the Colonial silver-smith never slipped away from his general habit of making useful articles, let him regard for a moment the handsome boxes made to hold comfits or sweet-meats. Five such boxes, described on page 49, remain to prove that the New England Puritan sometimes allowed himself luxuries. These boxes, which are the work of John Coney and Edward Winslow (Plate VIII), must date chiefly from the late seventeenth or the early eighteenth century, and are patterned after similar English boxes of a somewhat earlier period.

Charming reminders of the days when ladies wore gowns of flowered brocade and gentlemen wore pe-rukes and lace jabots and embroidered waistcoats are found in the little silver boxes for patches or snuff, which are often treasured among family heirlooms or find their place in collections of early silver. That shown in the illustration (Plate LXII) is heart-shaped, and bears on its lid a conventionalized tulip and on its base the touching sentiment: "This is Thine and Thou art Mine," with the initials A K and the date 1734. It bears the mark of William Whittemore, a Boston silversmith, and is now in the collection of Mrs. Miles White, Jr.

The simple designs that occur on other patch and snuff boxes are suggested by the line drawings below. Conventionalized flowers, especially the tulip and sun-flower, were favorites, and are not unlike those found on early chests and other furniture. Names, dates, and other inscriptions lend an added charm and personal-

[352]

ity and prove that these tiny things were, as one would expect, very personal possessions, and often the symbols of great esteem and affection.

There have also survived numerous early tobacco-boxes, which usually have a more dignified and less

FIGURE 33. Early American Boxes

intimate type of decoration. A number are engraved with the owner's coat of arms.

Silversmiths were sometimes called upon to make boxes for presentation to public personages. Many of those which have come to light are gold boxes made to contain a certificate engrossed on vellum presenting the freedom of the City of New York to some illustrious citizen or visitor. Charles Le Roux, who became official silversmith of the city in 1713, was commissioned to make numerous boxes of this sort. A later silversmith, Samuel Johnson, made the gold box (Plate

[353]

LXII) presented in 1784 to John Jay. Under date of September 11, 1784, it is ordered by the Common Council "that five respectful Addresses from this Corporation be presented with the freedom of this City in Gold Boxes, one to his Excellency, the Governor, one to his Excellency General Washington, one to the hon^ble John Jay Esq., one to the hon^ble the Marquis Delafayette, and one to Major General Baron Steuben."[1] Samuel Johnson made the box and marked it with his initials, but the seal of the City of New York and the inscription: "Presented by the Corporation of the City of New York with the Freedom of the City to John Jay, Esq." were engraved by Peter Maverick, as his signature on the lid proves. Maverick was one of the most prominent engravers in the city at the period. He frequently advertised and engaged to do various sorts of engraving and chasing. "Ladies may have their tea-table plate engraved in the most elegant manner and in the newest fashion, resembling the flat-chasing." The gold box presented to John Jay now belongs to a descendant, John C. Jay. Another freedom box, also made by Samuel Johnson and engraved by Maverick, is in the collection of Francis P. Garvan.

Reference has already been made (page 208) to the large circular silver box made by Louis Boudo, a Charleston silversmith, which was presented to Lafayette in 1825 by Governor Manning of South Carolina, and which contains a map of the State. It is one of the historic pieces included in the Clearwater collection.

[1] I. N. Phelps Stokes, "Iconography of Manhattan Island."

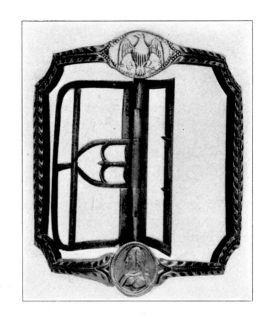

PLATE LXII

See pages 352, 353

PATCH BOX BY WILLIAM WHITTEMORE
BUCKLE WITH HEAD OF WASHINGTON
FREEDOM BOX BY SAMUEL JOHNSON

Evolution of Forms in American Silver

XXI. SPOONS

English silver spoons of the Middle Ages were vastly different in form from the modern. Their bowls were generally fig-shaped with the narrower end near the handle. The handle was relatively short, straight, and most frequently of hexagonal section and terminated in some ornamental feature, such as the figure of an apostle, a lion, a seal or fruit. By the middle of the seventeenth century a transformation was in progress, by which the modern form was eventually attained. In the course of the development, the bowl changed from one with its narrower end near the handle, through the stage of an oval, into a bowl with the narrower end farthest from the handle. The handle meantime changed from one of thick square or hexagonal form through one which was flat and uniform throughout its length to one which was thinner in section, broadened out at its tip, and more or less curved when viewed from the side.

This transformation was apparently under way when the American silversmiths began to work. The earliest styles extant are represented in the work of John Hull (1624–1683) and John Coney (1655–1722) (Plate III). Characteristically the bowl is ovoid, the handle straight, flat, and cut off rather squarely at its end, and at the junction of bowl and handle there is a short triangular tongue which runs down on the bowl.

The succeeding style is represented by the spoon by Van der Spiegel (Plate XXVI) and by the two spoons at the upper left of Plate LXIII. The Van der Spiegel spoon is furnished with balls or rattles because it was designed for a child but its trifid handle follows English styles of the second half of the seventeenth century. The bowl is becoming somewhat more egg-shaped and is usually ornamented with a long triangular ridge or tongue, often flanked by scrolls in low relief. Spoons with trifid end handles were made by Edward Winslow, John Edwards, John Coney, William Cowell, Everardus Bogardus, and others. The fashion undoubtedly lasted over into the early eighteenth century in America.

During the reign of William III in England spoon handles were often made without the clefts at the end and are described as wavy-end. Examples of this style are also to be found in Colonial silver.

Early in the eighteenth century the common type of spoon was one with a handle rounded and upcurved at its tip, with a long, distinct mid-ridge on its face and a concave space at either side of this ridge. The lower portion of the handle had ceased to be flat and had become more or less circular in section. The bowl was narrower than before and was furnished with a long rat-tail on the underside. A Colonial spoon of this style is illustrated in Plate LXIII, top row center.

The next stage dates from the second quarter of the eighteenth century when the rat-tail is superseded by a double-drop and the end of the handle, which is still upcurved, is marked by only a faint mid-ridge. The progressive steps in this whole development are indicated in Plate LXIII. The rococo styles of the mid-century occasioned the use of shell or scroll ornaments on the back of the bowl.

[356]

Evolution of Forms in American Silver

Another change occurred, probably about 1760–70, when the end of the handle, instead of being upcurved, began to turn down. The whole spoon became much lighter, thinner, and more delicate in appearance, the bowl became increasingly pointed, and the end of the handle was either rounded or somewhat pointed. The first two spoons at the left in the bottom row of Plate LXIII show the early stages of this development while the third spoon from the left shows the late eighteenth century styles. Spoons at this time, like other silver, were usually decorated with bright-cut engraving.

The three spoons at the right in the bottom row of Plate LXIII represent early nineteenth century styles, two having what is termed a coffin end and the last a fiddle handle. Spoons made about 1830 were often ornamented on the back of the bowl with a sheaf of wheat or a basket of flowers.

XXII. FORKS

Spoons had been accepted as a desirable and necessary feature of table equipment for some centuries before forks came to be so regarded. An English visitor

[357]

to Italy at the beginning of the seventeenth century noted with curiosity and interest the use of forks there and proceeded to imitate the custom upon his return home. Many of the earliest forms were probably for "suckets" or sweetmeats and for small fruits such as strawberries or mulberries. Table forks did not become common until sometime after the Restoration in England and were not generally made in sets until the early eighteenth century.

The rarity of early English forks is more than equalled by that of Colonial. Among the articles of silver brought to Pennsylvania by William Penn were six spoons, five sweetmeat spoons, six spoons "with a Cross on them yt are used in the kitching," six others brought from Walthamstow, and six egg-spoons. In sharp contrast to the number and variety of these spoons are the two forks mentioned in the list.

The early silver forks have handles corresponding in shape to spoons of the same period. Perhaps the earliest style of which an example has survived is the little two-tined fork with wavy end and engraved handle made by John Coney and now belonging to Dudley L. Pickman. Its length—4¼″—suggests that it was used as a berry or sweetmeat fork, in conjunction with a spoon of the same design. A pair of larger forks (length 7½″), also with wavy ends, were made by John Noyes (1674–1749) and bear the initials H A, for Hannah Arnold, to whom they were presented upon her marriage in 1719 to the Reverend Samuel Welles. They now belong to the Museum of Fine Arts.

A small fork with three tines and rounded handle-

See pages 355–357

PLATE LXIII

SERIES OF SPOONS ILLUSTRATING THE CHRONOLOGICAL
DEVELOPMENT OF STYLES

Evolution of Forms in American Silver

end in the style of the early eighteenth century is by an unknown American silversmith and now belongs to the Metropolitan Museum. The mid-eighteenth century saw many pistol-handled knives and forks. Miss Ella Parsons owns several pistol-handled forks, some with two tines, some with three, made by Joseph Richardson of Philadelphia and by John Le Roux of New York, and also owns knives of corresponding style made by John Hastier and William Anderson of New York.

Numerous advertisements in Colonial newspapers in the third quarter of the eighteenth century suggest that both knives and forks with ornamental handles of bone, ivory or porcelain were deemed very fashionable and were extensively imported. In 1752 John Smith advertises in the "New York Gazette" "Ivory Handle Knives and Forks" which he has imported from London. In the same newspaper for this year occurs the advertisement of Reuben Warren Thompson, announcing his importation of "china handl'd knives and forks mounted in silver in shagreen cases."

BIBLIOGRAPHICAL NOTE

THE volume of source material which may profitably be consulted in connection with the study of early American silver is so enormous that no attempt is here made to list the items. Suffice it to say that old newspapers; public records of baptisms, marriages, deaths; wills, inventories, diaries, land records and others of all sorts yield a vast amount of information concerning specific silversmiths and their customers and concerning general conditions which affected the production and use of American silverware. The best histories of the various localities will give the beginner in this field a general grasp of political, economic, social, and religious conditions and such histories usually contain suggestive bibliographies, including source material. The latter may be consulted to whatever degree the student's time and inclination dictate.

The following list notes the more important publications, exclusive of magazine articles, which have thus far appeared on the subject of early American silver. A number have already been commented upon in the Foreword.

Bigelow, Francis Hill. *Historic Silver of the Colonies and its Makers.* 1917.
Boston, Museum of Fine Arts. *American Silver, the Work of Seventeenth and Eighteenth Century Silversmiths, exhibited . . .* 1906. (With an introduction by R. T. H. Halsey, technical description of objects by J. H. Buck.) 1906.
American Church Silver of the Seventeenth and Eighteenth Centuries with a few pieces of domestic plate, exhibited . . . 1911. (With an introduction on Early

[361]

Bibliographical Note

Silversmiths of Connecticut, by George Munson Curtis.) 1911.

Brix, Maurice. *List of Philadelphia Silversmiths and Allied Artificers from 1682 to 1850.* 1920.

Buck, J. H. *Old Plate, its Makers and Marks.* 1903.

Curtis, George Munson. *Early Silver of Connecticut and its Makers.* 1913.

Dow, George Francis. *The Arts and Crafts in New England, 1704–1775. Gleanings from Boston Newspapers* . . . 1927.

Ensko, Stephen G. C. *American Silversmiths and their Marks.* 1927.

Hartford, Connecticut, Wadsworth Atheneum and Morgan Memorial. *The Early Plate in Connecticut Churches Prior to 1850, collected by The Connecticut Society of the Colonial Dames of America, catalogued by Florence Paull Berger.* 1919.

Jones, E. Alfred. *Old Silver of American Churches.* Privately printed for the National Society of Colonial Dames of America. 1913.

Old Silver of Europe and America. 1928.

Miller, William Davis. *The Silversmiths of Little Rest* (Rhode Island). 1928.

New York, Metropolitan Museum of Art. *The Hudson-Fulton Celebration, Catalogue of an Exhibition Held* . . . MCMIX. Vol. 2 part III, *American Silver.*

Catalogue of an Exhibition of Silver Used in New York, New Jersey, and the South, with a note on early New York Silversmiths by R. T. H. Halsey. New York. 1911.

American Silver of the XVII and XVIII Centuries; a study based on the Clearwater Collection, by C. Louise Avery. 1920.

Philadelphia, Pennsylvania Museum. *Exhibition of Old American and English Silver.* 1917.

Bulletin, No. 68, June 1921, Catalogue of Loan Exhibition of Silver, American and European.

Pleasants, J. Hall. *Maryland Silversmiths, 1715–1830, with*

Bibliographical Note

illustrations of their silver and their marks and with a facsimile of the design book of William Faris. (In press.)

Walpole Society. *A List of Early American Silversmiths and their Marks* (by Hollis French) with a silver collectors' glossary. 1917.

Arts and Crafts in Philadelphia, Maryland, and South Carolina, 1721–1785. Gleanings from newspapers, collected by Alfred Coxe Prime. 1929.

Washington, D. C., National Gallery of Art. *Exhibition of Early American Paintings, Miniatures, and Silver.* 1925.

Woolsey, Theodore S. *Old Silver.* Reprinted from Harper's Magazine. 1896.

Worcester, Massachusetts, Art Museum. *Old Silver Owned in Worcester County.* 1913.

If the student is interested in tracing the sources of American silver design, the following books will prove of assistance:

Begeer, Carel J. A. *Inleiding tot de Geschiedenis der Nederlandsche Edelsmeedkunst.*

Burlington Fine Arts Club. *Exhibition of a Collection of Silversmiths' Work of European Origin.* (With an introduction by J. Starkie Gardner.) 1901.

Carrington, John Bodman, and George Ravensworth Hughes. *The Plate of the Worshipful Company of Goldsmiths.* 1926.

Cripps, Wilfred Joseph. *Old English Plate, Ecclesiastical, Decorative, and Domestic; its makers and marks.* 1914.

Gardner, J. Starkie. *Old Silver-work, chiefly English, from the XVth to the XVIIIth Centuries;* a catalogue of the unique loan collection exhibited in 1902. 1903.

Jackson, Charles James. *English Goldsmiths and their Marks; a history of the goldsmiths and plate-workers of England, Scotland, and Ireland; with over thirteen thousand marks, reproduced in facsimile.* 1921.

An Illustrated History of English Plate, Ecclesiastical

Bibliographical Note

and Secular . . . from the earliest . . . examples to the latest of the Georgian period . . . 1911. 2 vols.

Jones, E. Alfred. *The Old Church Plate of the Isle of Man.* 1907.
The Old Silver Sacramental Vessels of Foreign Protestant Churches in England. 1908.
The Old Plate of the Cambridge Colleges . . . 1910.

Leeuwarden (Holland). *Friesch genootschap van geschied-oudheid- en taalkunde-Museum. Antiek nederlandsch goud- en zilversmidswerk . . . opname van* W. A. Slager. 1902.

Oxford. *Catalogue of a Loan Exhibition of Silver Plate Belonging to the Colleges of the University of Oxford.* November, 1928.

London. *Catalogue of a Loan Exhibition of Old English Plate and Decorations and Orders.* March, 1929.

London. *Queen Charlotte's Loan Exhibition of Old Silver, English, Irish, and Scottish, all proir to* 1739, *with examples of present day work.* 1929.

Moffatt, Harold Charles. *Old Oxford Plate.* 1906.

Watts, W. W. *Old English Silver.* 1924.

INDEX

Index

Boelen, Aefje, 160
 Anneke (Cours), 159
 Bayken (Arents), 159
 Catharina (Klock), 159
 Hendrick, 159
 Henricus, 132, 145, 159–61
 Jacob, 132–34, 136, 149, 159–60,
  161, 228, 253–54, 264
 Jannetje (Waldron), 159
Bogardus, Everardus, 141, 144,
 356
Bolting, Monoply, New York, 120,
 160
Bontecou, Timothy, 115
Book-plates, 249, 270–72
Borders, foliate, 103, 131, 134,
 145–46
Bosch, Albert, 159
Boston, Mass.:
 Brattle Street Church, 63, 67,
  82, 287, 311
 First Church, 17, 18, 19, 22, 23,
  25, 42, 130, 280, 284, 312
 Hollis Street Church, 292, 312
 King's Chapel, 101, 310, 312
 Lynde Street Church, 67, 313
 Museum of Fine Arts, 39, 49,
  55, 63, 67, 68, 72, 77, 80, 82,
  88, 148, 291, 311, 339, 358;
  exhibitions, xiv
 Old South Church, 17, 19, 25,
  130, 268, 312
 Second Church, 311, 312
 West Church, *see* Lynde Street
  Church
Boucher, Louis and Sarah (Mid-
 dlecott), 344
Boudinot, Elias, 183, 308
Boudo, Louis, 208
Bowditch, Mrs. Ernest W., 70
Bowes, William, 340
Bowls:
 Bleeding or barber-surgeons',
  47
 New York, 136–37
 Punch, 70, 337–40
 Sugar, 73, 80, 87, 151, 329–30
 see also Porringers

Boxes:
 Comfit or sweetmeat, 32, 49–50,
  352
 Freedom, 160, 162, 163, 353–54
 Various, 352–54
Boyer, Daniel, 100
Boyer, Peter, 340
Boylston, Edward, 63
Braddock, General, 187
Bradlee, Mrs. S. H., 294
Branson, William, 179
Braziers or chafing dishes, 60, 69,
 333–36
Brenton, Benjamin, 102, 104, 312
Brevoort, John, 150, 227
Bridge, John, 312
Bridges, Margaret, 290
Brigden, Zachariah, 281
Bright-cutting, 84, 86, 248, 272
Bristol, R. I., First Congregational
 Church, 100, 103
Bristol, R. I., St. Michael's
 Church, 101, 104
Britannia Standard, 58, 61, 74, 234
Brix, Maurice, xviii
Brooklyn, N. Y., New Utrecht
 Reformed Church, 132
Brown, Moses, 230
Brown University, 328
Browne, Nathaniel, 93
Buck, J. H., xiii
Buel, Abel, 115
Buffing, 241
Buichle, Louis, 203
Burger, Nicholas, 227
Burlington, N. J., 168, 196
Burlington, St. Mary's Church,
 130–31
Burnishing, 239
Burrill, Samuel, 311
Burt, Benjamin, 233, 254, 304
 John, 74, 231–33, 301, 334,
  351
 Samuel, 233
 William, 233
Byrnes, Thomas, 196

Cadwalader, Mrs. John, 189

[366]

Index

[367]

Index

Index

Index

Index

Index

Index

Index

Index

Portsmouth, N. H., South Parish, 301
Posset and posset-cups, 30, 288
Pots, *see* Tea-pots, Coffee-pots, Chocolate-pots, Jugs, etc.
Potwine, John, 115, 301, 312, 332, 334
Prime, Alfred Coxe, xviii, 203
Prince, Job, 113
Privateering, 95, 120
Processes, 233 ff.
Providence, R. I.:
 Rhode Island School of Design, Exhibition, xv
 St. John's Church (King's), 101, 104, 312
Provoost arms, 271
Pruyn, Foster, 140
P.V.B., 140, 143–45, 148, 164

Quaigh, Scottish, 330
Quakers, 92, 97, 99, 165, 168–69, 173, 182, 186, 333
Quality of colonial silver, 37, 217–22, 234
Quary, Robert, 131, 177
Quincy, Anna, 49
 Daniel, 56
 Norton, 229
 Arms, 269–70
Quincy, Mass., First Congregational Society, 26, 292
Quintard, Peter, 114, 289

Raising, 236–37, 246
Randolph, Benjamin, 172
Rantoul, Mrs. Lois, 64, 295
Rattle, Child's, 153
Rensselaerwyck, 117
Revere, Paul, Sr., 55, 212, 334
 Paul, Jr., 77, 80, 81, 85–88, 249, 312, 339
 Bill of, 230
 Career, 226
 Mark, 254–55
Reynolds, Thomas, 251
Rhode Island bills of credit, 109

Rhode Island Silver, Exhibition of, xv
Rhode Island School of Design, xv
Richardson, Francis, 174, 178, 179, 195, 308
 John, 179
 Joseph, Sr., 179, 185, 190, 195, 221, 328, 359
 Joseph & Nathaniel, 179, 190–91, 193–94, 224, 253–54
Ridout, George, 214, 351
Rings, dish, 336
Rivoire, Apollos, *see* Revere, Paul, Sr.
Robert, Christopher, 164
Robeson, Sarah, 221
Robinson, William, 98
Rocaille, 75
Rochester, N. Y., Reformed Church in Accord, 135
Rococo styles, 74–82
Roelofse, Cathrina, 134
Rogers, Daniel, 105
Roosevelt, Nicholas, 164
Rose, Jennie Haskell, 207–208
Russell, Mrs. C. F., 86, 327
 Daniel, 100, 102, 103
 Moody, 74, 317, 347
 Richard, 298

Salem, Mass.:
 Essex Institute, 26
 First Congregational Society, 280, 313
 First Baptist Church, 313
Salem, N. J., 168, 196
Salisbury, Josiah, 103
Salt-cellars, 31, 39, 68, 81, 148, 342–45
Saltonstall, Governor, 248
 Mrs. Mary, 268
Salts, standing, 31, 39, 341
Salvers, 81
Sanders family, 135, 161
Sanders, J. Glen, 135
 Robert, 134

Index

Index

Index